Luminos is the Open Access monograph publishing program
from UC Press. Luminos provides a framework for preserving and
reinvigorating monograph publishing for the future and increases
the reach and visibility of important scholarly work. Titles
published in the UC Press Luminos model are published with the
same high standards for selection, peer review, production, and
marketing as those in our traditional program. www.luminosoa.org

Creating the Intellectual

The publisher and the University of California Press Foundation gratefully acknowledge the generous support of the Sue Tsao Endowment Fund in Chinese Studies.

Creating the Intellectual

Chinese Communism and the Rise of a Classification

———

Eddy U

UNIVERSITY OF CALIFORNIA PRESS

University of California Press, one of the most distinguished university presses in the United States, enriches lives around the world by advancing scholarship in the humanities, social sciences, and natural sciences. Its activities are supported by the UC Press Foundation and by philanthropic contributions from individuals and institutions. For more information, visit www.ucpress.edu.

University of California Press
Oakland, California

Suggested citation: U, E. *Creating the Intellectual: Chinese Communism and the Rise of a Classification*. Oakland: University of California Press, 2019. DOI: https://doi.org/10.1525/luminos.68

Library of Congress Cataloging-in-Publication Data

Names: U, Eddy, author.
Title: Creating the intellectual : Chinese communism and the rise of a classification / Eddy U.
Description: Oakland, California : University of California Press, [2019] | Includes bibliographical references and index. | This work is licensed under a Creative Commons CC BY license. To view a copy of the license, visit http://creativecommons.org/licenses. |
Identifiers: LCCN 2018055941 (print) | LCCN 2018059316 (ebook) | ISBN 9780520972827 (Ebook) | ISBN 9780520303690 (pbk. : alk. paper)
Subjects: LCSH: China—Intellectual life—1949–1976. | Communism and intellectuals—China—History—20th century. | Social stratification—China—History—20th century.
Classification: LCC DS777.6 (ebook) | LCC DS777.6 .U23 2019 (print) | DDC 305.5/5095109045—dc23
LC record available at https://lccn.loc.gov/2018055941

27   26   25   24   23   22   21   20   19
10   9   8   7   6   5   4   3   2   1

For Lauren

The word intellectual *strikes me as odd. Personally, I've never met any intellectuals. I've met people who write novels, others who treat the sick. People who work in economics and others who write electronic music. I've met people who teach, people who paint, and people of whom I have never really understood what they do. But intellectuals, never.*

On the other hand, I've met a lot of people who talk about "the intellectual." And, listening to them, I've got some idea of what such an animal could be. It's not difficult—he's quite personified. He's guilty about pretty well everything: about speaking out and about keeping silent, about doing nothing and about getting involved in everything. . . . In short, the intellectual is raw material for a verdict, a sentence, a condemnation, an exclusion . . .

—Michel Foucault interviewed by Le Monde, April 6–7, 1980

CONTENTS

ILLUSTRATIONS

FIGURES

TABLES

This book grew out of a sociology graduate seminar that I took more than twenty-five years ago at the University of California at Berkeley. Titled *Intellectuals and Politics,* the course was inspiring not only because it included different research approaches and fascinating studies, but also because none of the writings seemed to be equipped conceptually to illuminate the dynamics leading up to the most violent episode against intellectuals in contemporary Chinese history. During the Great Proletarian Cultural Revolution initiated by Chairman Mao in the mid-1960s, countless intellectuals were attacked by student Red Guards. The victims included every conceivable type of person found in the literature on intellectuals produced inside and outside academia, such as reputed scholars and writers, university deans, state officials, and factory managers as well as primary school teachers, journalists, and performing artists. Although the precise number of fatalities would never be known, tens of thousands at least were beaten to death or hounded to suicide. The rest of the victims endured various combinations of corporal punishment, coerced labor, and public humiliation. Besides college, secondary, and even primary students, the attackers included peers of the victims. Some of these peer assailants placed themselves at the forefront of the assaults; some plotted behind the scenes; some joined unfolding attacks to keep themselves safe. The boundaries between attackers and the attacked shifted back and forth while a reign of terror consumed property, dignity, and lives nationwide.

During the last sixteen years, I published a series of articles that explore the historical background behind the brutality against intellectuals during the Cultural Revolution. The articles focus on two things. First, the evolution of *zhishifenzi* (the intellectual or intellectuals) from a little-known expression in China during the

1920s to a primary social identity of a heterogeneous population of people after the 1949 communist revolution. Second, the postrevolutionary struggle across state and society to define the roles and responsibilities of intellectuals as well as the social composition of this population. I trace how "intellectuals" as individuals and a population were constructed under the Chinese Communist Party, in contradistinction to conventional approaches that predefine the subject as critical thinkers, professional experts, or other kinds of persons. The articles reveal that individuals and organizations encountered the intellectual increasingly on many levels. As a subject matter, the intellectual turned up in party policies and leadership speeches, bureaucratic rules and personnel reports, newspapers and textbooks, government notices and pamphlets, radio shows and theatrical performances, and other mediums. As a person, the intellectual was eventually locatable across a wide range of circumstances: during high-level assemblies, political reeducation classes, land reform activities, and registration drives as well as within the state, the neighborhood, the family, and all sorts of workplaces. Under the party, the intellectual was woven into the fabric of everyday life, carrying in bodily, literary, aural, artistic, and other forms meanings and symbolisms inscribed upon the subject. Although I tried to connect the articles together thematically and analytically, what remained elusive was a genuinely coherent picture on how the intellectual was constituted, let alone one that clarifies twists and turns of the process and its implications for the violence of the Cultural Revolution. Each of the articles had been developed as an independent publication. They were not published in the order of the events. The study as a whole was always a work-in-progress.

Building upon those articles, this book investigates the intellectual in twentieth-century China first and foremost as a classification of people deployed by the Chinese Communist Party on behalf of its revolutionary project. The latter, which I call Chinese Communism, was inspired as much as any other contemporary project of communism by Karl Marx's understanding of class struggle as the motivating force of history. Launched with the party's formation in the early 1920s, Chinese Communism grew in fits and starts before maturing into a national military takeover led by Mao during the mid-century. The revolutionary project became a state pursuit and produced shortly afterward a nationwide elimination of private ownership and changes of governance at all levels. The party's emphasis on class struggle fluctuated, reaching feverish heights during the Cultural Revolution before fading by the early 1980s, not long after the Chairman's demise. From beginning to end, Chinese Communism nonetheless involved a top-down reordering of people into class subjects based on Marxian thought or, as Mao stressed early on, as a revolutionary separation of friends from enemies. "Capitalist" and "landlord" were major classifications of those identified as members of the exploiting classes; the markers each cast the individual as a target of economic expropriation and political suppression. "Worker" and "poor peasant" defined those so categorized as victims of class exploitation and part of the backbone of the revolutionary project.

In comparison, "intellectual," which became the primary classification of many writers, officials, schoolteachers, technicians, and others, signaled that they each were situated somewhere between the exploiting and the exploited classes, possessing knowledge and skills valuable to Chinese Communism as well as values, beliefs, and habits harmful to its development. The deployment of this marker by the party, unlike the other Marxian classifications, captured its modernizing as much as revolutionary impulses or the intention to achieve an industrialized China through class struggle.

The main message that runs through this book is the mutually constitutive relationship between the intellectual and Chinese Communism—that is, their power to influence politics and governance, work and leisure, association and identity, and other aspects of life through influencing each other. Scholarly as well as official accounts have long maintained that Chinese Communism arose because of the efforts of revolutionary intellectuals and then encountered support and resistance from intellectuals with different persuasions. The studies have illuminated political, organizational, and experiential features of the revolutionary project, but have also greatly simplified its relations with the intellectual. As Chinese Communism grew, the methods and measures of revolution and governance promoted by the party, along with its Marxian accounts of Chinese society, nurtured, supported, and ultimately normalized the intellectual as a classification of people. An ever-increasing number of men and women appeared locally as "intellectuals," or visible subjects who allegedly possessed similar class characteristics and hence similar political, moral, and economic influence on Chinese Communism. An even larger number of people found themselves potentially within the scope of the classification, because of its ambiguity and fluidity in terms of conceptualization and application respectively. At the same time, how to harness the knowledge and skills of such a diverse, dispersed, and growing population of intellectuals and to limit their adverse impact on class struggle became a constant concern of the party. Intense efforts at forging revolutionary theory, governing approaches, administrative arrangements, and mechanisms of mobilization and regulation persisted. The outcomes of representation, organization, and negotiation shaped patterns of authority and opportunity, workplace makeups and priorities, and social interaction and individual calculus, or the collective and individual experience of the revolutionary project.

Put differently, this book shows that the intellectual as an analytical object has significantly more to offer with regard to understanding contemporary Chinese society than previous studies have demonstrated. Under Chinese Communism, the intellectual was not simply a political visionary, an outspoken writer, a browbeaten schoolteacher, or any kind of person pushing for or coping with unprecedented change. The revolutionary project turned the intellectual into a primary classification of people. The spread of the classification critically redefined ways of thinking, seeing, feeling, and acting, and therefore the structure and culture of Chinese society. This book is about the historic voyage that the classification and Chinese society traveled together—until it was on the verge of the Cultural Revolution.

My desire to reexamine the intellectual in contemporary Chinese society arose while I was a graduate student. I received encouragement and advice from Peter Evans, Thomas Gold, Neil Fligstein, and Wen-hsin Yeh. For more than two decades, Wen-hsin supported my zigzagging effort and interrogated my half-baked claims and ideas. Helen Dunstan is an exceptionally generous scholar. She read and commented on earlier versions of some of the chapters. She provided hundreds of in-depth comments on how to refine the book manuscript. Stephen A. Smith's insightful reading of an early draft of the opening chapter left me with no choice but to revise the content dramatically. Robert J. Culp read the revision and earlier drafts of chapters 3 and 5 and helped me improve the substance. Frederick Teiwes has shared his thoughts with me on how to improve the research. A global authority in the study of China's intellectuals, Timothy Cheek has been especially kind with his unflagging encouragement. Even before he invited me to spend a month at the Peter Wall Institute of Advanced Studies at the University of British Columbia during the early 2000s, he knew perfectly well that I was exploring an analytical approach different from how he and his teachers had studied the intellectual in China. Richard Madsen and another reviewer of the manuscript offered excellent advice.

I have been fortunate in getting advice and encouragement from scholars in various disciplines. Neil Diamant, Xiaomei Chen, Thomas Mullaney, Andrea Goldman, Jeffrey Wasserstrom, Allison Rottman, Bruce Haynes, John Hall, Kwai Ng, Ching Kwan Lee, Rana Mitter, Luo Suwen, Julia Strauss, Kate Lawn Chouta, Michael McQuarrie, Linus Huang, David Gundry, David Faure, Brian DeMare, Derek Herforth, Michael Schoenhals, Yiyan Wang, Edmund Fung, and the late Glen Dudbridge offered helpful suggestions. Ming-cheng Lo, Thomas Beamish, and Stephanie Mudge repeatedly asked me to rethink my assumptions and the research's significance. I am grateful to the participants in the China seminars at the University of Oxford, the University of California, Los Angeles, and the Shanghai Academy of Social Sciences. I thank the participants in the sociology seminars at the University of California, San Diego and at Nanjing University and in the cross-disciplinary workshops at Tsinghua University and Peking University. I benefited from the history seminar organized by Xu Jilin at East China Normal University. I thank the participants of "Organized Knowledge and State Socialism in Mao's China" held at the University of California, Berkeley. I enjoyed the hospitality of Jimmy Chan, Pui Shan Li, Bao Xiaoqun, and Zhao Nianquo when I was conducting research in Shanghai.

Many institutions supported the research and writing of this book. During the mid-2000s, I received a multiyear fellowship from the Chiang Ching-kuo Foundation for International Scholarly Exchange that allowed me to travel to pertinent historic sites, talk to people, and collect documents. I am grateful to the University of California, Davis, the University of Sydney, the University of Oxford, and the University of California, Berkeley for generous funding. I received assistance from the staff of the Shanghai Municipal Archives, Beijing Municipal Archives, and Xi'an Municipal Archives as well as the Shanghai Municipal Library, the history library of the Shanghai Academy of Social Sciences, the C. V. Starr Library at the University of California, Berkeley, the Menzies Library at the Australian National University, the Chinese library of the University of Sydney, the Universities Service Centre at the Chinese University of Hong Kong, and the Shields Library at the University of California, Davis. Without the generous sub-vention from the UC Davis Library, this would not have been an open access book. Ben Alexander is a wonderful copy editor. Last but not least, I thank Reed Malcolm and his staff at University of California Press. He has been very supportive of the project. He shepherded the manuscript through review and production with care and advice that exemplifies the utmost professionalism of a veteran editor.

Chapters 2 to 7 contain journal article material reprinted with permission.

Chapter 2: "Reification of the Chinese Intellectual: On the Origins of the CCP Concept of *Zhishifenzi*," *Modern China* 35, no. 6 (2009): 604–31.

Chapter 3: "Reifications of the Intellectual: Representations, Organization, and Agency in Revolutionary China," *British Journal of Sociology* 64, no. 4 (2013): 617–42, and "The Formation of 'Intellectuals' in Yan'an," in *Knowledge Acts in Modern China: Ideas, Institutions, and Identities,* ed. Robert J. Culp, Eddy U, and Wen-hsin Yeh, China Monograph Series 73 (Institute of East Asian Studies, University of Californian, Berkeley, 2016), 328–54.

Chapter 4: "The Making of Zhishifenzi: The Critical Impact of the Registration of Unemployed Intellectuals in the Early PRC," *China Quarterly* 173 (2003): 100–21.

Chapter 5: "Rise of Marxist Classes: Bureaucratic Classification and Class Formation in Early Socialist China," *European Journal of Sociology* 57, no. 1 (2016): 1–29.

Chapter 6: "Intellectuals and Alternative Socialist Paths in the Early Mao Years," *China Journal* 70 (2013): 1–23.

Chapter 7: "Third Sister Liu and the Making of the Intellectual in Socialist China," *Journal of Asian Studies* 69, no. 1 (2010): 57–83.

CCP   Chinese Communist Party
CPPCC   Chinese People's Political Consultative Conference
GMD   Guomindang (The Nationalist Party of China)
NPC   National People's Progress
PLA   People's Liberation Army
PRC   People's Republic of China
SBE   Shanghai Municipal Bureau of Education
SCHUI   Shanghai Municipal Commission for Handling Unemployed
        Intellectuals

Reexamining the Intellectual and Chinese Communism

Bian Zhongyun (1916–1966) is notable in contemporary Chinese history for a ghastly reason. On August 5, 1966, this Beijing schoolteacher, a "bourgeois intellectual" according to the increasingly belligerent ideology of the state, became one of the first of many victims beaten to death by student Red Guards during the Cultural Revolution (1966–1976). Her ordeal had started weeks before with forms of severe humiliation and violent abuse once meted out to rural landlords expropriated under Chinese Communism, the revolutionary project initiated by the Chinese Communist Party (CCP) when it was founded in the early 1920s. The torment culminated in a brutal beating that lasted between two and three hours, while onlookers were too fearful to intervene on her behalf. The irony in her murder is obvious in retrospect. Bian was an ardent supporter of Chinese Communism. She joined the party during the early 1940s while it was still waging revolution from the countryside, or daringly earlier than most others did. Upon graduating from college a few years later, she began to work full-time for the revolution. After the CCP seized power in 1949, she was assigned to teach at the girls' secondary school attached to the Beijing Normal University, a privileged appointment insofar as schoolteachers were concerned. Located less than a mile from Zhongnanhai, where Chairman Mao and other party leaders worked, the campus was attended by their daughters and those of other senior officials. Thanks to her excellent work as an educator and a party cadre, Bian was promoted repeatedly. By the late 1950s, she had become the vice principal and the party secretary of the renowned campus. She met some of the leaders and even received words of appreciation from them for educating their daughters. On the eve of her demise, however, Bian was known to her attackers, among other things, as a "vanguard of opposition to the party," a "bastard of the capitalist class," a "leader of black gangs" seeking to restore class exploitation, a "despotic dog," and a "poisonous snake," and by names circulating in the official media in support of a hunt of class enemies within state and society.[1]

To objectify, according to the *Oxford English Dictionary*, is to express something abstract in a concrete form, identify a person with a stereotype, or degrade a person or a class of people to the status of an object.[2] As Chinese Communism grew, the intellectual became extraordinarily objectified in each of these manners. The CCP leadership drew on the political thought of Marx and Lenin to identify *intellectuals* as an integral part of the class structure and the political reality of Chinese society, along with *capitalists, poor peasants,* and other social categories. The leadership broadcast what it considered to be the class characteristics of intellectuals beneficial as well as harmful to the revolutionary project, or their previously acquired "petty-bourgeois" or "bourgeois" approaches or attitudes toward life. Through a myriad of activities in multiple areas of revolution and governance (such as propaganda, political training, economic reorganization, and workplace surveillance), the party turned notable as well as ordinary people into locally and even nationally recognized "intellectuals." The affected, who were then used and abused in particular ways, included party leaders and state officials, scientists and artists, office workers and industrial technicians, military officers, college students, housewives, former workers, and others. Like Bian, some of them did not survive the objectification of the intellectual under Chinese Communism.

Even more remarkable is how rapidly the objectification of the intellectual spread across China after the 1949 revolution. *Zhishifenzi,* the Chinese equivalent of "intellectuals," was a neologism of the early twentieth century with strong foreign roots. For more than two decades after its appearance, the term remained as one of many expressions used within literary and political circles to refer to educated persons or the educated population.[3] The debate on the intellectual within those circles was not unlike what occurred then and later in other societies, as the relatively small number of interlocutors focused on defining what intellectuals were and their moral and political responsibilities to the nation. Shortly after the revolution, however, residents in urban areas could generally identify intellectuals within the local population with little difficulty, before such subjects were virtually locatable everywhere across the nation. Otherwise perfectly ordinary people considered themselves intellectuals and supported, accepted, or challenged official evaluations of their class characteristics. How did "intellectuals" evolve from an obscure expression to a term for readily identifiable subjects? How did individuals and organizations handle this objectification of the intellectual? What was the impact of the objectification on Chinese Communism?

To address these influential yet underexamined changes in Chinese society, this book begins with an unconventional conception of the intellectual—that is, as a classification of people used across different cultures since the late nineteenth century for political control, social analysis, moral intervention, status struggle, or other purposes. Research has typically defined intellectuals as "persons with advanced educations, producers or transmitters of culture or ideas, or members of either category who engage in public issues."[4] The definitions have anchored insightful studies of the impact of such people on revolution, modernization, democratization, and other historic processes. Within research on twentieth-century communisms, however, the use of the definitions has obscured what, precisely, was distinct about the intellectual under such systems of rule. For the communist regimes constituted a rare breed in global political history that relied on Marxian thought to define, identify, and govern individuals and populations formally as "intellectuals." In the epigraph of this book, Michel Foucault speaks of the intellectual as a fictional yet recognizable person as well as raw material for orchestrating punishment and assaults. He asks us to reconsider what the intellectual is. He probably had in mind the ferociousness with which "intellectuals" were attacked during the Cultural Revolution, if not also the widespread denunciation, reeducation, and persecution of those identified as such under the Soviet Union and elsewhere.[5] This book takes Foucault's crisp insight on the intellectual to an analytically logical conclusion, one that recounts the rise of the classification under Chinese Communism and how the process devolved toward fatal outcomes on a mass scale.

This book is therefore about social classification and its consequences under Chinese Communism. How the CCP or other communist regimes categorized individuals, families, and occupations based on Marx's understanding of class struggle, or established what Christopher Browning and Lewis Siegelbaum call "frameworks for social engineering," has long invited analysis of the dynamics.[6] Overall, the studies focus on what I call conception, administration, reorganization, and negotiation, or more concretely the origins and meanings of the classifications, the execution of classification campaigns, the reconfiguration of local society, and the tactics and strategies used by individuals to deal with their own classification and those of others.[7] I extend this analytical tradition in two distinct directions. First, this book uses a diachronic study that involves multiple sites as a method to illustrate the rise of the intellectual as a classification of people under Chinese Communism, or how ordinary people were objectified as "intellectuals." That is, I treat the study of the intellectual as the study of social classification, because little is known about how the CCP or other regimes deployed this central marker in Marxian ideology in their reclassification of the general population when compared with "landlord," "rich peasant," or other labels. Second, this book describes the impact of the party's use of the intellectual classification on Chinese Communism, that is, the institutions and practices as well as outlooks and feelings that flourished. I am interested in how the classification's deployment affected social and political life, similar to what others have illustrated with respect to the spread of "capitalist" and other labels under communist regimes. From the beginning to the end of Chinese Communism, the intellectual was arguably the most important, most ambiguous, and thus most intriguing classification adopted by the party to reinterpret, reorganize, and reinvent China.

The following section explains the analytical framework that I have assembled to examine anew the relations between the intellectual and Chinese Communism. I rely on insights from studies of social classification, including those related to communist societies. Because the ruling regimes of such societies can be "best construed as mutations of a single genus" formed on the basis of Marxian ideology,[8] the framework is appropriate for exploring the intellectual classification under other communist systems, although their political and other characteristics must be taken into account. Readers who wish to skip specialized debates on classification and communism are welcome to skip the discussion. I then summarize the central argument of this book, namely that the intellectual and Chinese Communism were mutually constitutive. As the revolutionary project expanded, a mixture of discursive, organizational, and interpersonal practice transformed the intellectual into a major classification of people. As the number of "intellectuals" multiplied under the project, top-down programs and measures designed to address their conflicting presence flourished and shaped official governance, workplace structures, social relations, and individual consciousness. The final section explains my strategies for investigating this interlocking development of the intellectual and Chinese Communism. I discuss the themes and arguments of the following chapters and stress that an abundance of events, organizations, and people as well as ideas, interests, and motives were involved in what was a multilayered and contentious process.

AN INSTITUTIONAL-CONSTRUCTIVIST APPROACH

Studies of the intellectual and Chinese Communism, a major subfield of research on Chinese society, tend to treat their relations primarily as being between people and regime. Three lines of inquiry are especially prominent. On the level of elite politics, emphasis is given either to how CCP leaders as intellectuals developed and promoted Chinese Communism or challenged its direction, or to the political, ideological, and aesthetic choices the leaders made at various junctures of the revolutionary project. In terms of organization, the emphasis is on how the party mobilized and dominated writers, scientists, and others *qua* intellectuals, using propaganda, privilege, and punishment to further revolutionary goals. With respect to political reactions, the accounts have described active support of the party as well as calculated accommodation, public dissent, and other behavior on the part of intellectuals and have traced these responses to Confucian tradition, professional ethics, contemporaneous social movements, and other sources. Such scholarship furnishes an invaluable window into Chinese Communism through illuminating ideas and controversies, rivalries and alliances, institutions and practices, and public and private experiences that made up the project.[9] Like the broader interdisciplinary literature on intellectuals, however, the accounts as a whole portray their central subject as little more than a population of relatively educated people.

My approach to reexamining the intellectual and Chinese Communism is built upon a distinct tradition of social inquiry that runs from French sociologist Emile Durkheim to Michel Foucault and Pierre Bourdieu and, more broadly, to the study of racial, ethnic, and gender classification across sociology, history, and other disciplines. Accounts in this tradition purposefully refrain from using official, folk, or other preexisting conceptions of groups or peoples as the analytical point of departure. The studies, instead, focus on the relations of power and the work of classification underlying the shared belief that a certain group exists due to its own properties and on why a particular system of partitioning and grasping the social world is adopted in the first place. Some of the accounts document resultant changes in the values, interests, and behavior of individuals or organizations. The scholarship reveals social structures, relations, and practices otherwise unaccounted for and analyzes how they serve to produce or reproduce the social order.[10] Historian Sheila Fitzpatrick has advanced this analytical tradition in the study of twentieth-century communisms as much as anyone else, through her research on the rise of categories of people based on Marxian ideology (e.g., rich peasants and petty bourgeoisie) in Lenin's and Stalin's Russia as "a matter of classification" orchestrated by the state, and on "self-reinventions" as individuals coped with unprecedented patterns of risk and opportunity.[11]

A small number of studies have highlighted the intellectual as a social classification. Historians have recovered dynamics that engendered the classification in France during the 1890s, or amid the Dreyfus affair regarding whether a Jewish army captain had been wrongly convicted of treason. Although the term *intellectuel* antedated the affair, it only entered into common usage then as a classification of people. Novelists, artists, lawyers, scientists, politicians, and students used the term to refer to themselves or to insult others. They supported their views by building upon entrenched assumptions about social differences and by probing or alluding to heated political issues. State support of higher education, freedom of the press, and print capitalism sustained a network of journals and salons that served to introduce the classification to a broad audience, along with intense arguments about French society. As a result, the classification acquired meanings and symbolisms that had little to do with issues of fairness and justice in the legal system. The narratives and imageries associated with the intellectual included incorruptible masculinity, hysterical femininity, and subhuman personality as well as poignant references to declining national health, military failure, crowd psychology, and social disorder.[12] A new social type, however inchoate its features were, entered the French popular consciousness. Other scholars have examined the intellectual in Europe, Russia, and elsewhere as a form of "self-definitions,"[13] a "cultural myth,"[14] "a relationship of attribution,"[15] and "a weapon in the intellectual field,"[16] or a social classification for establishing identity, claiming difference, gaining authority, or achieving other purposes.

In this book I regard the intellectual as a classification of people deployed by the CCP for the purposes of remaking Chinese society, a marker of the class location of the individual based on the Marxian ideology of the party. I define *institutions* broadly as rules and regulations as well as regular and regulated practices found under Chinese Communism. This is necessary for capturing the wide range of patterned activities that served to normalize the classification while being affected by its normalization. Examples of the institutions were top-level announcements and instructions, state policies and programs, official reports and statistics, literary works and cinematic productions, and recurring patterns of social association and individual conduct. In other words, the first half of my analytical approach emphasizes the institutions of classification that objectified the intellectual and their institutional consequences for Chinese Communism. In comparison, the constructivist half of my approach highlights the values, ideas, and meanings as well as the symbolisms and boundaries associated with the intellectual classification. Where did they come from and how did they change across time and space? How did they inform the use of the classification? I also draw attention to the thoughts, interests, and calculations of individuals and organizations as they responded to the objectification of the intellectual, or the impact of those views on the revolutionary project. In short, the second half of my approach takes the political, moral, and demographic interpretations of the intellectual and their implications as an object of analysis.

My analytical approach is therefore set up to address both the objective and subjective dimensions of the objectification of the intellectual under Chinese Communism. This objectification was part of the reordering of Chinese society by the CCP elites according to their images, or their progressive and spectacular reduction of the massive population of an industrializing society into a relatively small number of social categories based on Marxian thought. The objectification presupposed, as well as engendered, decisive changes in social structures, dispositions, and behavior. More concretely, my investigation proceeds along three distinct axes: official representation of the intellectual, local identification of the subject, and informal negotiation of the classification. There are three reasons behind these choices. First, official representation, local identification, and informal negotiation are major themes in the research on social classification; they have been shown to be vital to understanding this ubiquitous process. Second, research on social classification under communist rule has spotlighted each of the activities when illustrating the local formation of landlords and other Marxian categories of people. Third, existing studies of the intellectual and Chinese Communism have largely bracketed these activities from analysis, through treating the intellectual as one or another type of person.

Official Representation of the Intellectual

Representation, as Stuart Hall has noted, is the use of "signs and symbols" to "stand for" concepts, ideas, and feelings, a central process in the production and reproduction of shared understandings.[17] Political regimes and other establishments (e.g., churches, universities, professional associations), Pierre Bourdieu indicates, commonly exploit their legitimacy, authority, and resources to represent people, things, and events—on behalf of their own dominance. Their representations influence the way people see, think, feel, and act, partly because of the already accepted and unequal "relations of meaning and communication" between the establishments and those whom they govern, lead, or serve.[18] Bourdieu calls this "power of constructing reality" held by the establishments "symbolic power,"[19] the exercise of which can "make appear as natural, inevitable, and thus apolitical, that which is a product of historical struggle and human invention."[20] The systems of social classification of the establishments signal how they assign attributes and differences to people and organizations, allocate roles and authority, and develop methods of governance. The classifications and their underlying values and meanings tend to extend across textual, visual, oral, architectural, and other substrates. Bourdieu stresses that no establishment, however organized or admired, has complete control over the reception of its representations or over how society is imagined or acted upon. To have the accounts or classifications accepted as true or valid, they must be "backed up by the order of things,"[21] that is, they must reflect existing viewpoints or resonate with social conditions already experienced to be real or accurate. To paraphrase Bourdieu, representations alone do not produce shared beliefs; any agreement with the representations happens within the relations between those who exercise symbolic power and those who submit to it.[22]

From the beginning, representations of Chinese society by the CCP were as challenging as they were necessary to the development of Chinese Communism. Not only was the party's vision of remaking China based on Marxism, a foreign ideology that claims society is composed of antagonistic classes of people; the vision also turned the contemporary understanding of status and prestige upside down. The party leadership considered those industrial workers and other manual laborers who were disadvantaged, deprived, and therefore often disparaged to be the most noble and valuable section of the Chinese population. Research has addressed how the CCP discourse of class struggle spread, through stressing the leadership's political, literary, and aesthetic ingenuity in combining history with ideology, narrative with emotion, and socialist ideals with traditional thought.[23] The scholarship delves into the broader context under which the representations spread, or the twentieth-century ecology of war and revolution that nurtured Chinese Communism,[24] as well as how the party used theater, cinema, and other channels to promote its views.[25] Building on these works, the first layer of my analysis focuses on what I call the methods, milieux, and mechanisms of the CCP's representation of the intellectual. How did the party elites combine historical,

cultural, and other symbolic resources with Marxist theory to define and redefine the intellectual? How did existing political and social conditions influence
the conceptions? And how did the party deploy offices and people and utilize the
media and other channels to publicize its understanding of the subject?

In other words, I illustrate how the CCP integrated words and things to represent the intellectual, or the tactics of symbolic power deployed by the party. In
her book on the Chinese socialist revolution, Elizabeth Perry suggests that *cultural positioning* conducted by the party leaders, or their "strategic deployment of a
range of symbolic resources (religion, ritual, rhetoric, dress, drama, art, and so on)
for purposes of political persuasion," was critical to the uprising's success.[26] From
early on, the leaders skillfully appropriated traditional and other values, mores,
and practices as means to rally support from underprivileged and other populations. This book extends the investigation of cultural positioning of the CCP elites
to their representations of the intellectual, or how they synthesized intellectual
assumptions, political sentiments, and social analyses as well as mobilized institutions and organizations to promote a Marxian view of the subject. The fact that
the party ultimately succeeded in constituting people who occupied distant social
spaces, or who had little similarity or interaction with one another, as comparable
subjects identified locally and nationally as intellectuals warrants an examination
of the role of official representation in this historic achievement.

Local Identification of the Subject

By local identification, I mean what Rogers Brubaker and Frederick Cooper call
external identification, or "the formalized, codified, and objectified system of categorization" developed by powerful establishments for governance or management
purposes.[27] Research has made great strides during the recent decades in illustrating the workings of local identification, which is vital to any influential system of
social classification. Local identification is often led by bureaucratic organizations
with full-time officials, experts, and staff. These persons conduct documentation, assessment, and other investigative tasks. They separate otherwise continu-
ous populations into discrete social categories, through registration, certification,
enrollment, or other acts of differentiation.[28] Such work of bureaucracy supports
division of labor, partition of space, allocation of privilege, imposition of restrictions, and other practices that reinforce recognition of the delineated categories. To
use a pair of well-known concepts, authoritative establishments often successfully
convert the *symbolic boundaries* that they use to divide a population conceptually
into various sections to readily perceptible *social boundaries* that separate those
sections in everyday life.[29] Sooner or later, the scholarship indicates, members of
the various sections thus produced will develop values, interests, and habits corresponding to their unequal experiences because of the inequality enforced by the
establishments. Such thinking and behavior will in turn reinforce the prescribed
divisions further.[30]

Chinese Communism ultimately evolved into a nationwide project of local identification: the CCP turned virtually everyone into a legible subject based on Marxian thought. Research has stressed this process and its consequences. During land reform campaigns, official documentation of property ownership and family connections, public announcements of land partition, and carefully planned spectacles of class struggle were channels through which party cadres and villagers learned the assigned class and political statuses of families and individuals. The emergence of "landlords" and other visible categories of people led to new forms of structure, behavior, and mentality that reinforced the introduced taxonomy, for example, the formation of "poor peasant associations" and the removal from party cells of those whom the local authorities regarded as undesirable elements.[31] Yet other than the broad picture of its classification schemes, exactly how the party turned city and town residents into identifiable class subjects remains murky. At the same time, research has alluded to institutional changes that both presupposed and reinforced the differentiation of such populations into capitalists, workers, and other Marxian categories, changes such as the expropriation of private enterprises, class-based enrollment in colleges, punishment of "counterrevolutionaries," and attitudinal changes in the matters of spousal selection and social association.[32] Specific events, for instance what the party called the thought reform of intellectuals, could not but lead to local identification of such subjects.[33]

The second layer of my analysis highlights the mechanisms and outcomes of local identification of "intellectuals" under the CCP. Compared to the landlord and other classifications of the party, the intellectual was conceptually elastic. The leadership frequently noted that intellectuals were part of the petty bourgeoisie, whose members focused on their own achievement and the welfare of their family. It stated that some intellectuals embraced the values and ideas of the exploiting classes, others endured hardships identical to those suffered by workers, and a small number were pioneers in advancing Chinese Communism. The classification, furthermore, was deployed across urban and rural areas, along the occupational hierarchy, and inside and outside the party. What were the official measures, procedures, and arrangements that served to distinguish "intellectuals" from other kinds of class subjects? Who were the people identified as intellectuals, and what did they have in common? What were the local practices and conditions that reinforced the local identification of the subjects? In short, I illustrate how the CCP representation of the intellectual was translated into formal methods of counting and accounting as well as informal institutions of categorization, or local instruments that produced and reproduced visible "intellectuals."

Informal Negotiation of the Classification

In their seminal work on social classification, Geoffrey Bowker and Susan Leigh Star state that no system of categorization, however established or elaborate, provides "total coverage of the world it describes."[34] Spaces and crevices of ambiguity

and indeterminacy are inevitable for conceptual, organizational, and other reasons. This is especially true with the categorization of people. Individuals pos-
sess many attributes as well as change or grow, and hence do not always fit into
predefined systems of classification. Standards and criteria of classification often
involve ambiguities and even contradictions and are periodically revised by the
authorities. Frontline agents of classification do not interpret or apply the standards or criteria uniformly, due to differences in their training, interests, and other
factors. The agents work around, alter, or ignore guidelines and even introduce
their own measurements. As a result, they sometimes classify people with similar
characteristics differently and sometimes place those with different traits in the
same category. Furthermore, as Brubaker and his colleagues have observed, "the
categorized themselves are chronic categorizers."[35] Individuals usually recognize
the potential consequences of classification for their own well-being and those of
others. They deploy "self-interested strategies of symbolic manipulation" to influence how they are categorized.[36] They use the classifications to characterize and
comprehend friends, colleagues, and others in ways that reproduce, revise, or contest official use of the markers. In practice, "classification systems from different
worlds meet, adjust, fracture, or merge."[37]

Research on Chinese Communism has highlighted the variability, capricious-
ness, and individual manipulation of official classification. In a study of land reform
in a village, Edward Friedman and his colleagues found that assignment of class
labels to families and individuals occurred three separate times because of policy
change as well as unevenly across the area. Official reliance on local consultation
and memory and the presence of favoritism and political strife engendered challenges to the assignments, as they often contradicted local understandings of fairness and justice.[38] Xiaojun Zhang discovered in his research on another village that
party cadres sometimes omitted the distinction between two official markers, and
sometimes created their own labels to fit their understanding of the class location
of the individual.[39] Evidence is available on self-reinventions as means of coping
with safety, career, and other concerns. Physical relocation, job change, alteration
of appearance, concealment of background, self-criticism, and vocal cooperation
were common, though not foolproof, tactics to fend off onerous labels.[40] Ip and
Perry have shown separately that even CCP leaders were not immune to the implications of the Marxian classifications that they had introduced. These otherwise
privileged men employed physical, narrative, and other strategies to craft images
conducive to the maintenance of their own authority within what they proclaimed
to be a proletarian revolution.[41]

My third layer of analysis focuses on the myriad ways in which CCP leaders
and cadres as well as ordinary people negotiated the intellectual classification.
Under Chinese Communism, every relatively educated person confronted a pre-
dicament at some point in a typical day because of the meanings and symbolisms
that the party inscribed upon the intellectual and other markers in its schema

of classes—or how to navigate this fateful grid of classification given their own background and the social location they occupied. On the one hand, I emphasize the conceptual ambiguities embedded in the CCP's understanding of the intellectual and challenges associated with the official identification of the subject, or gaps and pathways in which the affected persons could navigate. On the other hand, I highlight the tactics and strategies used by these individuals to deal with what they saw as risks and opportunities. Put differently, existing accounts on how party leaders, professors, artists, and others qua intellectuals supported, accepted, or resisted Chinese Communism have captured merely a small slice of their conduct of political negotiation, which quickly became an everyday performance of a class or a political identity vital to achieving authority, mobility, security, or other purposes valued by the individual.

In a nutshell, my institutional-constructivist approach brings together two main threads of research on Chinese Communism. Studies of intellectuals have illustrated the behavior of writers, schoolteachers, and others, but not how they were incorporated into the intellectual category of the party. Accounts of social classification have described dynamics surrounding the local appearance of landlords, counterrevolutionaries, and other subjects, but not of intellectuals. My synthesis stresses the institutions that objectified the intellectual and ways of seeing, thinking, feeling, and acting that followed. The approach promises an original account of the intellectual and Chinese Communism as well as a deepened understanding of the CCP's remaking of China.

THE ARGUMENT

This book contends that the intellectual and Chinese Communism were mutually constitutive. That is, the revolutionary project turned the intellectual into a primary classification of people as much as its deployment shaped how the project was organized and hence experienced. To put this in even stronger terms, one cannot fully understand either Chinese Communism or the intellectual without understanding their impact on each other. Entirely intertwined were their origins, extension, and even decline. This book hence contains two analytical movements, as it were. The first movement illustrates how the revolutionary project produced and altered the meanings, symbolisms, and boundaries that constituted the classification as well as its extension to various levels of Chinese society. The other movement describes how the deployment of the classification transformed authority relations, organizational structures, social identities, and individual conduct, or the impact of the objectification of the intellectual on Chinese Communism.

Reinterpreting the intellectual

My account begins with the May Fourth movement of the early 1920s, the heady days in Chinese politics when a variety of political activists grappled with foreign encroachment, warlord rule, mass poverty, and other national crises. The term *zhishifenzi* had yet to enter political debate, let alone the vernacular. The leadership of the newly founded CCP would skillfully recombine assumptions, arguments, and sentiments from three influential discourses to support its interpretation of the intellectual. The first of these discourses was the traditional understanding of social hierarchy, which saw the level of education and type of vocation of the individual as natural bases of social division. The second discourse was the heated contemporary debate on reform and revolution, which promoted the political participation of educated people but blamed their self-centeredness, apathy, and cowardice for the crises mentioned above. The third of those discourses was the spreading Marxist-Leninist view of class struggle, which suggested that scientists, accountants, technicians, and other white-collar or skilled personnel constituted a population of intellectuals between the exploiting and the exploited classes in modern societies. Once *zhishifenzi* entered the CCP lexicon, possession of formal learning, a self-centered personality, and resistance to revolutionary change became core meanings of the term. Together with "capitalist," "landlord," and other markers, the intellectual became a major component of the Marxian system of social classification of the party.

As Chinese Communism expanded, the organizational programs and measures of the CCP extended the intellectual classification to the local level, while newspapers, meetings, reports, and other events and arrangements organized by the party promoted its interpretation of China's class structure. Two types of programs and measures, in particular, penetrated a widening sphere of activities even as the leadership's understanding of "intellectuals" fluctuated. The first type was aimed at harnessing the knowledge and skills of these persons for economic development, educational growth, political propaganda, and other purposes of organization. The other type sought to curb the harmful influence of these individuals on the revolutionary project or rein in their "petty-bourgeois" and "bourgeois" approaches to life and politics. The programs and measures involved many kinds of bureaucratic routines with classification effects, such as promulgation of instructions and regulations, verification of qualifications, recruitment and appointment, assignment of responsibilities, stipulation of rights and privileges, political reeducation, investigation and supervision, punishment, and compilation of reports. The activities produced an increasingly dense web of texts, signs, and cues that promoted the intellectual as a classification of people, on top of the impact of official propaganda. In other words, the discourse and practice generated meanings and boundaries that indicated to party cadres and ordinary people alike who the intellectuals were in Chinese society and their supposed beliefs, habits, and dispositions.

Like landlords and other official categories of people that appeared under Chinese Communism, the population of intellectuals thus formed had persistently fuzzy boundaries. Conceptually, the intellectual was but one of the classifications deployed by the CCP to pinpoint the location of the individual in a predefined social order. Some of those classifiable as intellectuals were identifiable, too, as other types of class subject (e.g., landlords or workers). How the party defined the intellectual, moreover, changed over time. Politically, the classification was a tool of domination from the beginning. Educated party leaders and cadres exploited their revolutionary authority to promote and even consecrate themselves as part of the working class and cast less powerful persons as unreliable intellectuals. In this regard, CCP leaders differed from Marx, Lenin, and other leaders of communist movements who had fewer reservations in seeing themselves as revolutionaries as well as intellectuals.[42] Organizationally, the party's agenda of harnessing the knowledge and skills of intellectuals and guarding against their negative influence constantly extended the classification to otherwise unaffected populations. In the end, every relatively educated person was classifiable as an intellectual.

A sea change of individual behavior further destabilized the boundaries of the population of intellectuals that emerged under Chinese Communism. For safety, career, or other reasons, many of those affected by the intellectual classification actively negotiated their social identity. They changed jobs, concocted stories, manipulated rules, and acted differently to cope with the positive and negative implications of the classification. They presented themselves as intellectuals with a particular political leaning or as another kind of class subject altogether, especially in front of the party authorities. The tactics and strategies of these persons varied with their backgrounds, situations, and goals, and so did the outcomes. Some benefited from the positive meanings of the classification and largely escaped the harm of the negatives ones. Some admitted to being intellectuals but found ways to protect and even improve their lives and livelihoods. Some escaped the classification by playing up their other qualifications or backgrounds. Some straddled between classifications (e.g., "intellectual" and "worker") and used each to their advantage. Some went from intellectuals to counterrevolutionaries and endured labor or prison sentences. Some, like Bian Zhongyun, lost their lives.

Reexamining Chinese Communism

If the first analytical movement of this book reveals the ontological transformation of the intellectual from a little-known expression adopted by the CCP to a primary social identity of many under the People's Republic of China (PRC), the second movement shows how the metamorphosis affected the collective and individual experience of Chinese Communism. To be sure, the party's deployment of "capitalist," "landlord," and other classifications from the same Marxian analysis of China led to organizational endeavors that altered life dramatically, such as the nationalization of industry after the 1949 revolution as well as rural land reform and campaigns against "counterrevolutionaries." Yet, the deployment of the intellectual classification was distinct on three registers. Politically, the leadership regarded intellectuals as class subjects par excellence that were both assets and liabilities of the revolutionary project, even though official assessment of this population fluctuated periodically. Spatially, the leadership believed that intellectuals existed throughout state and society and held influential positions across industrial production, scientific research, secondary education, popular entertainment, and, more generally, the entire system of production and reproduction. Organizationally, the leadership was determined to develop China economically and therefore could not remove these persons completely from their posts regardless of their real or imagined threats to the project, unlike how the party dispensed with the "capitalists" or "landlords." In brief, once the party defined professors, factory managers, journalists, and others as intellectuals, their incorporation into Chinese Communism became a persistent challenge.

The CCP's efforts to harness the rational, constructive, and essential knowledge and expertise of "intellectuals" and to defend against their corruptive, contagious, and endless threats became a principal raison d'être of Chinese Communism. However the party leadership represented intellectuals—as utterly incorrigible, ideologically rectifiable, or, most of the time, somewhere in between—corresponding revolutionary paradigms, policies, and programs followed. Indeed, every major shift of the direction of the revolutionary project came after a top-down reinterpretation of the intellectual or a revision of the meanings and symbolisms that the leadership inscribed upon the classification. The turn from urban revolution to rural insurgency during the late 1920s captured a powerful rejection of the previous view that intellectuals were critical to the success of Chinese Communism. In contrast, the Yan'an phase (1937–1948) of the project epitomized the leadership's determination to involve as well as reeducate such people. After 1949, the leadership turned the Yan'an approach to intellectuals into a foundation for building a socialist and industrialized China. Before the Great Leap Forward of the late 1950s, the leadership had called into question again the value of intellectuals to the revolutionary project. Official denunciations of such subjects intensified further before the Cultural Revolution scorched the nation.

More concretely, once the intellectual emerged as a classification of people of the CCP, the imagined subject became a fulcrum of revolutionary practice, a basis on which the symbolic power and administrative capability of the party developed. On the ideological front, political rhetoric, narratives, and theories based on Marxist thought flourished. The party elites promoted the political and moral superiority of Chinese Communism and of themselves by tirelessly discrediting worldviews and ideas they attributed to "intellectuals" as well as the lifestyles and behavior of such persons. Their critiques took on traditional philosophies and all kinds of contemporary political thought (e.g., constitutionalism, social democracy, anarchism) and political and organizational practices traceable to these ideas. The critiques also targeted what Italian Marxist Antonio Gramsci called "common sense," or popular values and beliefs considered antithetical to the socialist revolution.[43] On the organizational front, an ever-growing system of governing approaches and programs as well as administrative measures and routines appeared, because of the constant effort of the elites to dictate the involve-ment of "intellectuals" in the revolutionary project. A variety of tasks multiplied wherever such subjects were located, especially those related to classification (e.g., documentation, investigation, identification), mobilization (e.g., propaganda, meetings, networking), reeducation (e.g., study class, self-criticism, evaluation), and supervision (e.g., appointment, reporting, discipline).

The extent to which the CCP deployment of the intellectual classification engen-dered intense ideological and organizational activities is revealed fully in three intertwined institutions that emerged before the party seized power and thrived afterward: workplace management by party cadres, ideological reeducation, and mass surveillance. To the party leadership, the knowledge and skills possessed by intellectuals and their enviable status and prestige enabled them to wield influence disproportionate to the size of their population, not to mention provide support to the exploiting classes and their political representatives. The advantages also permitted the intellectuals to move across sectors and space with relative ease, and to articulate defense of their beliefs and even challenge the party's views, policies, and measures. Wherever intellectuals clustered under Chinese Communism (e.g., schools, publishing houses, research institutes), management by trained party cad-res was considered vital to maintaining official control and tackling any sabotage or subversion of the project. Ideological reeducation emerged as indispensable to curbing the negative influence of the "petty-bourgeois" and "bourgeois" habits and dispositions of intellectuals. And mass surveillance was ultimately adopted, because meticulous investigation, observation, and documentation would reveal the strengths and weaknesses of these persons and thus how each one of them should be incorporated into the project. Each of the institutions produced pro-cedures, processes, and posts that shaped authority structures and organizational behavior and therefore life under Chinese Communism. Each served to reproduce a ruling population of party cadres and a dominated population of intellectuals, notwithstanding the fuzzy boundaries between these two types of people.

The CCP deployment of the intellectual classification had another major impact on Chinese Communism: it supplied heretofore unavailable rationales and vocabulary for those who otherwise occupied different social and physical space (e.g., reputed professors, regional officials, company clerks, college students, local artists) to develop oppositional collective identities. The ideological, organiza-tional, and interpersonal minefields that these persons were forced to navigate, or their shared experience of how the party defined, degraded, and dominated them, created "an objective potentiality of unity."[44] They interpreted their subjugation with various kinds of political thinking, besides the values and ideas promoted by the party. Some challenged the conduct of the party and its cadres and even the direction of the revolutionary project. However short-lived or disparate were the protests and however tragic the results, the complaints and grievances as well as the proposals and suggestions had a potential audience as broad and dispersed as the extent to which the party had constructed the category of intellectuals. In other words, the success of Chinese Communism transformed the treacherous intellectuals initially prowling on paper to an ever-growing population of real and potential adversaries of the project. For the party elites, the project had to be reconstituted repeatedly to stamp out the perfidy. The upheavals of Chinese Communism were inseparable from its objectification of the intellectual.

OVERVIEW OF THE BOOK

This book examines the mutual constitution of the intellectual and Chinese Communism from the early 1920s to the end of 1964, that is, from the time right after the CCP's founding when the classification was about to appear to the period shortly before the Cultural Revolution became the official priority of the revolutionary project. Even with these boundaries, it is impossible to produce any exhaustive account of the dynamics, which progressively spread across virtually every aspect of political and social life. The following chapters feature critical pathways and episodes for grasping how the intellectual was objectified and the consequences. This alone requires a multipronged journey that inspects inter alia political discourses, revolutionary strategies, rural activities, work arrangements, state registrations, organized protests, cinematic productions, and individual conduct, thus an analysis that reveals the multiplicity of the elements underlying the objectification as well as the breadth and depth of its impact. My account is based on many kinds of empirical material, including official declarations of the CCP and speeches of its leaders; policy statements, directives, reports, and statistics from various offices under the party; articles from newspapers, magazines, and specialized journals; films and plays; personal testimonies and biographies; and existing scholarly analyses. If the resulting picture makes sense, it is not because the thousands of pieces of evidence are uniformly accurate or reliable, as they were originally gathered or interpreted by a variety of people under different and sometimes unknown circumstances. Rather, it is because the gestalt recovers a historic feature of Chinese Communism, the objectification of the intellectual, the consequences of which for Chinese politics, society, and culture are still visible today, almost forty years after the project started to decline.

Put another way, this book illuminates the politics, policies, and practices that preceded the abuses during the Cultural Revolution against those who were decried as "bourgeois intellectuals" and against those among them who had allegedly morphed into enemies of the people. How that mass movement extended the objectification of the intellectual, how the objectification continued to affect the constitution of Chinese Communism, and how the classification and the project evolved after the Cultural Revolution deserve a separate study.

Two additional caveats before we move on. First, when *the intellectual* or *intellectuals* appear in this book, they do not denote any kind of persons that I have in mind. The appearances, instead, demonstrate that the terms have been used in multiple ways by the CCP, party authorities, and others and that they have flexible political, moral, and demographic meanings tied to the politics, interests, and circumstances in question. Second, my argument that the intellectual and Chinese Communism were mutually constitutive does not imply that their impact on each another was uniform across space, especially after the CCP gained sovereign control over China. Not only did the objectification of the intellectual vary spatially, but individuals and organizations responded to the objectification with different combinations of what symbolic and material resources they could muster. In other words, a tapestry of discourse and practice made up the relations between the classification and the project.

The next chapter describes the origins of the term *zhishifenzi* and its appropriation by early CCP elites as a classification of people, or "a revolution in the order of words" that preceded "revolutions in the order of things."[45] My focus is on a poignant debate about "the intellectual class" (*zhishi jieji*) that permeated urban political and literary circles during the early 1920s, at the height of the iconoclasm of the May Fourth movement, which redefined the relations of Chinese society with tradition and knowledge and hence politics and revolution. The debate centered on an alleged lack of political courage and moral integrity of members of the intellectual class, and its need to overcome such weaknesses if China was to be saved from foreign occupation, economic backwardness, and other crises. The ontological presuppositions, ethical assessments, and political sentiments underlying the powerful condemnations of the intellectual class would become foundations on which the CCP elites conceptualized the intellectual. I show that after the Communist International sponsored by the Soviet Union intervened in the building of the party in China, party leaders, who had participated in the debate and considered themselves part of the intellectual class, reinterpreted their relations to this population with a Marxian analysis. The intellectual class reappeared as the main ideological enemy of Chinese Communism, while the leaders began to depict themselves as proletarian revolutionaries. The leaders therefore created an insurmountable division under the project, which they believed reflected their relations to other educated people in Chinese society. Soon to be labeled "intellectuals," these people would become the Other, and thus threats to Chinese Communism.

Chapter 3 takes up another critical juncture in the mutual constitution of the intellectual and Chinese Communism, The setting is Yan'an, the rural town in northwestern China in which Mao and others set up the headquarters of the CCP during the late 1930s, and from which the party would wage its eventually successful takeover of China. Armed with the modified view that intellectuals, though untrustworthy, were vital to the revolutionary project because of their possession of knowledge and skills, the leadership recruited a heterogeneous population of educated people to the remote town. Ensuing establishment of organizations, allocation of responsibilities, and division of space produced and reproduced social boundaries that bolstered the official representation of the newcomers as a distinct population of "intellectuals." Workplace management by party cadres, ideological reeducation, and mass surveillance intensified and reinforced the portrayal of these intellectuals as inferior class subjects. I stress that negotiations of the intellectual classification flourished. Educated party leaders and cadres, not to mention the newcomers, altered their conduct and appearance to minimize real or potential stigmatization. Their responses not only strengthened the leadership's critical representation of intellectuals, but also muddied the boundaries of this objectified category of people.

In chapter 4 I illustrate the spread of the intellectual classification in post-revolutionary Shanghai and the concurrent extension of the symbolic power and administrative capacity of the newly found socialist state. My focus is an early 1950s official drive to register "unemployed intellectuals." The state wanted to reduce unemployment through harnessing unused knowledge and skills for national reconstruction purposes. The registration drive involved the establishment of procedures and mechanisms for identifying candidates; the formation of local offices and training of resident teams for promotional, documentation, and other tasks; and the mobilization of hundreds of trade and other associations for certification assistance, as well as placement efforts. The event became a collective exercise through which the state educated officials and ordinary people alike about its Marxian understanding of the intellectual and how to use the classification in everyday life. Meanwhile, recent discriminatory recruitments and dismissals by the state and other job losses pushed former government officials and military officers, as well as others with dubious records from the official perspective, to sign up as unemployed intellectuals in large numbers, sometimes even through fraudulent means. As the drive proceeded, official surveillance intensified within the city and across the establishments required to offer work or training to unemployed intellectuals. For the state, the registration became another instance that confirmed intellectuals as being unreliable subjects when it came to advancing Chinese Communism.

Chapter 5 focuses on the central role that the postrevolutionary workplace played in objectifying the intellectual and the kinds of social relations and organizational culture that arose as a result. The locus of analysis is the secondary education profession in Shanghai, a sector officially declared to be filled with unreliable intellectuals. Progressively intense domination of the sector by CCP cadres, through their official assignment to authoritative positions, created an abundance of textual, verbal, and physical cues that cast the faculty and staff precisely as such subjects. The domination enabled the state to collect sufficient information to distinguish each of the "intellectuals" as a class subject with particular habits and dispositions as well as separate them into different subtypes for political and professional purposes. I stress that the cadres, most of whom were educated and thus had been treated by colleagues and superiors as intellectuals, exploited their authority to promote themselves as proletarian revolutionaries. They shifted the moral burden that they had carried under Chinese Communism to those whom they now ruled. Their treatment of ordinary faculty and staff members involved disrespect, disregard, and distancing. For the faculty and staff, learning their own class identity dictated by the state entailed fear and anxiety, resentment and resistance, and maneuvers to cope with threats to their safety and livelihood. At the workplace level, I conclude, the mutual constitution of the intellectual and Chinese Communism led to schisms, grievances, and political disaffection.

Tensions and frictions stemming from the objectification of the intellectual under Chinese Communism came to a head during the 1957 Rectification Campaign, when the state urged professors, scientists, and others whom it regarded as intellectuals to evaluate its performance. Chapter 6 discusses three major perspectives on the intellectual and Chinese Communism that appeared, each of which confirms that they had become inseparable in political thinking inside and outside the state. Scholars, writers, and other social notables saw a faltering socialist project because of the ineptitude of party cadres. They built upon the Confucian literati tradition, defined themselves as intellectuals, and called for a broad involvement of people like themselves in decision-making. College students used Marxist and other political ideas to launch an even more intense attack against Chinese Communism. They disputed the official view of class struggle and socialist development in China, and wanted intellectuals like themselves to lead the revolutionary project away from CCP domination. When the state hit back, it proposed to expand the pool of usable and reliable intellectuals by supporting the work of professional workers and the training of college students and by deepening their ideological reeducation. The state wanted to extend professional education to select factory workers and other manual laborers and turn them into engineers and other kinds of skilled personnel. I emphasize that none of these efforts to redefine the intellectual and Chinese Communism became reality. The project, instead, took a dark turn when the party denigrated the intellectual further.

Chapter 7 uses theater and cinema production to illustrate the mutual constitution of the intellectual and Chinese Communism from 1958 to 1964. To legitimize the Great Leap Forward (1958–1960), the ambitious production campaign that discarded scientific reason and rational planning, the state widened its attack against "intellectuals" and their knowledge and skills. The making of the famous musical drama *Third Sister Liu* reveals how the state mobilized local populations to create, circulate, and consume degrading ideas and images about intellectuals, all the while relying on educated party cadres, scriptwriters, and other professional workers to organize and promote the anti-intellectual propaganda. Behind the musical's success, the rift between the cadres and the professional workers deepened, as the former used the production to attack the latter even though both populations were denigrated by it. I then turn to the notable film *Early Spring in February* to highlight the struggle to redefine the intellectual after the Leap's failure. While some party leaders mobilized people, symbols, and other resources to depict educated people in a favorable light, or invested positive meanings into the intellectual classification, others did the opposite. The film challenged the Leap's disparagement of intellectuals, but became a target of attack nationwide. Although audience reactions suggest that college students and others were confused by the official denunciations, another layer of virulent ideas, idioms, and imageries about intellectuals saturated the nation shortly before the onset of the Cultural Revolution.

The final chapter summarizes the mutual constitution of the intellectual and Chinese Communism from the 1920s to the early 1960s. I emphasize that my analytical approach can help recover critical but underexamined aspects of social classification, bureaucratic organization, political division, social interaction, and individual calculus under the CCP. Fascinating questions about the classification and the revolutionary project await exploration. In the second half of the chapter, I turn to the highly visible legacy of the objectification of the intellectual under Chinese Communism. Since the 1980s, the CCP has abandoned Marxism and Leninism, but not their functional and structural assumptions about intellectuals. Official propaganda and governance continue to objectify the intellectual into a usable subject and a political threat for China's development as well as to revive the kinds of divisions among educated people that first emerged under Chinese Communism. Meanwhile, political relaxation and economic liberalization have prompted scholars and writers to reinterpret the intellectual in various ways. The twenty-first-century Chinese struggle to define the intellectual, unlike those in other countries, permeates state and society.

The Birth of a Classification

From what I have seen, China's intellectual class has the worst ethos for mutual cooperation and solidarity. In moral terms, China's intellectual class is significantly less ethical than other classes. For example, [its members are] maliciously competitive, brashly frivolous, and divisively opinionated; [they] spread rumors and falsehoods, shamelessly ingratiate themselves with the powerful, and so on.

—ZHANG DONGSUN, "*ZHONGGUO ZHISHI JIEJI DE JIEFANG YU GAIZAO,*"
1919

Since the 1989 Tiananmen protest movement, writings on intellectuals have flourished in China, thanks to the relaxation of official control over media and academia designed to diffuse state-society tensions caused by the bloodshed, imprisonments, and executions that followed the mass demonstration. The interlocutors include well-known figures such as the late Nobel Peace Prize laureate Liu Xiaobo (1955–2017), the prolific intellectual historian Xu Jilin (1957–), and the exiled critics Wei Jingsheng (1950–) and Yu Jie (1973–).[1] The diversity of viewpoints is unprecedented in the history of the PRC. The accounts reflect and reinforce existing analytical approaches and narratives in the transnational literature on China's intellectuals. Some studies trace the conduct and dispositions of contemporary intellectuals and their pedigrees to the imperial traditions of state service and dissent of literati. These works show the political, ideological, and moral choices that intellectuals made from the late nineteenth century to the 1949 Chinese Communist takeover amid crises of political transition, war, and revolution. Some accounts describe the mistreatment of intellectuals under the PRC as well as their courage, complicity, and resilience. Others identify challenges that intellectuals have faced in a globalized China, or how markets and professions under authoritarian governance have influenced the outlook and behavior of such persons, especially in relation to the state and matters of social justice.

Any definition of a social category, Geoffrey Bowker and Susan Leigh Star tell us, privileges one point of view while marginalizing others.[2] The narrative of the endless struggle of China's intellectuals, both as a population and as individuals, obscures how *zhishifenzi* (the intellectual) became a primary classification of people and a central concern of rulers, organizations, and ordinary people under Chinese Communism. This chapter begins our pursuit of an alternative history of the intellectual in contemporary China. I start with the relations, processes, and discourses that nurtured the intellectual classification, conditions comparable to what happened with *les intellectuels* in France during the Dreyfus affair. During the famous May Fourth movement of the late 1910s and the early 1920s, a debate on *zhishi jieji* (the intellectual class) permeated literary and political circles, when *zhishifenzi* had yet to enter the vernacular. Participants denounced members of the intellectual class for failing the nation because of their lack of political courage and moral integrity. The assumptions, arguments, and analyses that saturated the debate would influence how the CCP elites defined, denounced, and deployed "intellectuals." While the debate raged on, the party was founded under the tutelage of the Third International (Comintern), sponsored by the Communist Party of the Soviet Union. Early CCP leaders, many of whom had been active in the debate and considered themselves part of the intellectual class, condemned this population further with a Marxist-Leninist understanding of class, party, and revolution. Former friends and allies reappeared with the rest of the educated population as ideological enemies of the incipient communist movement, while the leaders promoted themselves as China's only genuine socialist revolutionaries.

Recovering this embryonic link between the intellectual and Chinese Communism is critical to understanding their entwined development thereafter. For one thing, key conceptual boundaries that would make up the influential classification existed before its deployment by the CCP, associated with a social category known within elite circles as the intellectual class. The latter was apprehended through the prism of core cultural values, beliefs, and ideals as well as the themes, imagery, and language of a stirring protest movement. That is, conventional and contemporary ethos formed the foundation of the emerging classification as much as the foreign ideology of class struggle to be accepted and promoted by the party. Equally significant is how the early party leaders shifted from identifying with to separating themselves from the intellectual class. Similar maneuvers by large numbers of educated party cadres with respect to what they saw as intellectuals would spread across the revolutionary project and muddle the local identification of such subjects. To borrow a biting remark from Foucault, this chapter helps us "catch a glimpse of the radiant city" of Yan'an, Beijing, and elsewhere after the CCP as ruling power declared what intellectuals were and what their role would be under Chinese Communism, hence the narratives and organizations as well as interests, interactions, and experiences to be found in those places.[3]

I begin with an etymology of *zhishifenzi*. Transnational research often traces the term to its Russian and French counterparts, or интеллигенция (intelligentsia) and *intellectuels*.[4] Such analyses are highly problematic. First, they present little linguistic evidence on how the Russian or the French expression morphed into *zhishifenzi.* Second, they draw from the terms their positive connotations such as the public-mindedness, civic engagement, or moral integrity of the individuals, but tend to ignore the negative meanings associated with the words from early on, for example, political conceit, effeminacy, or intellectual deformity.[5] Most importantly, the analyses gloss over why the May Fourth generation of scholars, writers, and students consistently used *zhishi jieji* (the intellectual class) to denote the educated when writing about Chinese or other societies, and why a broad shift to *zhishifenzi* (intellectuals or, literally, members of the educated population) occurred subsequently. I indicate that during the May Fourth movement, the conventional ordering of the Chinese people into *jieji* (class) categories and the popularity of European socialist ideologies based on analysis of relations between economic classes inflected the reception of foreign concepts of intellectuals. This is evidenced by the Chinese rendering of интеллигенция, *intellectuels,* and *intellectuals* into *zhishi jieji,* even by political parties. Within the CCP, improved understanding of the Marxist concept of class would guide the leaders to replace *zhishi jieji* with *zhishifenzi.* By the early 1930s, the party had largely removed implications that educated people constitute a class of their own from its official language.

I then describe the May Fourth understanding of the intellectual class in Chinese society. Research on the historic movement has long laid out its immense impact on science, literature, romance, political thought, and other areas of life.[6] The scholarship explains how scholars, writers, and college students responded to national crises of foreign encroachment, warlord rule, economic backwardness, and stagnant traditions. Yet, insufficient attention has been paid to how these educated people, including those who would join the CCP, portrayed themselves or the broader educated population. Their representations of the intellectual class feature three major characterizations: (1) it is a politically and morally objectionable population; (2) its members must overcome their weaknesses and lead workers, peasants, and others in the struggle to overcome grave national problems of culture, inequality, and governance; and (3) some, especially the younger, members of the intellectual class are better equipped ethically and intellectually than other members to lead the struggle.

It is well known that under Comintern influence early CCP leaders adopted an unprecedented revolutionary identity built upon Marx's and Lenin's teachings on class struggle, labor movements, and the dictatorship of the proletariat.[7] In the third section of this chapter, I show that the leaders combined those teachings with May Fourth ideas in novel ways and introduced a radical separation between themselves and the intellectual class. The leaders accepted the May Fourth vision that the intellectual class was a distinct population, but rejected the idea that it could develop into a benign and decisive transformative force. They portrayed the intellectual class, instead, as a tool of oppression of the ruling classes. At the same time, the leaders declared themselves genuine socialist revolutionaries as well as part of the working class, that is, proletarian leaders of the struggle to end class exploitation in Chinese society. In other words, the intellectual class became the Other in the discourse of the budding party, an enemy of Chinese Communism.

FROM "THE INTELLECTUAL CLASS" TO "INTELLECTUALS"

Compared to its Russian, French, and English counterparts, the term *zhishifenzi* appeared relatively late. As far as we know, it first appeared in print in November 1920 in the inaugural issue of *The Communist* (*Gongchandang*), in an article titled "Commemorating the Third Anniversary of the Founding of the Russian Communist Government." That periodical, the first in China devoted to promoting communism, was published by a small group of communists in Shanghai with help from Grigori Voitinsky (1893–1953), head of the Far East Bureau of the Comintern. *Zhishifenzi* does not seem to have appeared in print again until January 1925, when the Chinese Communist Youth League issued its "Resolution on Propaganda and Agitation" during its third national congress.[8] From then on, the expression appeared repeatedly in the resolutions, instructions, reports, and meeting records of the CCP and its sponsored periodicals. Existing research does not offer any evidence on how *zhishifenzi* was used outside communist circles after the mid-1920s. Judging from the term's appearance in the titles of published essays—at least four times in four different periodicals between 1928 and 1932 and another eight times in seven different periodicals during 1933 and 1934—scholars, writers, and students apparently had started to use the term with some regularity by the early 1930s.[9]

Wang Zengjin, who has studied the etymology of *zhishifenzi*, shows that it is not a direct translation of any Russian, French, or English word. The term, instead, was derived from another Chinese term, *zhishi jieji*, which political parties, scholars, and others used during the May Fourth era to denote the educated population in China and elsewhere.[10] *Zhishi jieji* is what Lydia Liu calls a "return graphic loan," that is, a classical Chinese character compound used by the Japanese to translate a modern European word and then reintroduced into the Chinese language.[11] These linguistic loans were very common during the late nineteenth and the early twentieth centuries because of intellectual traffic between China and Japan, facilitated especially by the return of thousands of Japanese-educated college students to China.[12] The Japanese expression in question is *chishiki kaikyū* (the intellectual class), a translation of the Russian word интеллигенция (intelligentsia). Japanese sociologists, socialists, and Marxists used *chishiki kaikyū* regularly from 1919 onward.[13] In China *zhishi jieji* had appeared in print before the 1919 May Fourth protest erupted in Beijing, Shanghai, and other cities. The flowering of literary and political journals that followed greatly increased the term's circulation. Between 1920 and 1925, more than thirty periodical and newspaper articles had "the intellectual class" in China or elsewhere as the central subject of their investigation.[14]

Both the CCP and the more influential Nationalist Party of China (*Zhongguo guomindang*) depicted the intellectual class as a core section of the Chinese population in their reports, resolutions, and instructions.[15] The term's popularity is confirmed by a 1929 translation of a book review from the U.S.-based *Saturday Review of Literature* by the influential magazine *Eastern Miscellany* (*Dongfang zazhi*) published in Shanghai. The book is the English translation of Julien Benda's notable *La Trahison des Clercs (The Treason of the Intellectuals)*, in which he lamented what he perceived as the abandonment by philosophers, artists, and others of truth, reason, and universal morality in favor of political passions and gains. *Eastern Miscellany* translated "intellectuals" as *zhishi jieji*, even though the editors were probably as aware as anyone of the less-used expression, *zhishifenzi*.[16]

A combination of structural, political, and cultural reasons explains why political parties, writers, and others used "the intellectual class" to denote educated populations in China and abroad during the early twentieth century. The abolition of the traditional civil service examinations and the demise of imperial rule shortly after the turn of the century, together with the rapid expansion of urban commerce and industry and the emergence of modern education as well as academic and professional disciplines, had broad linguistic impact. The changes rendered usage of *shi* (literati), *wenren* (literati or scholars), *dushu ren* (men of letters), and other traditional designations for educated people problematic. These terms, which signal the knowledge of Confucian scriptures of the individuals and their common aspiration to public office, did not capture the growing diversity of training, careers, and ambitions of the educated population. Occupation-based classifications reflecting differentiation within this population were widespread by the late teens. The notion of "occupational circles" (*jie*), another return graphic loan, was used regularly in periodicals and newspapers to separate educated personnel into sections such as "academic circles" (*xueshu jie*), "intellectual circles" (*sixiang jie*), "journalistic circles" (*xinwen jie*), and "medical circles" (*yixue jie*). Within this fluid linguistic environment, "the intellectual class" became an umbrella term denoting the constantly evolving population of educated people. At the same time, the term serves to link members of this population in the cultural terms of ancestry, status, and dispositions to previous generations of Confucian literati, as some of the educated continued to study the scriptures and aspire to public office.[17]

The use of "the intellectual class" within literary and political circles, furthermore, reflected their members' exploration of European socialist thought and, especially, class analyses. Introduced into China largely via Japan since the last years of the Qing dynasty (1644–1912), different strands of socialist thinking, including social anarchism, guild socialism, trade unionism, syndicalism, social democracy, Marxism, Bolshevism, and state socialism, received immense attention after the May Fourth demonstrations, so much so that a "belief in socialism of one variety or another was shared across the political spectrum."[18] Underlying the enthusiasm were momentous developments inside and outside China. For two decades before the demonstrations, political groups, scholars, and students in China had been using their newly acquired knowledge of Western values and institutions to condemn traditional ethics, political thought, and institutions as sources of national weakness in the emerging global system of nations and political competition.[19] Urban industrialization had created new kinds of economic inequality and labor militancy that heightened such discontent with the status quo.[20] Globally, World War I (1914–1918) was often seen as evidence of the bankruptcy of Western capitalism with its brutal pursuit of land, profit, and power. By contrast, the 1917 Russian Revolution, though still poorly understood within China and elsewhere, was perceived positively and even as a harbinger of further revolutions.[21] Within these contexts, participants in the May Fourth and later debates on reform and revolution adopted the language of class from European socialist thought to articulate their views—and argued about the role of *the intellectual class* in the struggle.

Most significantly, the use of "the intellectual class" by political parties, scholars, and students suggests that they drew on conventional approaches to social classification in their attempts to understand recent changes in Chinese society. According to Philip Kuhn, *jieji* (class) had been a common term since the Han Dynasty (206 BCE–220 CE). It denotes "a system of social ranks," "fixed degrees on a continuum," a rank within "an accepted hierarchy of status distinctions," or "the gradient that separated social groups," before acquiring during the twentieth century meanings related to ownership in production based on European socialist thought.[22] China's political and cultural elites had long combined *jieji* with other terms to order the general population into functional and hierarchical categories, often with ethical and political implications. A prominent example is the Confucian division of "commoners" into classes of scholars, peasants, artisans, and merchants according to "the social usefulness of their vocations" and a remaining class of "mean" people that included butchers, actors, and others who were classified as such "by the virtue of the stigma of [their] occupational or inherited status."[23] When political groups, writers, and others mentioned the intellectual class or, for that matter, any other category of *jieji* (especially during the May Fourth era), conventional ideas about the social rank and status of the population and the vocation of its members came into play. This was probably the case, too, when "the intellectual class" was used in analyses of European and other societies, that is, traditional Chinese values partly informed the analysis of those other educated populations.

Put differently, during the May Fourth era, scholars, students, activists, and others considered the intellectual class a population integral to Chinese society. For centuries, China had reproduced a population of literati with distinct status, offices, and careers. After the demise of the civil service examination, modern secondary and higher education and their privileged graduates embodied this elitist legacy. In 1915, for example, China had over four hundred million people, but only 90,000 secondary school students.[24] Competing descriptions of the membership of the intellectual class existed, to be sure, even among early CCP leaders, because of the diverse culture of intellectual and political inquiry of the period. Zhang Guotao (1897–1979), one of the party's founders, included secondary school students in the intellectual class, but not existing officials, whom he assigned to a "scholar-official" (*shidafu*) class because he believed that their characters were as offensive as those of officials under imperial rule.[25] Qu Qiubai (1899–1935), another party leader, was also critical of existing officials. However, he placed such individuals in an *old* intellectual class that he characterized as a legacy of ruinous imperial rule, and classified schoolteachers and students and others who worked in banks, railroad companies, and other modern establishments as part of a somewhat promising *new* intellectual class.[26] Other definitions of the intellectual class persisted outside Communist circles, often with emphasis on modern education. The 1930 *Wang Yunwu Dictionary* defines the intellectual class as "ordinary individuals who have received higher education."[27] Jiang Tingfu (1895–1965), a reputed history professor at the famous Tsinghua University, included in the category only professionals and experts whose work produces or disseminates knowledge.[28] In 1940, another authoritative dictionary, *Sea of Words* (*Cihai*), provided two definitions of the intellectual class: people who have received education and those who use such training to earn their livelihoods, such as schoolteachers and lawyers.[29] Neither of the dictionaries has an entry for *zhishifenzi*, even though it had already become a key element in the Marxian schema of social classification of the CCP as well as a term used regularly by some scholars and writers outside the party.[30]

How, then, did the obscure expression *zhishifenzi* (intellectuals) replace the term *zhishi jieji* (the intellectual class) so thoroughly that the latter was "hardly used at all" after 1949, as Wang Zengjin has correctly pointed out? Wang contends that the switch was purely a linguistic matter, resolved well before the CCP takeover of China. *Zhishifenzi*, he indicates, is composed of two common terms, *zhishi* (knowledge) and *fenzi* (part of a population or social type). Compared to the collective noun *zhishi jieji*, *zhishifenzi* is a "substantially more flexible and useful" term that denotes the educated both as a population and as individuals.[31] But Wang's argument is only partly correct. Throughout the 1930s and 1940s, scholars and writers used "the intellectual class" as a singular as well as a plural noun, referring at times to "this intellectual class" or the "middle-age intellectual classes," or observing that "most of the intellectual classes want reform."[32] The context in which the expression was used (rather than its literal meaning) dictated whether the intellectual class was presented as a social type, a collection of individuals, or a specific person. Furthermore, *zhishi jieji* did not fade away after the term *zhishifenzi* appeared, especially within literary circles. "On the Intellectual Class," "On the Intellectual Class and Its Responsibilities," and "On the Fate of the Intellectual Class" are titles of periodical pieces published shortly before the 1949 revolution.[33] By then, some of the authors who wrote about the intellectual class, such as the famous sociologist and anthropologist Fei Xiaotong (1910–2005), were certainly aware of the Marxist concept of class and its emphasis on ownership in production. Nonetheless, they continued to use "the intellectual class" in their writings because the term captures the traditional belief that Chinese society is composed of categories of people with different functions and levels of prestige. As the next section suggests, the term also expressed ethical expectations toward the educated and their involvement in public affairs based on convention.

The rise of *zhishifenzi* in the Chinese language must be understood together with the growth of Chinese Communism, or how the CCP elites increasingly deployed the Marxist concept of class to promote their revolutionary cause. When the party was founded in 1921, its leaders had been using "the intellectual class" as others did to refer to educated people. As Comintern influence deepened within the party, the leaders drew on Marxism and Leninism to discuss class struggle and revolution *and* continued to refer to "the intellectual class," even though according to Marxist-Leninist thinking educated people do not constitute an independent social class comparable to the capitalists, the workers, or others. An editor of major CCP periodicals, Qu Qiubai was arguably most knowledgeable about Marxism and Leninism among the party leaders. He spent years studying Russian language and philosophy and had written from Moscow about Lenin, the October Revolution, and the Soviet Union. Yet, in a January 1923 essay, he used a mixture of traditional and Marxian language to refer to educated people in China as an intellectual class. In the article, *zhishi jieji* appeared with "the peasant class," "the labor class," and "the merchant class" as a primary population that made up Chinese society. Also, he presented *zhishi jieji* as involved in the class struggle between capitalists and workers, but not a social class by itself. Though its members benefited from "surplus labor of production and the blood and sweat of the working masses," "the intellectual class," Qu wrote, "will under no circumstances become the main body (*zhuti*) of society." Instead, the politicians and other "high-class hooligans" within the social category would serve as functionaries of warlords and magnates, while the most progressive secondary and college students would become a "sharp weapon of the laboring masses."[34] For Qu, as for other party leaders, the intellectual class was situated between the exploiting and the exploited classes, with its members adopting various political stances.

By the early 1930s, the CCP elites had mostly switched to "intellectuals" in their essays, announcements, instructions, and reports.[35] *Zhishifenzi* had become a primary classification of people under Chinese Communism. No evidence is available to suggest that the elites deliberated on the terminological change. In all likelihood, as the revolutionary project progressed, its leaders recognized that "the intellectual class" was conceptually and semantically incompatible with Marxist-Leninist teachings on class struggle. Institutional transformations within the party reinforced the switch to "intellectuals." Two stages of change are noteworthy. Before the Nationalist Party ended its cooperation in the United Front with the CCP in 1927 by massacring CCP members and followers, a development that the next chapter will address, the CCP elites had largely overcome the "regionalist attitudes and study-society modes of operation" that had originally given shape to the Chinese Communist movement.[36] Leninist emphasis on central institutions and formal procedures as well as internal discipline, supervision, and political education had become part of the CCP's operational norms, even as the party elites continued to deploy traditional values, mores, and practices to approach and organize workers, peasants, and others. After the massacre, some leaders blamed the bloodshed on what they saw as the leadership's lack of understanding of Marxist-Leninist teachings on class, party, and revolution. The organization of the CCP shifted further toward a centralized leadership, an official party line, and use of Marxism and Leninism as a legitimation and communication device.[37] "The intellectual class" did not surface again as a significant term in the party's lexicon thereafter. When the CCP seized power in 1949, "the intellectual class" was cast into the dustbin of history practically by fiat.[38]

THE INTELLECTUAL CLASS IN MAY FOURTH IMAGINATIONS

For May Fourth activists, the intellectual class not only objectively existed—it was an objectionable population. The activists extended a trope from the late Qing, when China had begun to experiment with new modes of governance to cope with defeats in the global system of nations and competition. Notable scholars such as Yan Fu (1854–1921) and Zhang Taiyan (1869–1936) had protested that literati in general and scholar-officials in particular lacked functional knowledge and moral fortitude for nation-building purposes, going so far as to label these people as greedy, useless, and dim-witted.[39] Attacks against the civil service examination and the literati legacy had been commonplace during the New Culture Movement (1915–1919), as scholars and students took aim at the Confucian tradition. Chen Duxiu (1879–1942), who would become the first general secretary of the CCP, founded the influential *Youth Magazine* (*Qingnian zazhi*) in 1915, which was renamed later as *New Youth* (*Xin qingnian*). He derided the traditional literati as "thugs in the middle level of society" who had kept China economically and politically weak as well as morally and legally underdeveloped, damaging China as much as the politicians at the top and the ruffians at the bottom.[40] Writing for the magazine, Fu Sinian (1896–1950), a student at the elite Peking University who would head the campus briefly almost three decades later, criticized China's scholars and scholarship ruthlessly. He ridiculed the scholars as superficial, stubborn, conceited, and narrow-minded, and the scholarship as unsystematic, lifeless, and backward-looking as well as useless compared with Western learning.[41]

As May Fourth activists established new periodicals to promote their political and other beliefs and interests, denunciations of the intellectual class multiplied. As before, the reproaches drew on assumptions about power and authority as well as relations of the individual to society in the Confucian tradition, even as that tradition was vehemently attacked. Many of the complaints, in effect, charged that educated people had abandoned the "perennial ideal of 'public-mindedness,'"[42] or the moral sensibilities and duties of the individual that were conventionally understood to furnish society with its coherence and harmony. Educated people had entered officialdom in large numbers to seek fame, wealth, and power. Their hypocrisy, lack of political courage, and apathy toward other sectors of the general population were the major reasons behind centuries of illiberal autocratic rule, or the reproduction of a political system that had condemned China to economic weakness and cultural backwardness compared with Japan and Western societies. After tracing the "sins" of "the intellectual class" since the Warring States Period (475–221 BCE), or how literati from his view had gained and exercised political authority at the expense of ordinary people as well as the structural and moral integrity of Chinese society, one writer observed that the existing intellectual class resembled its predecessors in the self-serving involvement of its members in national politics.

> To satisfy their lust for political power, members of the modern intellectual class create parties and associations and recruit lackeys and underlings. To allay their anger at political defeat, they make use of warlords and instigate wars. To attract lapdogs, they talk loudly about political thought and study theories and doctrines. To maintain their own dignity, they fabricate mass opinions and use higher instructions as excuses. The truth is that they engage in such conduct because they long to have a spacious Western-style house, a fast and roomy car, and a beautiful and tender concubine. . . . Whatever others regard as poisoning the thinking of the Chinese people or tearing families apart, they consider necessary means for the pursuit of their own joy, pleasure, lust, and indulgence.[43]

Outside officialdom too, the activists declared, members of the intellectual class used their training and knowledge for personal gain. Beneath this complaint lies the moral ideal of education in the Confucian tradition, or the belief that the purpose of education is to foster self-discipline and self-realization as well as moral responsibility and humane government.[44] For one critic, few now pursued higher education for moral enlightenment or even intellectual purposes, still less the edification of the nation. Those who studied abroad went there to "have fun" for two or three years, purchased a sham doctorate or other degree, and flaunted themselves as scholars after returning home. Some stitched various foreign ideas and passages together into "absolutely nonsensical" books and proclaimed themselves leaders of particular schools of thought. Some rushed out pitifully incompetent translations of emerging theories and academic thought and haughtily presented themselves as experts.[45] Modern education at other levels, another critic concluded, failed to have ennobling impact on the intellectual class. Although secondary and college students endlessly professed devotion to honorable causes, after graduation they turned their attention immediately to landing a well-paying job, so much so that they resorted to flattery, factionalism, and other dubious and even offensive tactics to achieve their goal.[46] The dramatic plea of another critic encapsulates the harshness of the complaints: "Oh, the intellectual class of China, there is no hiding the fact that your character is bankrupt. Your scandalous decline in society is almost beyond redemption. Please start afresh now in earnest if you want to rescue yourselves from perpetual infamy."[47]

Despite their denunciations of the intellectual class, May Fourth activists insisted that its members be on the frontline of national improvement, through promoting science and democracy, spearheading social movements, and pursuing other changes. This paradoxical confidence in the moral, intellectual, and organizational leadership of the intellectual class also embodied major elements of conventional and contemporary thinking, three of which are noteworthy. First, the confidence reflected an enduring moral-cum-analytical assumption in Chinese society. The Confucian tradition stresses the role of the educated in governance, their moral capacity and responsibility for criticizing mistaken policies and priorities as well as inappropriate attitudes and conduct, but dismisses similar potentials in other populations. As Jerome Grieder observes, in the vast Confucian literature "the peasant never spoke—save in the inchoate cries of rebellion."[48] Second, the recent New Culture Movement was built upon the same assumption about the transformative potential of educated people. Scholar and student activists sought reform of the Chinese language and culture, of scholarship and education, and of other matters by rallying support from the broader educated population. Third, even though the activists increasingly used socialist thought to promote awareness of the importance of labor and sought to learn from labor movements, they never imagined relinquishing social or political authority to industrial workers or other laborers. Even those who were drawn to social anarchism, the socialist philosophy most opposed to social hierarchy, did not share the anti-intellectualism of European or Russian anarchism.[49] May Fourth activists believed in their own civilizing missions, that is, they considered themselves responsible for assisting peasants, workers, and others and ultimately helping China to escape from feudal traditions, backward beliefs, warlord rule, and therefore foreign domination.

The following examples reveal the extent of agreement about leadership among May Fourth activists. Zheng Zhenduo (1898–1958), a college student who would become a famous writer, championed a transition to socialism through social movements. But he was skeptical that Chinese workers and laborers would initiate, or make sacrifices for, any kinds of movement, let alone provide leadership comparable to what their counterparts had done in Russia or Europe: "When we traveled ten *li* [about 3 miles] outside the city of Beijing to see the original inhabitants there, we found them virtually living in ancient times! Their extent of stubbornness and foolishness reaches the highest level. They do not have any basic knowledge of science, not to mention the new tides of intellectual thought!"[50] He ended another essay with this English remark, an obvious plea to the intellectual class: "Go, seek the [people], live among them, educate them, and with their confidence, if you want to get rid of the yoke of autocracy."[51] Qu Qiubai had written about social movements, too. While he was optimistic about popular participation, his understanding of leadership qualities, which apparently included academic training, limited the leaders to those who were members of the intellectual class. The leader, he stated, must have "a positive sense of skepticism, unflappable dedication to research, and unwavering perseverance. He doubts, and therefore he is awakened [to the crises of Chinese society]. The outcome of his research can engender new beliefs and worldviews; his determination can smash old habits and institutions."[52] Philosopher Zhang Dongsun (1886–1973), shortly before switching from supporting socialism in China to favoring capitalist development, insisted that positive change must start with the intellectual class. Its members must undergo "character reform" to replace selfishness and other flaws with moral standards that nurture sacrifices to nation-building. They must organize social movements and teach, support, and join forces with ordinary people, to such an extent that the intellectual class and the laboring class would become indistinguishable.[53]

A central question for May Fourth activists was, therefore, who among the objectionable intellectual class were reliable allies? Or, who within officialdom, academia, or other occupational circles could help build broad-based movements to improve Chinese society? Given their ideological differences and oscillations, the activists disagreed on the transformation the country needed. Whatever solidarity they had exhibited during the 1919 demonstrations dissipated as political rivalry and animosity emerged. Yet, the activists shared an ethical-cum-intellectual criterion, at least on paper, for separating friends from foes or potential allies from potential enemies—that is, whether the person had achieved *juewu* (awakening). *Juewu* is an age-old concept with Buddhist roots. It means a realization of truth which leads one to act properly henceforth, giving up unseemly thinking, habits, and ways of life. Chen Duxiu and other proponents of the New Culture Movement had invoked *juewu* as well as *zijue* (self-awakening) widely to muster support for their proposed literary and other reforms.[54] Across May Fourth writings, *juewu* carried multiple layers of meanings of what educated people should do. First and foremost, they must recognize the moral failings plaguing the intellectual class and overcome those marring their own outlook and behavior. On this foundation, they must awaken others, including workers and peasants, to the sorry state of knowledge, ethics, and governance in China. Equally important, they must study the history, structure, and dynamics of Chinese society as means to identify the proper tactics and procedures to improve its conditions. Wang Guangqi (1892–1936), who was influenced by anarchist and socialist ideologies, believed that the awakened within the intellectual class and other classes should join forces to produce a classless society.[55] Yun Daiying (1895–1931), who would join the CCP soon after its establishment, suggested that the awakened must cooperate with their foreign counterparts to combat imperialism, a problem that May Fourth activists regarded as foundational to China's political and economic difficulties.[56]

Chen Chengze (1885–1922), an editor of newspapers and periodicals who had studied in Japan, disagreed with Chen Duxiu and others who wanted to reorganize China on the basis of anarchism, communism, or other radical political thought. Nonetheless, he shared the *juewu* approach to societal change, or the need for a mass awakening led by educated people who would critically interrogate their own thinking and conduct so as to articulate proper courses for national transformation. The problems of China, he asserted, did not stem from hostilities involving social classes or ethnic groups, as they did in Western societies. Instead, the enduring lack of such conflicts in China had fostered "a focus on the self." This ethic had stunted the development of community, civic, and other forms of associational life, as well as of a national consciousness, and therefore had served to perpetuate imperial rule. Meanwhile, members of the intellectual class had exploited lofty rhetoric and other tactics to empower and enrich themselves. For Chen, any radical political ventures such as social revolution, universal suffrage, or decentralization of authority to provinces would merely redistribute power among those who already held it. The "truly awakened" would not promote grandiose solutions, reckless boycotts, or other forms of rebellion based on manipulation of the passions and naïveté of the populace. Instead, they would patiently develop self-governance and basic literacy across towns and villages as well as nurture labor cooperatives and other grassroots organizations as means to foster a popular agreement on the national developmental path.[57]

It is a well-known fact that May Fourth activists carried forward the New Culture Movement's adulation of young people as political subjects.[58] For our purposes, this adulation represents another feature in May Fourth interpretations of the intellectual class: that educated young people were imagined as sharing an unparalleled potential to achieve self-awakening and thus deserving a leading role in reform or revolution. While this belief challenged the understanding of moral and intellectual authority in the Confucian tradition, it reproduced the traditional vision of government as an elite-led, moral enterprise built upon an authoritative set of knowledge. The activists replaced Confucian scholarship with Western political and intellectual approaches, and scholar-officials with young people who could adopt such approaches to reorganize Chinese society. To be sure, educated young people were accorded such a privileged position within May Fourth thinking, not simply because modern education was believed to have potential to empower them to challenge conventions or even because some had already led attacks on such conventions. A persistent fear existed among May Fourth activists, as among New Culture advocates, that educated young people would slide into self-interested pursuits of power, wealth, and fame, replicating the behavior of older members of the intellectual class and previous generations of scholar-officials. Faith was therefore necessary to sustain the view that educated young people would somehow play a leading moral, intellectual, and organizational role in the transformation of Chinese society.

Early CCP leaders were among the May Fourth activists who assumed that educated young people represented the hope of Chinese society. As late as December 1922, or eighteen months after the CCP was founded, for example, Zhang Guotao, used the recent political and labor protests in urban areas to argue that "an extremely small number of members of the intellectual class" had proven to have "the strongest revolutionary spirit." He proceeded to describe what he considered another disappointing trend unfolding among secondary and college students, or their self-absorption.

> As of now, their revolutionary ardor is dimming day by day. Although they have made many tactical mistakes, the biggest reason is that they have been taken in by the hubbub of the movement in the cultural sector. What are the outcomes there? Students who have announced that they would fight for national salvation are pushed back into the classroom. Leaders of the May Fourth movement are learning to publish poetry and essays in the vernacular, going abroad to study, researching literature, philosophy, and science in the university, and applying themselves to reorganization of national cultural heritage.[59]

Rather than giving up on such young people, Zhang reaffirmed their place in revolutionary change. Peasants everywhere were waiting to be led out of the "fiery pit" of bandit and warlord oppression, and workers in foreign-owned plants were "ceaselessly calling for help." The role of educated young people, he stated, was to go to "every village, every factory, every shop, every school, and every site" to promote and organize the occupants for revolutionary struggle.

THE INTELLECTUAL CLASS AS THE OTHER

In July 1921, slightly two years after the May Fourth demonstrations, the CCP was formally established in Shanghai. As Arif Dirlik observed, Grigori Voitinsky of the Comintern, who had arrived in China in March 1920, was crucial to the party's founding. He met with Chen Duxiu, Li Dazhao (1888–1927), and others who would become the party's initial leaders. He discussed with them Marxism and class struggle, the October Revolution and the Soviet Union, and the Russian Communist Party and the Comintern. His visit stimulated the formation of Marxist study societies in Beijing, Shanghai, Guangzhou, and other places. Until then, Chinese reception of Marxism, mainly via translations of Japanese works, had been lukewarm. Writings on Marxism formed but a small part of the rapidly growing modern political literature. They emphasized Marx's economic interpretation of history and society, focusing on such concepts as wage labor, surplus value, and capital accumulation, but not his theory that class struggle drives history forward. The theory, which conjures up sectional interests and rivalries as well as violent revolution followed by the imposition of new forms of state control, squared poorly with influential proposals to improve China through reforms of education, politics, and cultural tradition, not to mention the deep-rooted Confucian emphasis on social harmony. Furthermore, class struggle as a principle contradicted the ideal of mutual aid and social unity underlying the anarchist vision of revolution, a main medium through which Chen, Li, and others had encountered Marxism.[60]

Under the Comintern's ideological, organizational, and sometimes economic support, the Marxist study societies promoted communism by translating and publishing Marxist works, launching periodicals, and growing their own membership. Chen Duxiu and others used their improved knowledge of Marxism and Leninism to engage fellow May Fourth activists in debate on issues of reform and revolution. Their goal was to elevate Marxism-Leninism above competing political thoughts, establish it as the theoretical orthodoxy among the increasing number of CCP members, and convert other socialists to their cause. The tone of their engagement with other socialists ranged from courteous to acrimonious, depending on the ideas and proposals under interrogation.[61] All the while, Chen and other party leaders could not but confront the question of the intellectual class within a new theoretical context—one dominated by Marxism and Leninism and markedly different from the Confucian and other intellectual traditions that had previously informed understandings of the social category. How did the intellectual class fit into the Marxist schema of classes? What were the relations of the intellectual class to class struggle and revolution? What roles would members of the class play after the revolution? And what were their own relations to the intellectual class as leaders of the CCP?

It is necessary to outline Marx's and Lenin's understandings of the relations of intellectuals to class, party, and revolution before explaining how the early CCP leaders combined these foreign views with May Fourth thinking to redefine the intellectual class as a social type. For Marx, classes are based on relations to the ownership of land, raw material, machines, and other resources shared by individuals in the realm of production.[62] Class struggle, which determines the acceptable form of ownership in a society, and classes are, respectively, the driving force and agents of social change. Marx provided no more than "brief and fugitive glosses" about the educated as a people in his class analysis.[63] Yet, what he said, did, and signaled had major influence on the organization of communist movements. His early work and political activities suggest that the transition of a workers' movement to a socialist revolution must be guided by the right kind of learned people, or those who understand the dynamics of class struggle in the society in question. These communists, as he and Friedrich Engels pronounced in the *Manifesto of the Communist Party,* "have no interests separate and apart from those of the proletariat as a whole"—but they do "have over the great mass of the proletariat the advantage of clearly understanding the line of march, the conditions, and the ultimate general results of the proletarian movement."[64] In addition, Marx stressed labor vigilance against other kinds of leaders involved in labor movements, "regarding his [ideological] adversary either as misguided by erroneous principles or as unscrupulously using principles as a disguise for selfish interests."[65] In particular, Marx believed, anarchists and other socialists "often wrought considerable havoc" on such movements, and writers, schoolteachers, and students usually lacked "revolutionary steadfastness." Even with proper intellectual guidance, socialist revolutions would occur only when workers have "gradually and painfully attained the level of class consciousness and political organization necessary for the overthrow of capitalism."[66]

In his reformulation of the relations of intellectuals to class, party, and revolution, Lenin resolved some of the gaps, tensions, and ambiguities in Marx's vision, but only to enunciate "a remarkable heresy."[67] Building on Marx's class analysis, Lenin indicated that professors, clerical staff, civil servants, technicians, and other white-collar workers form an intelligentsia between the exploiting and the exploited classes in capitalist societies. This heterogeneous population of educated people generally do not own any means of production or engage in direct production like workers or peasants. Instead, they obtain their livelihoods through services to the major classes and occupy the interstices of the class structure. Like Marx, Lenin believed that the working class is the agent of the socialist revolution. Unlike Marx, however, he insisted that workers on their own would develop at best "trade-union consciousness," or a bargaining and compromising mentality that impedes insurgent movements, not to mention the socialist revolution. Revolutionary thinking must be brought to labor by a revolutionary socialist intelligentsia, or communists who are trained in theory and organization and who serve as "the ultimate guardian" of the revolution. The communist party is the tool for uniting "revolutionaries from the intelligentsia" with "worker-revolutionaries."[68]

Furthermore, Lenin extended Marx's attack against the politics and dispositions of other educated people. Not only did Lenin disparage the kinds of reform or revolution proposed by ideological competitors; he persistently criticized ordinary educated people.[69] His famous work *One Step Forward, Two Steps Back* was written in 1904, amid his struggle with fellow Russian revolutionaries to define the organization of the communist party. The following passage captures the crux of his attack. His view anticipated the extensive role that the party assumed in controlling and reforming educated people after the October Revolution of 1917.

> No one will venture to deny that *the intelligentsia, as a special stratum* of modern capitalist society, is characterized, by and large, *precisely by individualism* and incapacity for discipline and organization. . . . This, incidentally, is a feature which unfavorably

distinguishes this social stratum from the proletariat; it is one of the reasons for the flabbiness and instability of the intellectual, which the proletariat so often feels; and this trait of the intelligentsia is intimately bound up with its customary mode of life, its mode of earning a livelihood, which in a great many respects approximates to the *petty-bourgeois mode of existence* (working in isolation or in very small groups, etc.). (Italics in the original)[70]

For all intents and purposes, Chen Duxiu and other early CCP leaders had switched from a May Fourth to a Marxist-Leninist interpretation of the intellectual class by mid-1923, as the party began to develop into a unified revolutionary organization guided by Marxist-Leninist teachings and a strong central leadership.[71] *New Youth,* which had become the party's flagship organ, did not publish any debate, if it occurred, on the change in perspective, nor did other forums used by the leaders to explain class struggle, worker revolutions, and the dictatorship of the proletariat. In a December 1923 article in which Chen analyzed China's class structure, he repeated much of Lenin's perspective on the intelligentsia. The article offered support to the Comintern policy that the CCP should form a united front with veteran revolutionary Sun Yatsen (1866–1925) and his Nationalist Party (*Guomindang*). The Comintern wanted the CCP to work with the Guomindang to wage a "democratic revolution" to remove foreign powers and warlords from China before mobilizing the working class in a socialist revolution. "The intellectual class," Chen wrote, was not "an independent class" with any "firm and unshakable" political character. It was part of the petty bourgeoisie with members furnishing ideological and other forms of support to landlords, capitalists, and warlords. Because the intellectual class lacked "any specific economic foundation" of its own, or the material basis for a shared class consciousness, some of the members supported reform and even revolution, but only with transient "romantic" sentiments and "fantasies of [themselves] transcending class interests." Nonetheless, Chen stated, members of the intellectual class would be critical for bringing together different sections of Chinese society in the democratic revolution.[72] A year later, Peng Shuzhi (1895–1983), who had worked at the Moscow branch of the CCP, pulled no punches on attacking "the intellectual class," stating that 80 to 90 percent of its members in capitalist societies were "lapdogs" of the bourgeoisie. Some of the members of China's intellectual class had "passionately" supported revolutionary efforts and even joined revolutionary organizations, only because these people shared "the psychology of the bourgeoisie" but had seen their financial and professional goals harmed by warlord rule and foreign occupation and themselves snubbed, insulted, and abused by these powers.[73]

In other words, CCP leaders extended the May Fourth attack on the intellectual class with a Marxist-Leninist logic. Their reinterpretation challenged the

May Fourth assumption that the intellectual class constituted a relatively autonomous political force and that some of its members, especially secondary and college students, could turn over a new leaf and lead the effort to transform Chinese
society. The intellectual class, the leaders concluded, had never been and would
not be a decisive transformative force. Under this interpretation, former friends
and allies who had been promoting anarchism and other forms of socialism reappeared alongside ordinary educated people as part of a global "intellectual class"
serving class exploitation and capitalist political rule in one way or another. For
example, the June 1923 special "Comintern" issue of *New Youth* carried lengthy
articles about capital-labor relations and the international communist movement as well as the October Revolution and the Soviet Union. In two successive
pieces, Qu Qiubai restated Lenin's and the Comintern's attacks on the "opportun-
ism," "economism," and "revisionism" of various socialist ideas and programs to
discredit their Chinese advocates. The ideas of Karl Kautsky, Eduard Bernstein,
Pierre-Joseph Proudhon, Henri de Saint-Simon, and other famous European and
Russian socialists and anarchists, and the activities of various European socialist
parties, were criticized for paying little attention to the history of class struggle, the
nature of capitalist development, and the revolutionary role of the working class.
Qu observed that members of "the intellectual class" who were active in politics
dreamed up "an ideal society" and sought to "implement the details" of organization that they had supplied. Anarchism was idealistic and utopian because its
"petty-bourgeois" proponents failed to understand the workings of politics. Social
democrats who pursued "class cooperation" were part of the "bourgeois" enemy.[74]
Labor unions, another article suggests, had become "the last refuge of the international bourgeoisie" and the tools of so-called reformers "to divide the working
class" and disrupt communist movements.[75] Vanished from these writings was the
courteousness that the CCP leaders had recently extended to some of their ideological rivals.

For CCP leaders, their reinterpretation of the intellectual class as a harmful
force for the socialist revolution could not but raise questions about their own
identities. Were they still part of the intellectual class, as they had previously suggested? Were they the revolutionary intellectuals who Lenin had stated must lead
communist movements? What were their relations to Chinese labor? The leaders
did not offer any definitive answers in the contemporary reports, analyses, and
declarations published by the party. Enough evidence, however, suggests that they
were assembling for themselves a novel revolutionary identity while attacking the
intellectual class with a Marxist-Leninist perspective. Their vehement attacks on
the politics and behavior of the intellectual class imply that they no longer identified themselves as part of that population. By their own definition, the intellectual class was at best an unreliable ally of the working class and an enemy at
worst. But the CCP leaders, unlike Lenin, did not claim with any consistency that

the educated persons leading communist movements constituted the genuinely revolutionary section of the intelligentsia. The leaders reserved the phrase "revolutionary members of the intellectual class" (*geming de zhishi jieji*) and "revolutionary intellectuals" (*geming de zhishifenzi*) mainly for other educated people within the party or working with it, while implying that these persons, though useful to Chinese Communism, harbored petty-bourgeois and even bourgeois values and habits that were obstacles to its success.[76]

The CCP leaders also did not seem to share Lenin's pessimism or even their own previous doubts about the revolutionary potential of labor. Their writings, instead, echoed Marx's view on how the socialist revolution would be won. Qu Qiubai proclaimed that the proletarians worldwide would combine their "basic inclination toward collectivism and organization with ability to use social science" (that is, Marxism) to arrive at "general and practical principles" to be deployed against capitalist rule.[77] Peng Shuzhi contended that Chinese workers could provide leadership to the democratic revolution that the CCP would sponsor together with the Guomindang before launching their own socialist revolution.[78] We arguably see a glimpse of how the leaders wanted to define their relations to the intellectual class, the working class, and the socialist revolution as early as July 1922. "We the proletariat have our own class interests," the Declaration of the Second Congress of the CCP announced, and the purpose of the CCP "is to organize the proletariat."[79] Although the party leaders had relatively privileged backgrounds and educations, they wanted to be recognized first and foremost as part of the proletariat and organizers of its revolution.

Put differently, early CCP leaders creatively combined Marxism, Leninism, and the May Fourth discourse in an effort to turn themselves into members-cum-leaders of the proletariat. From Marxism, the leaders accepted the idea of the revolutionary proletariat, that is, that the working class would ultimately acquire the class consciousness and organizational skills needed for the socialist revolution. From Leninism, they borrowed the notion of the revolutionary vanguard, which expects the communist party and its leadership to guide, nurture, and organize the proletariat. From May Fourth discourse, they adopted self-awakening as a prerequisite for leadership in social change. They asserted that through their studies of politics and society they alone recognized the revolutionary path that China must follow to save itself from foreign encroachment, economic backwardness, political tyranny, and other crises, all considered to be consequences of class exploitation and its recent intensification under capitalist development in Chinese society. The leaders suggested that they constituted an entirely different category of educated people compared with scholars, officials, college students, and other educated people. They were the proletarians and communists at the forefront of the Chinese socialist revolution; the others were members of the intellectual class, working against it in one way or another. The political ideas and ideologies of the intellectual class, however sensible they might seem, had to be defeated along with its members. For the CCP leadership, the intellectual class became the Other, an enemy of Chinese Communism.

The fact that millions of Chinese categorized themselves and were classified by the state as intellectuals during the Mao era has nothing to do with the changes that occurred in China's division of labor after the 1949 revolution. Like other industrializing countries, China saw a diversification of work, skills, and careers, which should have impeded the assignment of this heterogeneous population to the same social category. Nor would the wide range of political or other conducts of these persons justify giving them a common classification. The transformation of these people into "intellectuals," instead, reflected an interplay of discourse, relations, and processes across Chinese society, in which the CCP played the dominant role. So objectified was the intellectual that many would deprecate themselves as embodiments of the inferior, greedy, and conceited subject as alleged by the state; so objectified that others protested as, with, and for intellectuals when there were opportunities to speak out; so objectified that otherwise perfectly ordinary people were hounded to death and even murdered publicly during the Cultural Revolution, because of an imagined fear that the scourge of intellectuals would incurably infect Chinese Communism.

A quarter of a century before the CCP takeover of China, key conceptual boundaries of the intellectual as an official classification of people had already emerged, associated with a social category known as the intellectual class. For the party leadership, the intellectual class was a diverse yet distinct population consisting of professors, writers, lawyers, schoolteachers, college students, and other educated personnel. Members of this population shared an intermediate position in the class structure, or one that fostered outlooks, ideas, and habits at odds with the objectives of Chinese Communism. Still, recent secondary school graduates and other young people in the population had potential for political and moral self-improvement. These boundaries that defined the intellectual class did not come only from Marxism and Leninism, the internationally influential revolutionary thought borrowed by the leadership to interpret and publicize the plight of a beleaguered nation; more importantly, the boundaries reflected deep-rooted cultural assumptions as well as powerful contemporary thinking about Chinese society, or ideas restated in innumerable accounts and analyses during the May Fourth movement. The Marxian synthesis of various political thoughts by the party leaders led them to assert a distinction between themselves and the intellectual class, even though the leaders were as educated and privileged as those whom they criticized. These conceptual boundaries would become foundations of revolutionary policy and later sovereign classification.

Formed at the cusp of the May Fourth movement, the Comintern's intervention in Chinese politics, and the CCP reception of Marxist-Leninist ideology, *zhishifenzi* as a social classification had an inauspicious beginning compared to the Russian *интеллигенция* or the French *intellectuel*. The Russian radicals, liberals, and conservatives who popularized the term *интеллигенция* during the late nineteenth century were undoubtedly divided about its meanings. The word nevertheless had multiple positive connotations: intellectual enlightenment, service to the people, superior moral qualities, and intelligence.[80] Likewise, the much-debated French term featured honor, civic engagement, incorruptibility, and moral authority in its original meanings. In comparison, "the intellectual class," the predecessor of *zhishifenzi*, was rife with negative imports such as selfishness, greed, vanity, timidity, and lack of discipline, reproaches against educated people popularized by the May Fourth movement. When the CCP leadership reinterpreted and further denigrated the intellectual class within a Marxist-Leninist framework of class, party, and revolution, the discourse conjured up the perception of a tenacious enemy of Chinese Communism—the intellectuals.

3

Visible Subjects in the Countryside

But after I became a revolutionary and lived with workers and peasants and with soldiers of the revolutionary army . . . I came to feel that compared with the workers and peasants the unremoulded intellectuals were not clean and that, in the last analysis, the workers and peasants were the cleanest people and, even though their hands were soiled and their feet smeared with cow-dung, they were really cleaner than the bourgeois and petty-bourgeois intellectuals. That is what is meant by a change in feelings, a change from one class to another. If our writers and artists who came from the intelligentsia want their works to be well received by the masses, they must change and remould their thinking and their feelings. Without such a change, without such remoulding, they can do nothing well and will be misfits.

—MAO ZEDONG, *SPEECH AT THE YAN'AN FORUM ON LITERATURE AND ART*, 1942

In the spring of 1939 Ma Hong (1920–2007), a 19-year-old, had an unforgettable encounter with Mao Zedong (1893–1976). Ma had recently joined the CCP and was studying at the Academy of Marxist-Leninist Studies (*Malie xueyuan*) in Yan'an, an impoverished town in northwestern China that housed the party's headquarters. The academy was set up across a row of loess caves traditionally used as residential spaces. It offered what the party leadership regarded as advanced theoretical and political training to select party members, some of whom had studied in college and even overseas. The training was designed to prepare these individuals for positions of authority in the ongoing project of Chinese Communism. On the day of the encounter, Mao arrived at the academy and paid a surprise visit to an office shared by students, before giving a prescheduled speech. As the party secretary of his class, Ma answered the Chairman's questions about life on campus on behalf of delighted classmates. Mao then inquired about the teenager's own background. Ma replied humbly that he had little formal education and therefore his "level of knowledge and learning" was not high, but he also stressed that he relished every opportunity to read books and newspapers. Before leaving the office, Mao excited the students further with three pieces of impromptu calligraphy that validated their sacrifices and hard work. One of these said "Reading books is good."[1]

Based on his daughter's recollection, Ma came from a poor rural family but was not as undereducated as he indicated to the Chairman. Although his parents did not send him to school, Ma learned to read and write so painlessly as a child that a village elder paid him to compile the local lineage genealogy and the county gazetteer. Ma used the earnings to attend primary school and completed it in fewer than four years. The school principal promptly hired this outstanding graduate to teach senior primary classes. Fellow villagers also considered Ma exceptionally talented, and helped him land a desk job in a railway management bureau when he was only 16.[2] His precociousness would be recognized at the academy. Within two years of meeting Mao, Ma penned two important essays that laid out the rationale, approach, and procedure for investigating and evaluating the class backgrounds and characters of party cadres, a political as well as literary achievement, and all the more so for a young adult.[3] In front of Mao, however, Ma did not disclose that he was a superior writer or former schoolteacher, or other parts of his life that would have led the Chairman to see him as an "intellectual." Ma's reaction suggests that he understood something unconventional, and even paradoxical, about the self-presentation of educated people under Chinese Communism. He recognized this, moreover, before others did during the famous 1942 Yan'an Forum on Literature and Art, when Mao put down "bourgeois and petty-bourgeois intellectuals," all the while flaunting his own literary achievement, aesthetic sensitivity, and cultural refinement within the rural town.

This chapter describes the rise of a visible, sizable, and stigmatized population of "intellectuals" and the spread of the institutions of workplace management by party cadres, ideological reeducation, and mass surveillance in Yan'an. Within the town, Chinese Communism enjoyed much-needed stability and security after a tumultuous decade marked by growth, fragmentation, and carnage. The party elites accepted Mao's leadership, however grudgingly, and his view that the revolutionary project badly needed the knowledge and skills obtainable from intellectuals even though they were untrustworthy. Exploiting the symbolic power and mobilization skills it had acquired since the early 1920s, the party recruited large numbers of relatively educated people to Yan'an. Ensuing partition of space, division of work, establishment of organizations, and other social and physical rearrangements engendered an abundance of signs and cues that reinforced the top-down representation of the newcomers as intellectuals. The virtually coercive Rectification Campaign (*Zhengfeng yundong*) (1942–1944) initiated by Mao normalized not only his view of the intellectual but also the triple institutions mentioned above. Instruction, confession, supervision, and other measures turned the newcomers and others into usable but unreliable "intellectuals" as well as subjects of education and objects of knowledge. Like the emergence of the intellectual classification shortly after the CCP's founding and the subsequent normalization of the classification under the PRC, the pursuit of revolutionary authority by edu-cated party members over others who were also educated was a central dynamic in the spread of the marker.

Although the above objectification of the intellectual occurred in a relatively enclosed environment organized by the CCP, it was not a uniform, clear-cut, or one-sided process. Conceptually, the party's definition of intellectuals—as a population of educated people situated between the exploiting and the exploited classes—did not capture the complexity of the backgrounds of the educated per-sons involved, some of whom could be counted as "workers," "poor peasants," or other kinds of subject under the official schema of classes. Organizationally, the hierarchical structure underlying workplace management by party cadres, ideo-logical reeducation, mass surveillance, and other political control mechanisms had uneven impact on social identity, as they tended to spotlight some as "intel-lectuals" more than others who were equally, if not more, educated. Furthermore, because the intellectual classification was laden with both positive and negative meanings, individual negotiations aimed at gaining authority and opportunity within the revolutionary town and minimizing stigmatization, like the conduct of Mao and Ma noted above, created ambiguity and difficulty in everyday identifica-tion. In fact, as Chinese Communism expanded, it furnished pathways for upper mobility, job change, and training that enabled many educated persons to improve their revolutionary images as well as to benefit from their academic or professional training. The revolutionary project created a myriad of social and ideological posi-tions and stimulated multiple strategies of "position-taking"[4] that muddied the boundaries of the population of intellectuals that emerged.

This chapter therefore gives an account of the evolution of the intellectual from a classification of people in early CCP ideology to the social identity of tens of thousands of revolutionaries in a rural society. It illustrates the corresponding transformation of institutions, organizations, and relations as well as personal val-ues, interests, and habits. Research on Yan'an has studied how the party leadership set up the town and the implications for Chinese Communism after 1949.[5] It has explored how writers, artists, and others as intellectuals supported or challenged the project.[6] Only limited attention has been given to arguably the most important achievement of Chinese Communism up till then, that is, what Pierre Bourdieu and Loic Wacquant would call the "collective work of construction of social real-ity" led by the party.[7] Yan'an revolutionaries came to apprehend, characterize, and distinguish themselves and others as class subjects based on a Marxian view.[8] At the heart of this success, this chapter reveals, was the top-down deployment of the "intellectual" marker. The deployment engendered discourses, processes, and relations that profoundly affected the revolutionary project in terms of structure and culture.

Before revisiting life in revolutionary Yan'an, it is necessary to summarize the relations between the intellectual and Chinese Communism from the early 1920s to mid-1930s. I draw attention to four interrelated trends, each of which would intensify within the headquarters town. First, the intellectual became a major classification used by the CCP to categorize and differentiate its members and supporters. Second, party leaders and cadres applied the classification to individuals from a variety of backgrounds, but represented themselves differently even if they were well educated. Third, the classification served as a powerful weapon in power struggles within the party leadership and at lower levels of the party. Fourth, provision of education and employment by the party and its mechanisms of control turned otherwise perfectly ordinary people into politically unreliable "intellectuals." The classification was therefore a foundation of organization, identity, and schism under Chinese Communism before it entered the Yan'an phase.

PRELUDE TO YAN'AN

Despite their denunciations of the character and politics of the educated, Chen Duxiu, Qu Qiubai, and other early CCP leaders believed that these persons were critical to the development of Chinese Communism. The belief reflected the background of the leaders as May Fourth activists seeking to modernize China as well as their subsequent embrace of the Bolshevik model of socialist development, which stressed use of professional knowledge and skills, especially after the socialist revolution. The Comintern-brokered United Front (1923–1927) between the Guomindang and the CCP provided the leaders with otherwise unavailable opportunities to advance Chinese Communism, with results that further reinforced that belief. Thanks to the work of educated men and sometimes women, CCP influence expanded quickly nationwide, albeit under a dominant partner with no interest in a proletarian revolution. CCP leaders and cadres developed and maintained labor unions and other supportive associations as well as orchestrated and assisted in labor strikes and other protests in Shanghai, Wuhan, Guangzhou, and elsewhere. In rural areas, efforts of propaganda and mobilization led to the formation of peasant associations and to social service reforms, rent and interest reductions, and the execution of landlords. Some leaders and cadres became soldiers and political commissars in the Guomindang military and helped to recruit factory workers and peasants into the forces. During the mid-1920s, CCP membership jumped from under 1,000 in January 1925 to almost 58,000 by April 1927.[9]

With their increasing exposure to Marxist-Leninist thought, early CCP leaders formally categorized some of the people working for Chinese Communism as intellectuals. In December 1926, the party stated that 60, 12, and 27 percent of its members in four regions (Hunan, Guangdong, Shanghai, and northern China) were respectively "workers, peasants, and intellectuals and others."[10] Four months later, the total number of CCP members who were intellectuals reportedly rose above 11,000.[11] The figures on intellectuals or other categories of class subjects reported by the party then or later (and many such numbers that appear in this book and elsewhere) do not point to any demographic subgroups that existed objectively because of their own characteristics. The figures, instead, were part of the objectifying practice of the CCP and the effort of its elites to remake China according to their image. We do not know the people, criteria, or methods involved in the compilation of those numbers mentioned above. In fact, the party leadership at that same time reported its inability to monitor this nationwide process of classification.[12] From what we have seen in the last chapter, the local party authorities probably categorized a wide range of personnel as intellectuals, for example, from professors and writers to college students and office clerks. Underlying the numbers was an emerging approach to revolutionary organization based on counting and identifying class subjects in general and intellectuals in particular.

When the Guomindang ended the United Front in 1927 by slaughtering nearly 30,000 CCP members and supporters, the intellectual acquired what would become another enduring feature under Chinese Communism: the classification became a weapon in intraparty struggles. Despite early CCP leaders' anti-intellectual rhetoric, educated people had gained prestige, authority, and opportunities within the revolutionary project. What happened at the Peasant Movement Institute in Guangzhou is an excellent example. Thanks to the United Front, the institute was established in 1924. The CCP elites tightly controlled the institute and used it to produce cadres to support the expansion of Chinese Communism into rural areas. During the institute's three years of operation, its instructors, successful graduates, and students were mostly educated men.[13] After the United Front debacle, however, political vitriol against "intellectuals" saturated the party, leading to its reorganization as well as an extension of its schema of classes across the teetering project. The new leadership, headed by Qu Qiubai at first and supported by the Comintern, attacked deposed leader Chen Duxiu and other cadres. The leadership alleged that these "petty-bourgeois intellectuals" had dominated "virtually every guiding body" of the party.[14] "They had not received training in Marxism-Leninism, were ignorant of the experiences of the international proletarian movements, and stood outside the class struggle of the workers and poor peasants. They had not reformed themselves into thorough *proletarian revolutionaries*. On the contrary, they have brought into the party such qualities as being politically infirm, incomplete, and irresolute in behavior, unorganized in style, together with other habits, temperaments, prejudices and fancies that are typical of petty bourgeois revolutionaries" (emphasis added).[15] Even before the United Front's collapse, ideological competitions among CCP leaders had been common and sometimes intense.[16] The denunciations afterward crossed another threshold. Defeated colleagues and former allies were cast as political obstacles, liabilities, and even enemies of Chinese Communism, or no better and sometimes even worse than "intellectuals" outside the party.

When Chinese Communism splintered into rural rebellions shortly thereafter, some CCP leaders and cadres acquired opportunities to solidify their claim of transformation to proletarian revolutionaries, the political identity they adopted when attacking other educated people inside or outside the party. During the United Front, hundreds of cadres had gained experience in rural organization and mobilization through the Peasant Movement Institute. They had molded and guided peasant interests, established schools and militias, and built layers of peasant associations across different provinces.[17] Some of these persons, including Mao Zedong, returned to the countryside in Jiangxi Province and elsewhere afterward and joined forces with local party cadres, many of whom were former students and schoolteachers. Together, they adopted local values, mores, and practices as well as peasant dialects, appearance, and habits, and worked with local strongmen and militia, bandit gangs, sworn brotherhoods, and ordinary villagers. Their newly formed guerilla units defended captured territories, raided landlords' properties, promoted mass uprisings, conducted land reform, and fought against incursions from the Guomindang military.[18] These party leaders and cadres thus assumed roles, personae, and ways of life dramatically different from those of the leaders or cadres who stayed in urban areas, not to mention the office workers or the college and secondary school students that the party disparaged as petty-bourgeois intellectuals.

Hung-yok Ip's study of Peng Pai (1896–1929) and Mao, both of whom were from well-to-do families and well educated, reveals further how some CCP leaders maneuvered to achieve a proletarian revolutionary identity. Peng and Mao were instrumental in developing the rural strategy of Chinese Communism. Although they touted the revolutionary capacity of poor peasants and farm hands to be even more advanced than that of industrial workers (and thus departed from Marx's and Lenin's teachings), they did not entrust their insurgencies to the peasantry any more than other party leaders handed over the organization of urban struggles to workers. Instead, Peng and Mao portrayed the peasantry as "deficient historical subjects,"[19] through exploiting their own symbolic power acquired from revolutionary leadership, urban experience, and privileged education, as well as the elitism of the Confucian tradition and the urban biases of May Fourth activism and Marxist-Leninist thought. Between Peng and Mao, a litany of problems of the peasantry purportedly reflecting values, habits, and ways of life in the countryside was identified as obstacles of the revolutionary project, or timidity, superstition, passivity, pessimism, ignorance, familism, localism, stubbornness, hedonism, incompetence, individualism, and lack of spirit, discipline, and organization.[20] Like the intellectual, the peasant became another figure that party leaders adapted from conventional and contemporary discourses and reintroduced into Chinese Communism to elevate their own status and authority, or consecrate themselves as proletarian revolutionaries.

As the CCP's rural strategy grew by leaps and bounds during the late 1920s and early 1930s, the use of the intellectual classification as a weapon in intraparty struggles intensified due to policy change and local conflict. After the United Front debacle, the CCP leadership, as noted earlier, demanded removals of "petty-bourgeois intellectuals" from positions of authority within the party. The leadership wanted "extensive appointment of workers to cadre positions" (*ganbu gongrenhua*) and recruitment of workers, poor peasants, and rural laborers into the party.[21] Much research is needed to clarify how local party organizations and members deployed the intellectual marker during this period of Chinese Communism. Still, trends are observable. Within the leadership, educated men continued to dominate policymaking despite elections of former workers to top positions.[22] At lower levels, attacks against cadres identified as intellectuals assumed unprecedented proportions even as the leadership warned against excessive actions. Educated men exploited the ideological shift to drive out political competitors and challengers, thereby announcing themselves essentially as proletarian revolutionaries. Some cadres relied on their touted worker backgrounds to attack colleagues whom they accused of being untrustworthy intellectuals. A 1933 CCP report indicates that leaders of the rural bases severely restricted the recruitment of "intellectuals" into the party.[23] Some local recruits who took up teaching responsibilities quickly became petty-bourgeois intellectuals in the authorities' eyes.[24] Even former workers and poor peasants who had received schooling organized by the party were sometimes put "on the enemy side of the ledger" by the local authorities.[25]

Across the rural bases, the objectification of the intellectual into embodied class subjects ultimately led to life-and-death consequences. During the early 1930s, fear and paranoia among the leaders about infiltration by Guomindang agents and hence decimation by Guomindang forces intermingled with power struggles and triggered a wave of brutal campaigns against "counterrevolutionaries." Imprisonment, torture, and executions of CCP leaders, cadres, and soldiers became commonplace. According to one estimate, the campaigns caused the deaths of tens of thousands of people.[26] For example, within the Red Army base that straddled Hubei, Henan, and Anhui Provinces (the E-Yu-Wan base area) and the western Fujian (Minxi) base area, "intellectuals" were designated as targets of investigation, along with former Guomindang personnel and others who had joined the insurgencies. Across the Hunan-Hubei-Jiangxi (Xiang-E-Gan) base area, over 5,000 people, most of them "rich peasants" and "intellectuals," were executed.[27] A former revolutionary remembered that in her Fujian location, "most of those who were intellectuals in their background were reportedly arrested."[28] How the detained, tortured, or executed intellectuals had been identified in any of the bases remains unclear. Another former revolutionary recalled that "anyone with a pen clipped on the shirt would be considered an intellectual and could face persecution; it was worse for those who wore glasses."[29] She probably described not so much the fate of the educated party leaders on the site, but what occurred at the rank-and-file level, in which former schoolteachers and secondary school students and even some with a few years of formal education became targets of abuse.

As fatal and other assaults raged across the rural rebel movements, their growth drew often unsuspecting people into the CCP category of intellectuals. Besides expanding the local Red Army forces and training their members, party leaders sought to develop industry, commerce, and education as well as art, finance, and medicine in the base areas as means to increase the legitimacy and influence of their insurgency. However fragile were the successes of these efforts, they turned many into technicians, artists, journalists, schoolteachers, and so on—or personnel describable as intellectuals from the party's perspective. What happened within the Jiangxi base led by Mao at one point is instructive. A multilevel system of classes, schools, and institutes emerged. Establishments designated as universities (e.g., the Red Army University and the Soviet University) enrolled military and administrative cadres for political and theoretical training. Thousands attended teacher-training classes and courses in finance, nursing, commerce, and drama and then served in those areas. Primary schools, evening schools, and newspaper reading classes offered basic education to children and adults. One estimate put the number of primary school teachers across fourteen counties at 2,535. As well, some rebels took over factories and maintained transportation and communication systems, printing presses, roads, and bridges. Others wrote for newspapers and journals; produced dramas, music, and folksongs; and published books on medicine, law, politics, and other topics.[30] These and other similar efforts at organization created a pool of revolutionaries who were classifiable by superiors and colleagues and even by themselves as intellectuals.

In sum, although the intellectual had become a major classification of people under Chinese Communism by the mid-1930s, who was recognized locally as an intellectual was not always obvious. Occupation and education, the principal criteria for distinguishing intellectuals expressed in CCP ideology, were important but not decisive factors. Having been a peasant or worker, or having authority within the party, did not always exempt one from the dubious marker. The identification was contextual rather than rule-based, shifting with relations of domination, organizational development, and changes in personal circumstances. Equally important, top-down deployment of the classification led to specific patterns of revolutionary authority, organization, and violence, most prominent of which were the self-consecration of some of the educated rebels as proletarian revolutionaries and their denunciation, exclusion, and even persecution of other educated people as treacherous intellectuals. These ideological and organizational trends would converge in Yan'an—and propel Chinese Communism and its objectification of the intellectual to new heights.

OBJECTIFYING ORGANIZATION OF A TOWN

Located in Shaanxi Province, Yan'an was a poor and remote town with roughly 3,000 people before CCP leaders established their headquarters there.[31] When the leaders arrived in Yan'an in early 1937, Chinese Communism had already under-gone important changes in response to a decade of internal turmoil and external aggression. First, the deadly purges that threatened leader safety and damaged revolutionary morale had been successfully halted; persuasion with moderate coercion, instead, had emerged as the primary means to handle intraparty con-flict.[32] Second, the Red Army forces had been rebuilt with nearby peasant support after their devastating Long March (1934–1935) from central to northwest China to escape annihilation by the Guomindang military. Third, thanks to his military prowess and political skills, Mao had risen to the top of the CCP with a precari-ous hold on the position. Most important for our purposes, the leadership had adjusted its stance on intellectuals, even though they were still considered flawed in political and moral terms. Mao subsequently articulated the position with the utmost clarity in a 1939 conference of senior party cadres in Yan'an. "The [Chinese Communist] revolution will not triumph without revolutionary intellectuals . . . Our army must take in large numbers of such intellectuals. We must convince worker-peasant cadres to accept and not be intimidated by them. Without the help of revolutionary intellectuals, peasants and workers will not improve their skills or knowledge. And we will not be able to rule the nation, the party, or the military. Our government and party offices as well as mass movements must also be set up to attract revolutionary intellectuals."[33]

The CCP's revised approach to intellectuals was consistent with what Lenin promoted before as well as after the October Revolution in Russia, that is, that the socialist revolution and, even more so, the building of a modern socialist soci-ety required the active participation of intellectuals.[34] The party's entrance into the Anti-Japanese War (1937–1945), or resistance against the Japanese invasion of China, reinforced the policy change, as the war would become the primary chan-nel through which the leadership promoted Chinese Communism to a national audience and, in particular, the educated. The new united front that the CCP established with the Guomindang because of the war also facilitated the execution of the revised approach. The political cooperation enabled the CCP to maintain control over Yan'an and the broader Shaanxi-Gansu-Ningxia (Shaan-Gan-Ning) base area as well as to conduct limited but meaningful political activities in Guomindang areas.

The CCP used its networks of members and supporters, military offices in vari-ous provinces, and newspaper advertisements to recruit "intellectuals" to come to Yan'an, especially young men and women, whom the Mao regime, like previous leaderships, considered less corrupted by Chinese tradition and capitalist ideol-ogy. The party promised the recruits, some of whom were from overseas, accom-modation, education, and an active role in war and revolution.[35] A December 1943 party report notes that roughly 40,000 intellectuals had entered Yan'an since the late 1930s. Given the party's broad definition of intellectuals, these newcom-ers unsurprisingly had a variety of backgrounds. Academically, 30 percent of the population had started but not finished junior high school; 21 and 31 percent had completed senior and junior high school, respectively; and 19 percent had post-secondary education.[36] Most of these recruits were men. A large number were recently secondary school students, to whom the leaders also referred to as intellectual youths (*zhishi qingnian*). There were professional experts such as professors and engineers, literary and art personnel such as playwrights and painters, and technical-support and white-collar workers such as automobile technicians and government clerks. A small number were former soldiers. Some had poor parents, some had had enviable upbringings, and many came from what the party called the petty-bourgeois households of small business owners, schoolteachers, or office workers.

Top-down labeling did not transform these recruits into widely recognized "intellectuals" any more than self-proclamation turned Mao and other CCP leaders into admired proletarian revolutionaries. How the leadership reorganized Yan'an and therefore Chinese Communism to receive the newcomers was crucial. Building on their revolutionary experience and authority, the leaders established an array of institutes bearing names that denoted professional or higher education to absorb the recruits, for example, Women's University of China, Northern Shaanxi Public Academy, Natural Science Research Institute, and Yan'an Ethnology Institute.[37] Though physically crude and poorly equipped, these institutes usually had their own grounds with residential space allocated nearby. The newcomers were therefore clustered in various parts of the town, separated from the leaders, who lived in relatively spacious compounds that they shared with one another, and from the stationed Red Army troops, who protected Yan'an on its perimeters. Surrounded by poverty and warfare, the faculty and students took classes, read books, and conducted discussions. They attended opening and graduation ceremonies and other activities related to teaching and learning. The education usually lasted from three months to two years and involved various combinations of professional, political, and military training.[38] Put differently, as the leaders jubilantly proclaimed the arrival of intellectuals, an asset that would strengthen the war effort of the party and its revolutionary capabilities, unprecedented changes overtook work, space, and life in the previously unremarkable town.

How the CCP operated the Lu Xun Academy of Arts (*Lu Xun yishu xueyuan*) exemplifies the changes in topography and work that spotlighted the newcomers as "intellectuals" as officially claimed. Named after the famous and recently deceased leftist writer, the academy opened its doors in April 1938 inside another newly established institute, the Lu Xun Normal School. Most of the Academy's instructors were writers and artists from Shanghai with no experience in rural insurgency. The students, whose levels of education ranged from primary school to college, were selected because of their interest in the fine arts or performing arts. Climbing enrollment led the authorities to relocate the campus quickly to one of the hills that made up the town. The faculty and students occupied almost twenty

FIGURE 1. Contemporary view of the church that once housed the Lu Xun Academy of Arts. (Photo by author)

existing loess caves. They dug two more rows of caves, erected a single-story building, and cleared a desolate area for residential, performance, and other purposes. In August 1939 the authorities moved the growing institute farther away from the town center, into an imposing Catholic church with two steeples (see figure 1). Many nearby loess caves were converted for residential use, as were some newly excavated ones.[39] Work within the academy reflected the leadership's emphasis on both education and revolution. The faculty and students concentrated on teaching and learning art, music, literature, and theater. They distinguished themselves further with use of Western sources, forms, and techniques foreign to the region and unfamiliar to ordinary party cadres and soldiers. They held exhibitions of their work and rehearsals for their productions and performed in front of cadres, soldiers, and students throughout Yan'an.[40]

These organizational measures allowed for preservation of the values and habits of the faculty and students acquired outside the rural milieu, the display of which distinguished them further from other Yan'an residents. The notable writer Mao Dun (1896–1981), who taught briefly in the academy during the early 1940s, described faculty residences with admiration: "Because writers and artists live here, each cave is decorated differently and expresses its occupant's unique character.

Every artist has used his clever inventiveness, his own hands, and extremely crude materials and turned the abode [cave] into an elegantly refined, brightly beautiful, or majestically special place."[41] In equally visible fashion, some faculty did not wear the military outfit provided to everyone who worked or studied in one or another of the institutes. They donned, instead, fedoras, woolen coats, and other urban-style or self-made clothing. Students wore the military outfit, but often with "personal flair." Young women often added a dickey underneath the shirt and pinned colorful swatches on their sleeves and shoes. Some students wore their caps stylishly like berets. Every evening, students and instructors strolled along a nearby riverbank, chatting, making friends, and even falling in love. The popularity of ballroom dancing in revolutionary Yan'an is well documented. Many recruits and even Mao and other party leaders enjoyed this activity. The Lu Xun Academy was an especially popular venue in this regard, hosting at one point dancing parties every Saturday evening. These involved live music by students and decorations by resident artists.[42]

Within the academy and other institutes, relations of domination established by the CCP leadership signaled further that the "intellectuals" who had traveled to Yan'an were different from the revolutionaries who had arrived there earlier. Mao and other party leaders periodically visited the institutes, lectured to the students, and sometimes instructed them on how to overcome their "petty-bourgeois" foibles qua intellectuals.[43] Party leaders served as heads of the institutes, while veteran cadres filled key administrative positions. These leaders and cadres were mostly well-educated men. In other words, the pattern of authority reflected and reinforced a social division that CCP leaders had been stressing shortly after the party's founding. Or, there were two kinds of educated people in Chinese society—those who had transformed themselves into proletarian revolutionaries and those who had not. For example, the head of the Academy of Marxist-Leninist Studies, Zhang Wentian (1900–1976), had a university-level education and had received theoretical training in Marxism in the Soviet Union. He briefly headed the CCP before Chinese Communism entered its Yan'an phase.[44] Thanks to his revolutionary experience, authority, and knowledge, this man could confidently claim to be a proletarian revolutionary in front of the faculty and students whom he oversaw. This was probably true, too, of the chief of instruction at the Lu Xun Academy, Xu Yixin (1911–1994), a revolutionary of ten years' standing who had received higher education in the Soviet Union.[45]

For practical and ideological reasons, the Mao leadership used the resources of some of the institutes to train separately newly arrived factory workers and other laborers as well as party cadres from nearby areas and other rural bases. Such visible arrangements further reinforced the official view that the recruits who were former writers or schoolteachers or other kinds of educated persons were "intellectuals." What happened at the Chinese People's Anti-Japanese Resistance University of Military and Politics Affairs (*Zhongguo renmin kangri junshi zhengzhi daxue*) is revealing. This institute, which produced tens of thousands of political, military, and other personnel, divided the constantly changing mix of trainees into brigades (*dui*). For example, the class that moved into Yan'an with the institute in early 1937 had fourteen brigades totaling almost 1,400 people. Senior and ordinary Red Army personnel filled eight of the brigades. The remaining six brigades, including one composed entirely of women, contained mostly recently arrived and relatively educated young people.[46] Across the institutes, even when the classes involved a mixture of trainees, the heads apparently wanted those who were party cadres or former workers to monitor the behavior of former office workers, college students, and others, and to remain on guard against their supposedly inevitable display of petty-bourgeois or other undesirable ideas and behavior.[47]

Job assignment within Yan'an also had classification impact. To strengthen the Shaan-Gan-Ning base for war and revolution, the CCP leadership used many recruits immediately after their arrival or upon their completion of training to expand education, art, industry, and other sectors. For example, the industrial workforce jumped from under 200 people before 1937 to over 12,000 by 1944.[48] The assignments not only turned many into engineers, schoolteachers, journalists, and other kinds of personnel that fit into the party's definition of intellectuals; the development of some of the sectors led to the further clustering of the recruits across the town. A place called Cultural Valley (*Wenhua gou*) quickly emerged as home to various writers' groups, literary associations, art troupes, a library, and other cultural and educational organizations. On Refreshing Mountain (*Qingliang shan*), which is a short distance away across the Yan River that runs through the town, the leadership created a media hub that included a news agency, a newspaper, a printing press, a radio station, and a bookstore, among other facilities. The establishment of Yan'an Central Hospital (*Yan'an zhongyang yiyuan*) during the late 1930s illustrates how this approach to job assignment brought those whom the leadership regarded as intellectuals together. The leadership approved the project, chose a site, and appointed as head a bespectacled man who had a doctorate of medicine from the University of Toulouse in France. Others with experience in medicine, nursing, and pharmacology were reassigned to work in the hospital. Physicians and other medical personnel were sent from elsewhere to the establishment, which also recruited and trained newly arrived women with secondary education to become nurses.[49]

NORMALIZATION OF A MARXIAN CLASSIFICATION

The Rectification Campaign sponsored by Mao was a watershed in the history of Chinese Communism. The campaign began in Yan'an, spread to other CCP bases, and served to consolidate Mao's leadership and strengthen ideological discipline. In their account of the campaign, David Apter and Tony Saich indicate that "a symbolically orchestrated tutelary regime"[50] built upon textual learning and other instructional techniques and backed by coercive power enveloped Yan'an. This regime served to propagate Mao's understanding of revolutionary ethics, Chinese society, and global history and at the same time to delegitimize other political narratives, visions, and strategies. For our purposes, at the center of this achievement was the Mao leadership's deployment of the intellectual classification. In fact, we cannot understand the campaign and its organization any more than we can fathom the topographical and institutional changes mentioned above without taking into account how the classification was used. Mao's view of the intellectual as a usable but unreliable subject defined the character of the campaign, while its success deepened the objectification of the intellectual and left behind an influential organizational legacy.

During Rectification, Mao and his deputies used the intellectual classification as a weapon to attack competitors and potential challengers, just as previous CCP leaders had done when embroiled in intraparty struggles. At the elite level, Mao's targets were the so-called Russian Returned Students led by Wang Ming (1904–1974), Bo Gu (1907–1946), and Zhang Wentian. These members of the party leadership had studied at the Soviet-sponsored Sun Yat-Sen University of the Toilers of China in Moscow during the 1920s. Through their work in the Comintern, they had developed close relations with the Soviet regime, which continued to exert influence over Chinese Communism, albeit with diminishing impact after rural insurgency became a main component of the project. Wang, Bo, and Zhang had each held the top post in the party before Mao's ascent. Each of them had lost a key ideological battle to Mao not long before he initiated the campaign. Known to be a Marxist theoretician and an essayist, Wang had promoted a Soviet-sanctioned model of a united front between the Guomindang and the CCP for the Anti-Japanese War in lieu of the one proposed by Mao.[51] Zhang and Bo had headed the critical work of revolutionary propaganda and cadre training as well as the party organ *Liberation Daily* (*Jiefang ribao*), but encountered Mao's rebuke for failing to highlight the uniqueness of Chinese society and of the Chinese revolutionary experience.[52]

Written by Mao shortly before Rectification spread across Yan'an, "Reform Our Study," "Rectify the Party's Style of Work," and "Oppose Stereotyped Party Writing" were important essays where he laid out the campaign's rationales and his dissatisfactions with particular types of conduct and thinking found under Chinese Communism.[53] Although the works unmistakably attacked revolutionaries who were well educated, none labeled Wang, Bo, Zhang, or any of the Russian Returned Students as petty-bourgeois or unreliable intellectuals. However, Mao's teeming complaints against party leaders and cadres who had researched, lectured, or written about Marxist theory and practice leave little doubt that he regarded the Returned Students as such subjects (rather than as proletarian revolutionaries like himself). In "Reform Our Study," Mao launched a thinly veiled attack against such individuals. He placed them together with other educated people within the party based on what he observed as their "subjectivist attitude" (*zhuguan zhuyi*) toward the socialist revolution and indicated why they all needed ideological reeducation.

> With this attitude, a person does not make a systematic and thorough study of the environment, but works by sheer subjective enthusiasm and has a blurred picture of the face of China today. With this attitude, he chops up history, knows only ancient Greece but not China and is in a fog about the China of yesterday and the day before yesterday. With this attitude, a person studies Marxist-Leninist theory in the abstract and without any aim . . . When making speeches, they [senior party cadres and even leaders] indulge in a long string of headings, A, B, C, D, 1, 2, 3, 4, and when writing articles, they turn out a lot of verbiage. They have no intention of seeking truth from facts, but only a desire to curry favour by claptrap. They are flashy without substance, brittle without solidity. They are always right; they are the Number One authority under Heaven, 'imperial envoys' [dispatched from Soviet Russia by the Comintern] who rush everywhere. Such is the style of work of some comrades in our ranks.[54]

Mao's attack against the Returned Students reminds us of Qu Qiubai's condemnation of Chen Duxiu and other CCP leaders during the late 1920s. That is, the victor of an intraparty struggle denounced the defeated as treacherous intellectuals. A critical difference, however, separates the attacks. Like Qu, the Returned Students had Comintern support and political training in Moscow. The fact that they became Mao's targets reveals that Soviet influence over Chinese Communism had declined significantly.

What happened to Zhang Wentian reveals how some defeated CCP leaders became self-denigrating "intellectuals" for others to see. A polyglot and a successful writer and translator, Zhang was one of the four Returned Students who had received advanced training in Marxist-Leninist thought from the Soviet regime. During the 1930s, he had used his training and leadership position to advocate passionately for the inclusion of "petty-bourgeois" writers and "intellectuals of petty-bourgeois background" in Chinese Communism.[55] His appointment as head of the Academy of Marxist-Leninist Studies in Yan'an reinforced his superior status as a Marxist theoretician and revolutionary. As Mao's attack against fellow leaders intensified, Zhang conceded that the Returned Students were ideologically unprepared to be proletarian revolutionaries. In September 1941, he indicated at a high-level CCP meeting that the Comintern had made a grave mistake by placing "cadres without actual experience in revolutionary work" in the party's upper echelons. He confessed that "subjectivism" and "dogmatism" had severely colored his understanding of Marxist thought, leading to among other things his "crude and cartoonish" interpretations of issues and problems facing Chinese Communism.[56] Responding to Mao's criticism and instruction, Zhang and other leaders embarked on a rural investigation trip in January 1942 to acquire what passed for genuine knowledge and experience about class and revolution in China. He and his team spent more than a year in northern Shaanxi studying and writing reports on economic and other village issues. His return to Yan'an brought forth further self-reproaches. In a March 1943 report to the CCP Central Committee, he implicated others, too, as usable but unreliable intellectuals who lacked basic knowledge of Chinese society. "In particular," he wrote, "the kind of intellectuals like ourselves [who wanted a socialist revolution] always love to 'hold our heads high and gaze at the sky' and find among the stars other-worldly, bizarre 'ideals' . . . We do not understand the most mundane, most common, and yet most essential issue facing the masses," or their pains and traumas stemming from rampant class exploitation.[57]

Outside the CCP leadership, the Rectification Campaign in Yan'an targeted the large numbers of recently arrived "intellectuals" and led to conspicuous growth of ideological reeducation, mass surveillance, and management by party cadres. To be sure, the campaign also attacked those regarded as former peasants (*nongmin*) and workers (*gongren*) among the revolutionary personnel, or the purportedly deleterious impact of class exploitation on these persons' thinking and behavior. The assault on the intellectuals, however, occurred on an entirely different scale. First, the Mao regime had inherited from previous leaderships a deep distrust of such subjects. Second, recently arrived writers, artists, and students had incurred the ire of Mao and other leaders by airing or supporting complaints about inequality and other problems of organization in the town.[58] The leadership combined Marxist-Leninist and May Fourth language with Maoist reproaches and declared intellectuals an obstacle to revolution if they should remain ideologically unreformed. The attacks appeared widely in speeches, directives, and reports as well as in *Liberation Daily*, which also reproduced the required readings of the campaign.[59] Many of the condemnations were drawn from Mao's writings, especially the above-mentioned essays; some were gleaned from other leaders' works, such as the notable piece written by Liu Shaoqi (1898–1969) in 1939, "How to Be a Good Communist."[60] Mao's scornful remarks on intellectuals quoted at the beginning of this chapter constitute but one example of the torrential attacks.

The Mao regime claimed to have unmasked intellectuals' dubious participation in Chinese Communism on three levels: how they understood the project, what they wanted from it, and how they behaved in it. On the first level, the leadership charged that intellectuals glossed over the importance of Marxism and Leninism. Their political thinking reflected, instead, valorization of personal experience, fixation on abstruse philosophies, and dogmatic use of Marxist-Leninist teachings. That is, they failed to understand what Chinese Communism stood for. On the second level, the leadership noted that self-centeredness was a central trait of intellectuals. Although they were involved in a socialist revolution, they pursued their own goals, sang their own praises, and aspired to become famous surgeons, educators, writers, and so on, exhibiting en masse "the syndrome of a self-styled hero" (*geren yingxiong zhuyi*). This conduct of theirs harmed the project's progress. On the third level, intellectuals therefore tended to dislike assignments incompatible with their own ambitions or interests. They lacked discipline, flouted orders, and sought to come and go as they pleased. At heart, the leadership proclaimed, this focus on personal interests, accomplishments, and liberties reflected the "petty-bourgeois" or "bourgeois" backgrounds of intellectuals, or ways of thinking antithetical to sacrifice, order, and collectivism, the very things that Chinese Communism allegedly needed if it was to succeed.[61]

Within Yan'an, a multilayered instructional apparatus emerged, turning revolutionaries at virtually all levels into subjects of education as well as objects of knowledge. Headed by Mao, the ad hoc General Study Commission of the CCP Central Committee (*Zhonggong zhongyang zhong xuexi weiyuanhui*) handled policymaking. Subarea study commissions controlled by party leaders and senior party cadres appeared in the Red Army, the Central Party School (*Zhongyang dangxiao*), the Shaan-Gan-Ning government, and the cultural, educational, and other sectors. The commissions drew up study plans based on the leadership's instructions and on considerations relevant to the sector in question. Writers, teachers, military officers, government officials, and others underwent three to five months of training, using part of the workday to study and discuss material preselected by the General Study Commission. Mao and his deputies visited various establishments and gave lectures, advice, and encouragement. The trainees were required to "interrogate deeply," "discuss fervently," and "understand and connect with the spirit and substance" of the material. They had to use the material to examine the establishment where they worked and to "reform thoroughly" its operation and their colleagues' workstyles and political thinking. They were instructed to reflect "comprehensively" on their own conduct, ideas, and experience and to identify, examine, and overcome their political and ideological mistakes. Everyone, including senior party leaders, was required to keep "study and discussion notes" (*biji*), and to write and rewrite "a political history of the self" (*zizhuan*) to demonstrate efforts and progress.[62]

Besides serving to amplify the Mao leadership's attack on "intellectuals," top-down deployment of "criticism and self-criticism" across the many institutes engendered a multitude of supposedly firsthand confirmations of the official view. Under the supervision of senior or other party cadres, students and instructors divulged, discussed, and denounced their own mistakes and those of others. They condemned themselves and one another for selfishness, lack of discipline, arrogance, and other shortcomings that the leadership stated were common among intellectuals. They reported that they had been seduced by incorrect or impractical political views, including "dogmatic" interpretations of Marxism-Leninism. They traced the shortcomings to their own "petty-bourgeois" or other backgrounds and the allegedly corresponding lifestyles and social ties. Some pored through their own writings, drawings, or other works as well as those of one another, and discovered and decried objectionable political views and expressions. The authorities within the institutes organized the publication of some of the mistakes on wall posters, bulletin boards, and newsletters to encourage further collective learning and individual disclosure. *Liberation Daily* published select self-criticisms by writers, artists, and students for the same purposes.[63]

Additional mechanisms of official surveillance were set up to ensure the success of ideological reeducation. Before Rectification spread across the institutes and sectors, the General Study Commission had provided administrative and ideological training to senior party cadres to prepare them to become supervisors. During the campaign, the cadres attended study and discussion sessions at lower levels and offered instructions and guidance. The commission established a traveling inspection team (*xunshi tuan*) with responsibility of reporting once a week on general issues and concerns. Members of the team visited discussion sessions and gave recommendations. They had the authority to examine study and discussion notes and mete out tests to gauge the participants' efforts and progress. At lower levels, inspection commissions were formed, too, to monitor participation in learning activities. Members of these commissions assumed various tasks, such as attending discussions, administering exams, checking study notes, and giving advice. Some establishments (e.g., the Central Military Commission, the Central Party School, the Shaan-Gan-Ning Government) created visiting teams (*canguan tuan*) that traveled to other sites to exchange learning experiences. The team members would meet with senior cadres on the site, read study notes, and talk to individual participants. Some establishments (such as Shaan-Gan-Ning Government) even arranged joint conferences (*lianxi huiyi*) between various agencies to address campaign issues and assess progress.[64]

Within Yan'an, Rectification thus led to a "total reeducation of the [revolutionary] community."[65] The intellectual as a classification of people doubled as a linchpin of the campaign and a substrate acted upon by it. Ideological reeducation, mass surveillance, and management by party cadres became the tripods and conduits through which the leadership normalized the meanings it inscribed on the marker and defined the authority structure of Chinese Communism. Henceforth, tens of thousands of revolutionaries recognized themselves or identified others as intellectuals based on the CCP discourse of class struggle. The objectification of the intellectual under Chinese Communism entered a new phase.

MANIPULATIONS OF SOCIAL IDENTITY

Although CCP domination produced in Yan'an a highly visible population of "intellectuals," its boundaries remained indeterminable in practice. The ambiguities embedded in the party's concept of intellectuals, the heterogeneous backgrounds of the revolutionaries, and the diverse training and opportunities they received ceaselessly affected how they regarded themselves and one another. Self-refashioning, which intensified after Rectification, further blurred the boundaries of the objectified population. While relatively educated persons had to deal with actual or potential stigmatization, they also had opportunities to acquire positions and authority as government, industry, and other sectors expanded in nearby areas controlled by the party. This tension between class identity and revolutionary career, or the moral and the functional view of the intellectual of the Mao regime, drove many to monitor and even modify their own image. The fact that every indicator used by the party to define or describe the intellectual as a class subject (i.e., education, occupation, political thinking, moral dispositions, and habits and lifestyle) was changeable or concealable on an individual basis only reinforced self-refashioning.

Overall, four sets of hierarchical divisions that reflected the ideology and organization of Chinese Communism formed the basis on which Yan'an revolutionaries sought to minimize stigmatization *and* benefit from their knowledge or skills. The divisions were those between the party elites and the rest of the revolutionary personnel, the military and the nonmilitary sector, "poor peasants" and "workers" and other Marxian categories of people, and party members and nonmembers. Since the 1920s, the CCP leadership had been investing the upper sections of these divisions with positive meanings, symbolisms, and imageries of class and revolution through speeches and statements, theater and literature, and other channels. An ascent to any of the upper sections would provide the revolutionary with symbolic resources for self-presentation, be they pertaining to his or her belief, behavior, or background. Upward mobility would not make one immune to being labeled an unreliable intellectual, as Mao's attack against Zhang Wentian and other Russian Returned Students evidenced. Nonetheless, the ascent would help the revolutionary separate herself symbolically, if not also physically, from the schoolteachers, journalists, and others working under Chinese Communism, for whom the leadership regarded ideological reeducation and discipline as most necessary, not to mention from the "petty-bourgeois" and "bourgeois" intellectuals outside the revolutionary project.

Based on memoirs and other material, we can divide Yan'an revolutionaries' strategies of self-refashioning broadly into three (non–mutually exclusive) types: self-consecration as proletarian revolutionary, deflection of the intellectual marker, and self-image makeover. As we have seen, self-consecration as proletarian revolutionary had been a strategy available to CCP leaders since the 1920s. The leaders exploited their revolutionary authority, organizational experience, and even literary skills to elevate themselves above the rest of the revolutionaries. The triumph of Mao during Rectification, and especially his attack against senior colleagues, greatly reduced the number of party leaders who could use the strategy. Timothy Cheek's study of the campaign offers clues to the kind of leaders who might still be able to present themselves as proletarian revolutionaries in words and deeds. Zhang Ruxin (1908–1976), Yang Shangkun (1907–1988), and Kang Sheng (1898–1975) had all studied in Moscow but had been supporting Mao before he initiated Rectification. During the campaign, Zhang, Yang, and Kang assumed leadership roles in the areas of propaganda, organization, and security respectively. Zhang and Yang reprimanded senior party cadres openly and instructed them on how to reform themselves ideologically; Kang was in charge of exposing and punishing "irredeemable enemies," including those among "intellectuals," and of delivering lectures to the cadres about such enemies.[66] Rectification thus elevated the three men above the cadres and even some party leaders. Equally telling is the case of the Red Army's commander in chief, Zhu De (1886–1976). Zhu came from a well-to-do family and had once enrolled in the University of Göttingen in Germany. By the late 1930s, a foreign correspondent observed, "Had it not been for his uniform, he could have passed for almost any peasant in any village in China."[67] During Rectification, Zhu exploited his revolutionary authority, military leadership, and physical transformation to attack writers and others, including those within the army, for lacking proletarian consciousness. He indicated that he "did not belong to the proletariat originally" but "had handed himself over to" (toujiang) and was willing to die for that class. In effect, he announced that he was a proletarian revolutionary.[68]

For other CCP leaders chastised by Mao or subjected to ideological reeducation, Rectification did not necessarily lead to their permanent stigmatization as unreliable intellectuals. Quite the contrary, their superior status within the party provided them with otherwise unavailable opportunities to reclaim their proletarian revolutionary identity—so long as they submitted to Mao's leadership. Let us revisit Zhang Wentian's return to Yan'an from rural investigation. In the reports to the CCP Central Committee, he recounted repeatedly how he had studied work and life using Mao's ideological approach (which included "seeking truth from facts," "going to the masses," "emphasizing typical examples," and focusing on production), and how he strove to purge himself of the subjective, dogmatic, and bureaucratic attitudes that the Chairman had condemned. In December 1943 he produced for Mao's perusal a lengthy volume, Notes from Self-Examination (Fanxing biji), in which, to the Chairman's delight, he again "conducted a systematic and profoundly revealing criticism" of his intellectual habits and political mistakes. From then on, Zhang returned to the center of the party's activities, while continuing to criticize himself in public forums, including the Seventh National Congress of the CCP held in Yan'an in 1945. His self-abnegation paid off. During the Congress, he was reelected to the Political Bureau, the party's highest body, which had only thirteen members.[69] Zhang did not regain the political capital that he had once had as head of the party; nonetheless, he had enough compared with most others under Chinese Communism to present himself as a proletarian revolutionary.

At lower levels, Rectification amplified existing efforts by revolutionaries to deflect the intellectual marker. Some of the revolutionaries were from poor families and did not want their academic training or professional experience to impede their advancement. Ma Hong, with whom I began this chapter, was an example.

For this precocious young man, the main challenge of self-presentation was how to draw attention to his disadvantaged background while benefiting from his excellent writing skills and education in a research institute run by the party. Ma emphasized his humble background and lack of schooling, and hence signaled that he was not another petty-bourgeois intellectual who had come to Yan'an to join the revolution. For revolutionaries like Ma, repeatedly referring to stints of manual labor that they had endured might help as well. What happened at the Anti-Japanese Resistance University during the late 1930s suggests that finger-pointing probably remained within the arsenal of self-representations of formerly underprivileged revolutionaries. When asked by superiors to screen and recruit recently arrived personnel into the party, some of the cadres staffing the campus balked. One of them remembers, "We were somewhat worried about absorbing into the party college students who used to wear long gowns and leather shoes. Almost all of those whom we had recruited until that point were young peasants or handicraft workers. I felt that those students did not behave as they should have in a revolution. Most of them had very complicated social ties and rather bad class backgrounds."[70] The cadres exploited their familiarity with the CCP rhetoric of class and played up the social distance between themselves and the students, even as this gap was closing because of their own improving access to education and job opportunities, and because the austere lifestyle in Yan'an was continuing to transform the appearance, habits, and routines of the students. In effect, the cadres indicated to themselves and their superiors that they were genuine revolutionaries and the others were unreliable intellectuals.

Likewise, the CCP cadres who had survived the bloody purges of "intellectuals" in rural revolutionary bases during the 1930s had little reason to want to be marked as such subjects. By Rectification, some of these cadres had been in the countryside for more than a decade. The discipline, labor, and valor needed to survive armed invasions, severe climates, and demanding terrains had left physical signs, or (to borrow from Foucault) "a bodily rhetoric of honor"[71] useful for self-presentation. For example, Long March veteran Cheng Fangwu (1897–1984), who headed the Northern Shaanxi Public Academy (*Shaanbei gongxue*) in Yan'an, was a May Fourth activist who had studied in Japan, taught in a university, and edited several journals, among other literary and intellectual activities. There was seemingly little in his everyday appearance that betrayed his superior education or previous privileges. As a former revolutionary recalls, Cheng was "of medium size, having a few whiskers and an always greasy face that he apparently seldom washed. He wore a cotton-padded jacket that looked filthy and glossy [from overuse]. Nowhere was Cheng close to resembling a cultured man [*wenhua ren*]; instead, he looked like a veteran cook."[72] Yang Guangchi (1905–1987), a former college student, had been a political officer in Red Army forces since the early 1930s. In Yan'an, he trained large numbers of secondary school and college recruits at the Anti-Japanese Resistance University. A former student recalls that Yang was a "completely experienced soldier" who wore "shining five-star medals" on his uniform and hardships on his face and had "the appearance of an ordinary worker."[73] Both Cheng and Yang adopted bodily strategies for self-presentation.

Self-image makeover was the most common strategy of refashioning employed by Yan'an revolutionaries after Rectification. Here stigmatized writers, students, and others performed commitment to the ideal version of a revolutionary as promoted by the Mao regime. Their goal was to gain symbolic and other resources that would help to alter their now-recognized identifications as petty-bourgeois intellectuals. Joining the Red Army was an approach for some, although a physically risky one. The CCP elites had built around the forces an aura of courage, loyalty, and discipline compared with the selfishness, impracticality, and other shortcomings ascribed to "intellectuals." Enlistment could bring one a military rank (such as platoon leader), a classification as military personnel (*junren*), and the accolade of "Red Army warrior" (*hongjun zhanshi*), all of which were symbolic assets.[74] Serving in an impoverished village inside or outside the region as deputy village chief (*fu xiangzhang*) or village clerk (*xiang wenshu*) helped other revolutionaries to improve their images. The party needed staff to expand propaganda and organizational work in the countryside. Austere as life was in Yan'an, conditions in such villages were worse, filled with risks to health and life itself.[75] By accepting a rural assignment, one practically announced willingness to rise above one's own "petty-bourgeois" desire for comfort and professional success. After Mao chastised writers and artists during the Yan'an Forum, many of them reportedly wanted to be sent to the countryside, or follow what the Chairman had asked them to do.[76] The notable poet Ai Qing (1910–1996) and other artists as well as some former schoolteachers and students even volunteered to join the Red Army.[77]

The CCP authorities did not support every enlistment or transfer request from writers, artists, or students, and thus decided in practice which "intellectuals" would receive such opportunities for self-refashioning. Chen Xuezhao (1906–1991), an accomplished writer with a PhD from the University of Paris, had come to Yan'an in 1938. After Rectification, the authorities assigned her as an editor at *Liberation Daily*. Chen expressed her desire to live and work among poor villagers "to reform [her] thinking and worldview and to produce literary works that would serve peasants, workers, and soldiers." Her repeated requests for transfer to the countryside were denied. Two years later and not yet a party member, she was reassigned to the Central Party School as a literacy teacher. Headed by party leaders, this institute specialized in providing select cadres with advanced political training.[78] Chen taught in the Fourth Division (*Sibu*). The enrollees were veteran cadres, military officers, and other cadres of "peasant" or "worker" origins who were chosen for their laudable service to Chinese Communism and their need for basic education for report-writing and other tasks.[79] Within this environment, Chen could not but be typecast as an intellectual because of her background and responsibilities (see Figure 2).

FIGURE 2. Commemorative inscription of Mao Zedong's message to college instructors counseling them to serve the revolution by fulfilling teaching responsibilities rather than by requesting to be sent to the frontline. (Photo by author)

Even writers, artists, and others who stayed in professional or literary posts after Rectification found ways to alleviate their stigma. The Mao leadership demanded that such revolutionaries improve their political consciousness and performance. Someone who received positive assessments in this respect from superiors stood a good chance of gaining a reassignment, an invitation to join the party, or a promotion in party rank—or symbolic resources for self-presentation. Displaying commitment to official ideology, watching one's words and deeds, and following orders were appropriate tactics. He Qifang (1912–1977) graduated from Peking University in 1935, and worked as a schoolteacher while publishing poetry and essays in newspapers before departing for Yan'an and joining the CCP during the late 1930s. When Rectification ended, the party decided to send him to Chongqing to liaise with novelists, essayists, playwrights, and others supportive of the revolutionary project. The city, which was in southwest China, had been designated by the Guomindang as the national capital. Hu Feng (1902–1985), a prominent writer among those who received He Qifang, remembered that the revolutionary used himself to illustrate the success of thought reform. He spoke with "a tone that made others feel he was proving he had already reformed himself into a genuine member of the proletariat," while indicating to his audience that they should mend their "petty-bourgeois" thinking and habits.[80]

Around the same time, Zhao Chaogou (1910–1992), a famous journalist who visited Yan'an with some others, noticed the following on his day of arrival: "Here the tinges of femininity are unusually light. Not even one woman wears a *qipao* [a close-fitting dress] or a perm, and no lovers strut around holding hands. Most female cadres put up little feminine affect and behavior (*jiaorou de zuozuo*). What they wear differs little from what male cadres wear. To exaggerate somewhat, Yan'an is probably the least sexy (*xinggan*) place [in China]."[81] Such departures from the multifaceted display of urban styles and habits in the town before Rectification occurred in other areas of life, too. Zhao spoke to notable writers but found that they did not mention any foreign literary theory during conversations on art and literature, quoting, instead, Mao's famous lectures on the topics. Most of the students he interviewed had studied in urban schools and even colleges but showed no obvious sign of having received a Western-style education. The students gave "standardized" replies not only to queries about politics and revolution, but also to those related to romance and personal life.[82] Their reactions undoubtedly reflected top-down pressure and tutelage and even fear. When considered with other flourishing tactics of self-refashioning, such conduct can be said also to reflect a desire to be seen as a committed revolutionary.

Participation in agricultural work, voluntary or not, was another channel for writers, artists, and other "petty-bourgeois intellectuals" to improve their own images. This form of adaptation had strong ideological, practical, and institutional support within Yan'an. The CCP leadership had praised the class character of poor peasants and farm laborers, such as their perseverance, humility, and righteousness, even as their habits and dispositions were criticized as tainted by exploitative traditions. Driven by necessity, large numbers of revolutionaries had participated in agricultural production before Rectification. After the campaign, the Mao regime deepened what it called the "to the village" (*xiaxiang*) movement, requiring "intellectuals" to raise their revolutionary consciousness through working and living with peasants. The leadership expanded farming in the Shaan-Gan-Ning base area to cope with Guomindang embargoes. Teachers, students, and others learned to sow grains, grow vegetables, raise livestock, chop wood, spin yarn, make tools, and so on.[83] Shen Xia (1921–1945) was Mao Dun's daughter. She was attending Yan'an University, another institute started by the party, when she heard that the campus would participate in the drive to produce farm and other goods. What she entered in her diary suggests that production activities were perceived by those stigmatized as intellectuals as opportunities to alter their class identity: "Now it is time to experience reality and temper myself through labor.

For someone who wants to train herself into a complete proletarian, genuinely taking part in labor has great import."[84]

In sum, Yan'an revolutionaries used occupational, physical, and linguistic strategies as well as institutional channels under Chinese Communism (e.g., official assignment, rank promotion, productive labor) to deflect the menace of the "intellectual" marker or mitigate its stigma. For these individuals, building a revolutionary career would entail managing their own biography, physical appearance, public conduct, social relations, and so on. The goal was to obviate or temper attacks against their political and moral character and garner approval from colleagues and superiors. As such, the maneuvers did not call into question the leadership's view of the intellectual as a usable yet unreliable subject. To the contrary, they further legitimized the view and objectified the intellectual.

In a 1990 lecture at the Collège de France, Bourdieu stated that if it seems easy to talk about a subject, it is because "we are in a certain sense penetrated by the very thing we have to study."[85] The conviction toward what the subject is becomes an obstacle to understanding its genuine nature. The intellectual under Chinese Communism is a case in point. Research relies on readily available concepts of intellectuals that emphasize the social function, cultural capital, or moral conduct of the educated, however they are defined. The studies mask the metamorphosis of the intellectual from an obscure classification adopted by the CCP to concrete political, ethical, and physical forms, or embodied subjects locatable eventually throughout state and society. Within Yan'an, the emergence of a population of "intellectuals" reflected as well as affected the organization of Chinese Communism. The CCP discourse of class and revolution and reorganization of political relations, division of labor, and space constituted the ontological foundation of the subjects. As revolutionaries were turned into usable but unreliable intellectuals, ideological reeducation, mass surveillance, and workplace management by party cadres intensified. The incorporation of the intellectuals into the revolutionary project enabled the party to pursue otherwise unachievable goals, such as expanding industrial production, deepening rural mobilization, developing multifaceted propaganda, and increasing literacy in the Red Army.

What happened in Yan'an was but a harbinger of the mutual constitution of the intellectual and Chinese Communism that would occur nationwide. After 1949, class subjects recognized as intellectuals appeared in every sector penetrated by the state. The multiplications, elaborations, and intensifications of the ruling tactics and strategies that had originally converged in the town altered local organization and thus subjectivities and social identities. Government offices, newspapers, villages, and many other sites each had intellectuals who were used and abused in particular ways. Yan'an was the fountainhead of such development in another respect. The Mao regime assigned many revolutionaries who were trained there to positions of authority. Whether these cadres had been denounced as intellectuals by the regime or not, they were familiar with its ideology and practice of class struggle. They spread the official view of the intellectual through meetings, reports, newspapers, and other channels. They helped to reorganize local authority structures and install political control mechanisms. Some even headed scientific, educational, industrial, and cultural establishments. In short, they became frontline agents in the objectification of the intellectual under the PRC.

4

The Self-Fulfilling Prophecy of a Registration Drive

Question: Can dance hostesses [wunü] who have graduated from junior high school or above register as unemployed intellectuals?

Answer: Dance hostesses and others who meet the official criteria can register as unemployed intellectuals.

—STAFF MANUAL OF THE SHANGHAI MUNICIPAL COMMISSION FOR
HANDLING UNEMPLOYED INTELLECTUALS, 1951

[She] became a Guomindang member during the Anti-Japanese War; husband teaches in a factory-run school. Not that sophisticated; saw great progress during training. Poor awareness in the past; now can criticize [political and ideological offenses and injustices]. Likes to help others and to laugh; not serious enough; has the gift of gab; straightforward.

—AN OFFICIAL ENTRY ON CHEN TAOZHEN, 32, A STATE-LABELED
UNEMPLOYED INTELLECTUAL LOOKING FOR WORK, 1952

On December 1, 1951, slightly over two years after the PRC's founding, the Shanghai government began a registration process for persons officially referred to as "unemployed intellectuals" (*shiye zhishifenzi*). Similar registrations occurred in Beijing and other major urban areas. The main purpose of the registrations was to locate educated but jobless people, ascertain their background and experience, and return as many of them as possible to work, especially in sectors and regions where replenishment or expansion of the labor force was needed. Because of two decades of war and revolution, unemployment had become a national problem. From the perspective of the new political leadership, the harnessing of otherwise unused knowledge and skills was not only vital to socialist development but also necessary for tackling joblessness. The registration drive in Shanghai lasted for fourteen months and overlapped with various highly charged national campaigns, including the Campaign to Suppress Counterrevolutionaries, the Resist-America-Aid-Korea

Campaign, the Three Anti and the Five Anti Campaign, and Thought Reform of Intellectuals. These other campaigns involved mass parades, public denunciations, incarcerations, executions, and other poignant dramas.[1] With the registration drive, there is apparently little to attract those scholarly lenses that routinely focus on the excesses of coercion or politicization of ordinary life by the Mao regime. In those rare instances when it is spotlighted, the registration is depicted as little more than a public welfare event, or else the official interpretation is presented.[2]

With this chapter, we begin our investigation of the mutual constitution of the intellectual and Chinese Communism in postrevolutionary China. In Shanghai, the registration of unemployed intellectuals turned out to be a key exercise across state and society that served to objectify the intellectual. To conduct the registration, the municipal government set up commissions and offices; printed instructions, regulations, and manuals; and devised application forms, assessment protocols, and identification cards. The government posted announcements in newspapers and other places and involved professional, trade, and other organizations. It arranged meetings, training sessions, and visits to local neighborhoods to educate CCP cadres and residents about unemployed intellectuals and official efforts to locate and assist these individuals. Eager to find paid work or help family members to do so, neighborhood residents sought information and studied eligibility criteria. Many gathered documents, filled out application forms, and prepared themselves for interviews. Cadres and residents thus learned how the state defined intellectuals in professional and academic terms, amid its complaints about the class character of these people and calls for them to learn from workers and peasants. Like the overlapping campaigns which advanced CCP control of government, industry, and other sectors, the registration drive helped the party extend its symbolic power and administrative capability into local neighborhoods. The drive furthered goals of the campaigns such as spreading the Marxian vision of Chinese society and the party's principles of social classification, recording and ascertaining the backgrounds of individuals, and mobilizing their participation in officially sponsored activities. Furthermore, the drive enabled the authorities to reach the unemployed, who otherwise had little incentive to observe state-mandated routines or procedures.

The boundaries of the category of intellectuals that emerged during the registration drive were no more clear or stable than those found in Yan'an a decade before, even though the CCP was much richer in resources for enforcing its system of social classification. Shanghai saw a proliferation and repeated replacement of rules and regulations governing registration eligibility, with contents that reflected varying official approaches to revolutionary justice, the allocation of opportunities, and the reduction of unemployment as much as changing official efforts to clarify the kinds of people to be considered unemployed intellectuals. Although the registration drive turned many unemployed people directly (as well as employed people indirectly) into locally recognizable "intellectuals," ambiguities regarding who the intellectuals were persisted. Meanwhile, some individuals used the drive for self-interested purposes, registering themselves or others who did not meet the criteria for recognition as unemployed intellectuals. In other words, in the lower reaches of the population of intellectuals formed under Chinese Communism, as in the upper echelons described in the last chapter, we encounter in sharp relief the political and social forces as well as individualized and institutionalized conduct that objectified some as intellectuals but not others who had similar backgrounds or even superior education. The category of intellectuals everywhere assumed a historical form that reflected the dynamics of Chinese Communism.

As unemployed intellectuals appeared en masse across Shanghai, official surveillance intensified in the local neighborhoods and the growing state sector. The city had been the major financial, industrial, and commercial center in China and home to political and official bodies sponsored by British, Japanese, and other foreign authorities and, not least, the Guomindang. Even without the citywide purges launched by the victorious CCP to rid government offices, colleges, and other sites of people confirmed or presumed to be staunch political enemies, many of the unemployed still had worked for other political regimes, foreign or domestic capital, or "vice" businesses eventually closed by the state such as nightclubs and cabarets. For the Shanghai authorities, among the unemployed intellectuals were many who had been involved in the political repression, economic exploitation, or moral corruption of the Chinese people. Clarifying the backgrounds of the intellectuals was necessary to forestall future problems of governance. Within the state-run establishments instructed to train or hire the intellectuals, the authorities used political and moral standards gleaned from official discourse to screen and select candidates. They investigated the chosen and monitored, documented, and categorized their behavior. The "petty-bourgeois" and "bourgeois" politics, habits, and dispositions of intellectuals described in official discourse were converted into visible realities and written records. The usable yet unreliable intellectual who had emerged in Yan'an not only migrated into the postrevolutionary workplace, but in many cases did so in the form of a figure detested by the local authorities.

To use Pierre Bourdieu's terminology, the intellectual appeared twice in *homologous* forms during the Shanghai registration of unemployed intellectuals, that is, both in the *objective structures* of the state and in the *mental structures* of ordinary people. The classification saturated various forms of official announcements, informed registration rules and activities, and led to specific mechanisms of domination within local neighborhoods and workplaces. Under these circumstances, government officials, registration staff, enterprise administrators, and neighborhood residents began to consider themselves and/or others as intellectuals, or a specific type of political subjects based on the Marxian understanding promoted by the state. What bridged the classification across two kinds of structure was the symbolic power and administrative capability of the Mao regime, both of which the registration drive helped to strengthen, notwithstanding that the concept of intellectuals remained unstable because of central adjustments of registration criteria and variations of local understanding. Before moving on, it is vital to highlight the dynamics of displacement and employment in Shanghai and nearby areas from the late 1940s to the early 1950s, which critically influenced the kinds of people who would claim to be unemployed intellectuals and therefore how the authorities reacted.

DYNAMICS OF PRESELECTION

Like other Chinese cities, Shanghai, with a population of approximately 5 million people, saw high unemployment while the civil war (1946–1950) raged between the CCP and the Guomindang.[3] The CCP takeover of the city, which began in late May 1949, was followed by capital flight, foreign economic sanctions, Guomindang air raids, a Guomindang naval blockade, and other challenges that intensified the problem of joblessness.[4] From March to May 1950, an additional 150,000 workers were laid off.[5] The municipal government followed central instructions and registered and organized assistance for the unemployed.[6] The recovering city was hit with economic decline again in the spring of 1952 because of the state-sponsored Five Anti Campaign, which attacked tax evasion, bribery, cheating on government contracts, and other economic wrongdoing in the commercial and industrial sectors. Many firms responded to the campaign by terminating, suspending, or cutting back operations, which led to a "wave of sackings" of white-collar and blue-collar workers and manual laborers.[7] Over 414,000 people reportedly signed up for unemployment assistance during 1952, and more than 300,000 remained on the registry two years later.[8] These figures do not include people who had some but inadequate work, homemakers and sojourners looking for work, and others who stayed away from all forms of official registration for one reason or another. In short, Shanghai's unemployment rate hovered above 10 and sometimes 20 percent during the early 1950s.[9]

Critical to our analysis are the forms of displacement that preselected those who would come forward during Shanghai's registration of unemployed intellectuals. In August 1948, the CCP implemented its personnel policy in northeast China when state agencies (including government departments, the military, the police, and the judiciary) and state-run establishments (such as schools, newspapers, and radio stations) were seized from the Guomindang. When the Red Army entered Beijing and Tianjin in January 1949, CCP cadres were directed to "shake up" existing state agencies, except those overseeing public utilities and public health. The cadres were asked to dismiss "reactionary elements, notoriously objectionable people, and unusable incompetents," assess the background and performance of the rest of the staff, and retain only the minority who were vital to everyday operation. Anyone who was rendered redundant but did not fall into any of those rebuked categories of people would be reassigned to another post or sent home with an allowance and an order to wait for official assignment. Across state-run establishments, the cadres were instructed to keep the workforce intact and dismiss only the most notorious, the steadfastly reactionary, and the incompetent employees. During the spring and summer of 1949, however, massive layoffs unanticipated by the Mao leadership occurred during the takeovers of Shanghai, Nanjing, and Hangzhou. Almost 27,000 people were cut from state agencies and state-run establishments.[10] In Shanghai, more than 6,000 people were laid off; another 800 were dismissed; a few thousand more were instructed to wait for assignment or to return to their native places, or simply resigned.[11] For example, almost 280 people, or 20 percent of the workforce, were removed from the public secondary school system.[12] The layoffs triggered "mass social unrest" and compelled a tactical retreat from the leadership. In September 1949, takeover cadres were directed to remove from office only "the minority of war criminals and special agents [of enemy regimes] and notoriously objectionable elements," and to even rehire some of the people who had been laid off.[13]

In practice, former officials and administrators and others who were most offensive to the CCP authorities were ousted from state agencies and state-run establishments during the Shanghai takeover. Among those removed were leaders of Guomindang organizations and staunch supporters of the fleeing regime; former political, military, and intelligence officers; and people who had reportedly committed serious acts of wrongdoing such as graft or embezzlement or violent crimes against CCP members or supporters. The removal of Wang Guocai, the head of discipline and instruction at Yangshupu Secondary School in the summer of 1949, is illustrative. Undercover CCP agents had studied this Guomindang member and discovered that he had been a political instructor at the Luoyang campus of the Central Army Officer Academy (*Zhongyang lujun junguan xuexiao*). They determined that he was "obviously reactionary" in his political thinking and behavior. Wang reportedly had gotten his post at the secondary school, not because of his educational credentials or pedagogical skills, but through his connection with and willingness to serve the school principal, an alleged Guomindang special agent who had already left for Taiwan. Wang was said to have been a Guomindang mouthpiece throughout the civil war and, especially, in front of his students.[14] Some of those removed from state agencies or state-run establishments would be arrested and even executed during the Campaign to Suppress Counterrevolutionaries (1950–1952); others would find work on their own or leave the city. The bulk would see the official registration of unemployed intellectuals as an opportunity to return to full-time employment.

In Shanghai, business closures pushed large numbers of office workers with different levels of knowledge and skills into the ranks of the unemployed. Between January and May 1950, 1,400, or more than 10 percent, of factories and 6,000, or 6 percent, of shops (*shangdian*) were closed. Although many of these establishments reopened in response to the surging demand created by China's involvement in the

Korean War (1950–1953), bumper crops nearby, and state economic intervention, a total of 1,800 factories and 7,800 shops applied for closure in 1950.[15] During the same period, more than 90 private banks and money houses (*qianzhuang*) were closed, or almost 60 percent of such establishments, because of the severe restrictions that the municipal government placed on financial exchange.[16] Likewise, between August 1949 and December 1950, almost 600 of 1,600 import-export companies went out of business because of state regulation or other reasons.[17] Private newspapers, news agencies, radio stations, publishing houses, and schools were forced to shut down or reorganize their operation to comply with new regulations.[18] For example, almost 40 private schools ceased operation during the first year of CCP rule.[19] Hotels, jewelry stores, dance halls, gambling venues, and other places that catered to a business clientele or encouraged consumerism also saw rapid declines due to official regulation. The Five Anti Campaign furthered closures of small and medium-sized enterprises.[20] By May 1952, "urban unemployment was again high and confidence in the prospects for urban employment growth again shattered,"[21] prompting the municipal government, already a main consumer of industrial products, to increase loans and orders to local factories and organize mergers and other economic activities to arrest job losses.[22]

Two other forms of displacement increased the number of educated people among the unemployed in Shanghai. First, land reform began in the suburbs in July 1950 and was relatively peaceful until the Korean War intensified within months. Besides public denunciations and confiscation of land, animals, crops, and other forms of property, landlords faced investigation, arrest, and summary execution. Meanwhile, the Campaign to Suppress Counterrevolutionaries, which led to false accusations and reckless executions, spread across rural areas.[23] Fengxian County, for example, located to the south of the city, saw 30 landlords sentenced to death and 129 given jail sentences.[24] We do not know how many landlords or their family members fled to Shanghai. But the threat of punishment likely pushed some of these people to seek refuge there, where anonymity and therefore personal safety was still possible. Some of these newcomers had attended traditional tutor schools (*sishu*), modern-style schools, and even colleges.[25] Second, closures and reductions of operation of various kinds of establishments within the city from the late 1940s to the early 1950s created tremendous pressure on household incomes, and drove homemakers who had received formal education to enter or return to the job market.

The way in which the CCP offered jobs and opportunities after seizing Shanghai depressed the average educational level of those who would register as unemployed intellectuals, especially among young men and women. To support its takeover of China, the party was determined to tap the "source of energy and enthusiasm" among secondary school and college students and recent graduates. This undertaking reflected the party's now-entrenched cult of youth. In practice, the Mao regime established many courses and centers to train young people for official service.[26] Soon after the takeover of Shanghai had started, the East China Military and Political University (*Huadong junzheng daxue*) run by the People's Liberation Army (PLA) (previously the Red Army) sought to enroll at its Suzhou and Nanjing campuses 30,000 people aged between 18 and 28 with at least a junior high education.[27] The PLA also wanted 3,000 "intellectual youths" from Shanghai, individuals between 18 and 30 years of age with that same education, to join the Southward-bound Service Corps and assist in propaganda, mobilization, and other tasks vital to the takeover of other cities or regions.[28] Many other opportunities for intellectual youths to join the PLA followed, with age restrictions varying across recruiting organizations. For example, the garrison near Shanghai planned to train 950 men and 50 women who had graduated from high school to become "cultural cadres."[29] Another unit needed 300 people to serve as "cultural and art workers."[30] The Ninth Regiment had 1,200 openings in communication, art, and other capacities.[31]

Other careers in government were available to educated young people. For example, the East China People's Revolutionary University (*Huadong renmin geming daxue*) enrolled thousands with the aim of training them to assist the CCP takeovers occurring elsewhere.[32] The East China branch of the Central Tax Administration Institute (*Zhongyang shuiwu xuexiao*) needed 500 people to learn to become "finance and tax cadres."[33] And the Shanghai Cadre Institute (*Shanghai ganbu xuexiao*) wanted to train 1,000 people for various positions in the central government.[34] There were opportunities for older educated adults. The positions, however, were often limited to those who had college education and professional experience and were willing to relocate. For example, representatives of the People's Government of Northeast China (*Dongbei renmin zhengfu*) were in Shanghai as early as September 1949 to recruit professors in various fields of science and technology as well as experts (*zhuanjia*) in similar areas and in law, politics, medicine, accounting, and so on.[35] The Central Ministry of Heavy Industry announced a few months later a plan to hire factory management and technical personnel with university or technical college educations.[36] The Dongbei government had almost 5,000 additional openings for various kinds of faculty, experts, and technical personnel.[37]

In sum, even though war and revolution had forced students in Shanghai to enter the labor market prematurely and increased the unemployment of recent graduates, many of these people did not need to use the subsequent official registration of unemployed intellectuals to return to work. Likewise, the knowledgeable but jobless had other channels to find work. The registration drive was destined to encounter large numbers of ordinary office workers, former Guomindang members and government officials, especially those whom the CCP had dismissed on political, moral, or even criminal grounds, and others who, for one reason or another, had not been able to take advantage of state-sponsored training or other opportunities.

STATE AND SOCIETY SEARCH FOR INTELLECTUALS

In January 1951, the State Council of the PRC issued a "Supplementary Instruction on the Handling of Unemployed Intellectuals" that directed regional governments to return such people to work "to the fullest extent possible."[38] The "instruction" followed months of assistance provided by the state to displaced office workers and technical personnel, unemployed graduates, and other educated people in the form of job placement or living subsidies, sometimes together with mandatory political reeducation. Reflecting its Marxian view of China's class structure, the state had been referring to these persons as unemployed intellectuals to distinguish them from unemployed workers (*shiye gongren*), whom it classified as part of the proletariat. Large numbers of such workers existed, and large shares of resources had been allocated to tackle their joblessness.[39] With that instruction noted above, the state adopted the goal of registering unemployed intellectuals systematically, educating them at people's revolutionary universities and other venues, and placing them in the educational, industrial, and other sectors. The instruction included a statement of individual eligibility designed to help the local authorities to identify unemployed intellectuals. Heretofore a principal classification of people under Chinese Communism, the intellectual acquired a concrete administrative definition. "The range of people to be handled as unemployed intellectuals is as follows: (1) those who have *at least graduated from senior high school* or have an equivalent education, but have lost their jobs or have been unable to find work since leaving school; and (2) those who have *considerable academic knowledge and prestige* in the local area and are *willing to serve the people*, but cannot take up hard work or support themselves due to old age or poor health" (emphasis added). To undermine political enemies and lawbreakers, the State Council declared that "the minority of intellectuals" who had "degenerated into special agents [of other political regimes] or vicious thugs (*eba*)" or had committed serious criminal acts were not eligible for assistance.[40] From the state's perspective, these intellectuals had apparently morphed into counterrevolutionaries or class enemies, or were no longer usable.

In Shanghai, the Shanghai Municipal Commission for Handling Unemployed Intellectuals (*Shanghaishi chuli shiye zhishifenzi weiyuanhui*) (SCHUI) was formed in October 1951. The commission was composed of officials from six municipal bureaus (education, personnel, civil affairs, labor, culture, and news and publications) and representatives from the General Office of the municipal government and the Shanghai branches of the Women's Federation, the Education Union, and the Communist Youth League. District (*qu*) branches of the commission were established to involve officials from corresponding district bureaus and representatives from an even broader array of organizations sponsored or sanctioned by the state, including political associations such as the China Democratic League (*Zhongguo minzhu tongmeng*) and the China Association for Promoting Democracy (*Zhongguo minzhu cujinhui*). The SCHUI formulated policies, procedures, and regulations for registering unemployed intellectuals, prepared applications forms and identification cards, and wrote press releases for newspapers. It organized classes to teach the district staff how to run the registration office, use bulletin boards, public assemblies, and other channels to publicize the registration drive, and handle applications. Manuals explaining official terminology, individual eligibility, standards of documentation, and other registration matters were printed and distributed.[41] A total of ten registration offices were set up across urban and suburban Shanghai.[42]

The Shanghai authorities used junior (instead of senior) high school graduation or its equivalent level of education as the minimum academic qualification for registering as unemployed intellectuals.[43] The change had apparently come from the State Council, as its subsequent instructions and decisions consistently defined unemployed intellectuals according to the relaxed criteria, which in effect increased manifold the number of people classifiable as intellectuals across China.[44] There were probably three reasons behind the change. First, jobless people with high school diplomas were too few to justify an official registration campaign. Second, the Mao regime had deemed less educated persons to be intellectuals during its Yan'an years. Third, many schoolteachers, accountants, and others who fit into the Marxian concept of intellectuals of the state were not high school graduates. Included in the SCHUI staff manual were additional regulations and statements about eligibility, which show that the state continued to grapple with how to use the intellectual as a classification in administrative matters. For example, peddlers, pedicab drivers, and dance hostesses who had the required education could register as unemployed intellectuals, but not instructors from traditional tutor schools, because these individuals "lacked knowledge of modern culture and science."[45] Others were disqualified on political grounds, for example, denounced landlords hiding in Shanghai, expellees of state-owned enterprises, and college students who had refused official assignments. The SCHUI also wanted those discovered to be counterrevolutionaries or criminals during the registration drive to be handed over to the Public Security Bureau for further investigation and punishment.[46]

Research has stressed the CCP's imposition of a Marxian system of social classification on state and society during the early 1950s. The Shanghai registration of unemployed intellectuals enabled the party to extend this system into urban neighborhoods. Applicants had to put down, many for the first time, their class background according to the official double markers of "family status" (*jiating chengfen*) (e.g., poor peasant, petty bourgeoisie, capitalist) and "individual origin" (*benren chushen*) (e.g., student, office worker, industrial worker). Other requirements captured growing state surveillance that seized upon particular aspects of social life as objects of analysis. Applicants were instructed to describe their involvement in political organizations (*zhengzhi qingkuang*) and the backgrounds of close friends and relatives (*shehui guanxi*). Everyone had to submit an autobiographical narrative (*zizhuan*) of his or her "individual experience, changes in political thinking, understanding of the PRC government, and personal strengths and weaknesses."[47] As we shall see, the collection of these materials helped the local authorities not only to pin down each applicant's own particularity as a class subject, as Foucault might have said, but also to describe the general traits of the applicants as well as compare between any two of them based on the official analytical framework.[48]

The SCHUI drew into the search for unemployed intellectuals many of the city's political, professional, trade, and other associations. The commission was expecting that some applicants had lost their academic diplomas, professional certificates, or letters of appointment because of war and displacement. It had thus asked prominent associations for assistance and trained their representatives in assessing and certifying educational achievements and employment histories.[49] Numerous cases of missing documents were reported shortly after the registration drive had started, so much so that the commission augmented the list of certifying associations to roughly 300. These associations included, for example, the Shanghai branches of the China Art Workers Association, the China Pharmacology Association, and the Sino-Soviet Friendship Association; the Shanghai Peasants Association and the Shanghai Homemakers Federation; and the district branches of various labor unions. Applicants without valid papers were instructed to approach an association related to their own occupation. The association was required to assign to each case two of its members, who would use their knowledge and familiarity with the applicant to evaluate that applicant's asserted qualifications, experience, and, if appropriate, class background, political involvement, and other matters that deserved attention. The association would then furnish a written report to SCHUI as to whether the applicant was an unemployed intellectual (see figure 3).[50]

In Shanghai, the search for unemployed intellectuals intensified further after their registration was integrated into the Unified Unemployment Registration (*shiye renyuan tongyi dengji*) in October 1952. A national event, the unified registration sought to address the rising urban unemployment that resulted from the Five Anti Campaign. The registration was also designed to enable local governments to ascertain, among other things, the backgrounds of the unemployed, a population quite challenging for the state to reach, let alone control. The Shanghai authorities had noted that some who could sign up as unemployed intellectuals had not done so for reasons such as fear of relocation or arrest.[51] Within every district, neighborhood unemployment registration committees (*lilong shiye renyuan dengji weiyuanhui*) were formed to publicize the registration drive and to document former officials and police officers as well as workers, homemakers, youths, and others who were jobless. Each committee normally contained seven to thirteen members who were residents of the neighborhood. The committees were supervised by the district's labor and employment commission, the members of which were drawn from various government offices.[52] For example, in the

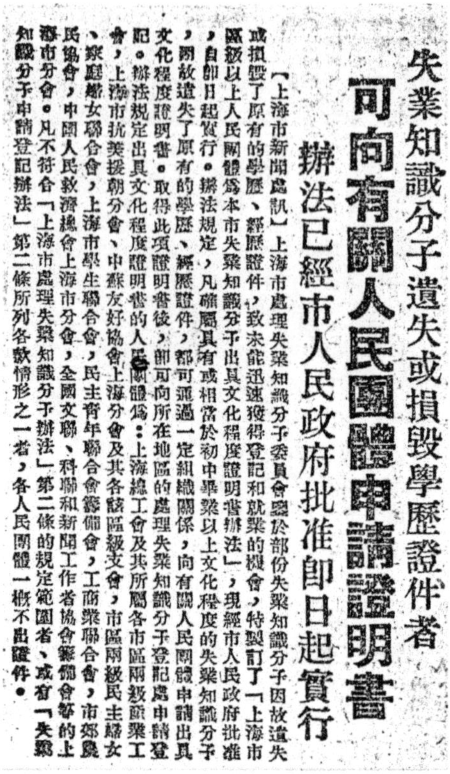

失業知識分子遺失或損毀學歷證件者
可向有關人民團體申請證明書
辦法已經市人民政府批准即日起實行

【上海市新聞處訊】上海市處理失業知識分子委員會鑒於部份失業知識分子因故遺失或損毀了原有的學歷、經歷證件，致未能迅速獲得登記和就業的機會，特製訂了「上海市區級以上人民團體爲本市失業知識分子出具文化程度證明書辦法」，現經市人民政府批准，自即日起實行。辦法規定，凡確屬具有或相當於初中畢業以上文化程度的失業知識分子，因故遺失了原有的學歷、經歷證件，都可通過一定組織關係，向有關人民團體申請出具文化程度證明書。取得此項證明書後，即可向所在地區的處理失業知識分子登記處申請登記。辦法規定出具文化程度證明書的人民團體爲：上海總工會及其所屬各市區兩級產業工會，上海市抗美援朝分會、中蘇友好協會上海分會及其各該區級支會，市區兩級民主婦女、家庭婦女聯合會，上海市學生聯合會，民主青年聯合會籌備會，工商業聯合會，市郊農民協會，中國人民救濟總會上海市分會，全國文聯、科聯和新聞工作者協會籌備會等的上海市分會。凡不符合「上海市處理失業知識分子辦法」第二條的規定範圍者、或有「失業知識分子申請登記辦法」第二條所列各款情形之一者，各人民團體一概不出證件。

FIGURE 3. An announcement of the certifying role of associations in *Wenhui Daily*, January 8, 1952.

industrial district of Yulin, the population of which exceeded 230,000, the commission trained more than 1,800 unemployed workers, homemakers, and others to staff the neighborhood committees. These persons took classes on registration procedures and requirements. They learned criteria for categorizing people as unemployed intellectuals. They practiced alongside the authorities and performed tasks such as promoting the registration through bulletin-board messages, visiting families to explain policies and eligibility, and verifying documents and checking submitted applications.[53]

The unified registration in Shanghai, which lasted until January 1953, involved rule and regulation changes that affected, once again, how state and society understood the category of intellectuals. Politically based barriers to registration were lifted for members of the following disfavored groups: former Guomindang military officers and state officials; expellees from the military, government offices, and state-owned establishments; former Christian clergymen, Buddhist monks, fortune-tellers, and "religious and superstitious practitioners" of other kinds. So long as they satisfied the educational and unemployment requirements, such people could register as unemployed intellectuals. If the changes helped the state locate such personnel, place them where they could be monitored, and alleviate unemployment, it also served to absorb these people squarely into the population of intellectuals. Rule changes adopted for other reasons had classification and career impact, too. In a reversal, the authorities stipulated that those who had completed junior high school but had been making ends meet in a blue-collar or unskilled position for an extended period were ineligible to register as unemployed intellectuals. A homemaker with such education was no longer automatically considered an unemployed intellectual; unless her family was in dire poverty, her application for assistance would be "put on record," or handled after unemployed men with comparable qualifications had been helped. By contrast, displaced workers who had sought education in part-time schools and achieved the equivalent of junior high school graduation could choose to register as unemployed workers or unemployed intellectuals.[54]

A procedure of collective appraisal (*pingyi*) of unemployment status was adopted by the Shanghai authorities. As the next section will show, during the registration drive organized by the SCHUI, the authorities had good reasons to doubt the truthfulness of the applicants and the propriety of the registration staff. Collective appraisal was inserted to assist local governments with obtaining accurate information about the unemployed and in deciding case by case whether to list applicants on the placement registry, recommend them for state relief, act on their job request at a later time, or even deliver them for prosecution for discovered wrongdoing. Each neighborhood registration committee was required to form an appraisal team of about twelve people including district officials, registration staff, and some of the unemployed, and to invite local residents to appraisal sessions. The procedure thus fostered further public learning of the official schema of classes, including use of the intellectual classification.

What happened in Baxian Lane in Songshan district, which the Shanghai Municipal Commission of Labor and Employment cited as exemplary in conducting the registration drive, is illuminating. Officials from the commission organized multiple meetings to encourage members of the local residents' committee, women's representatives in the neighborhood, homemakers, the unemployed, and others to attend the appraisals. The local registration committee had already conducted pilot research and established appraisal procedures. The latter included discussion by the committee members of information provided by the unemployed; appearance of the unemployed before the committee to explain their background and experience; and feedback and questions from attending residents. The committee even asked the unemployed to evaluate one another's statuses.[55] In short, the appraisals served as neighborhood forums in which officials and residents alike grappled with the class identity of each unemployed person with guidance from

TABLE 1 Number of *Wenhui Daily* Articles with Specific Terms for Educated Persons, 1938–1957

	1938	1946	1952	1957
Zhishifenzi (intellectuals)*	27	53	798	1,511
Xuezhe (scholars)	210	285	141	317
Wenren (literati)	93	113	26	80
Wenhua ren (cultural personnel)	25	113	12	9
Dushu ren (men of letters)	9	25	9	19

SOURCE: Electronic database of *Wenhui Daily* at Shanghai Municipal Library.
*The figures include both *zhi1shifenzi* and *zhi4shifenzi*. The second one was dropped by the newspaper after the 1949 takeover.

the state. The exercise led all of the participants to consider their own class identities and those of their friends and relatives, if they had not already done so.

In Shanghai, these registrations played a unique role in turning the intellectual into a primary classification of people. For more than a year, every district was involved in studying the concept and locating unemployed intellectuals. Table 1 illustrates this development from a linguistic perspective. *Wenhui Daily* (*Wenhui bao*) was founded in Shanghai in 1938 and quickly became a major newspaper and channel for political and intellectual debate. Before 1949, the term *zhishifenzi* was used significantly less than other terms denoting educated people (which, unlike *zhishifenzi*, often signaled the basis of their knowledge). After 1949, CCP control of the media produced a surge in the use of *zhishifenzi*, as the party considered the other categories of people as subsets of intellectuals. The registrations and Thought Reform of Intellectuals overlapped in 1952 and pushed the use of the term to new heights, while it also circulated in abundance in radio, cinema, magazines, and public meetings—right when "intellectuals" were locatable in every neighborhood.

A SELF-FULFILLING PROPHECY

Between the two registration drives, the Shanghai authorities signed up 40,000 unemployed intellectuals.[56] Table 2 indicates the self-reported ages and educational attainments of 34,100 people who registered during the first eleven months of the events. Half of the registrants merely satisfied the official minimum educational requirements. The two youngest cohorts contained the smallest proportion of college-educated members for reasons discussed above. Overall, only 12 percent had college education. Because educated homemakers could register as unemployed intellectuals during the SCHUI registration, women constituted a moderate majority (57 percent). In terms of professional knowledge, the largest proportion (35 percent) did not report any specific skills; 23 percent mentioned

TABLE 2 Educational Attainments of "Unemployed Intellectuals" by Age (with Percentage), 1952

	18–25	26–35	36–45	46–60	Above 60	Total
Junior high	8,008	6,398	2,129	637	32	17,204
	(62.5)	(45.3)	(41.0)	(35.2)	(18.2)	(50.4)
Senior high	4,235	5,823	2,096	588	51	12,793
	(33.1)	(41.2)	(40.3)	(32.5)	(29.0)	(37.5)
College	568	1,898	953	536	65	4,020
	(4.4)	(13.4)	(18.3)	(29.6)	(36.9)	(11.8)
Other	3	16	20	50	28	117
	(0.0)	(0.1)	(0.4)	(2.7)	(15.9)	(0.3)
Total	12,814	14,135	5,198	1,811	176	34,134
	(100.0)	(100.0)	(100.0)	(100.0)	(100.0)	(100.0)

SOURCE: SMA B1–1–1121, 206.
NOTES: "College" refers to at least two years of postsecondary vocational training. "Other" refers to the possession of professional expertise or recognized knowledge and local reputation but not formal academic credentials.

experience in finance or economics, but mainly as bookkeepers or elementary learners of accounting; 19 percent were former schoolteachers or had worked in education, arts, literature, or the news media; another 7 percent were former clerical workers.[57]

Having expected to find a substantial number of knowledgeable and skillful people—for example, physicians, surveyors, factory supervisors, and mechanical engineers—the registration authorities were disappointed. "Many of the registrants are of low cultural level; only a small number have high academic or professional achievements . . . Although our methods of classification and figures suggest that we have a number of technical personnel, rarely do these people have genuine expertise or robust learning. The majority have acquired their skills and knowledge from part-time school, have been jobless because of chronic illness, or have not worked before."[58] In hindsight, this outcome was inevitable. The state had set junior high school graduation or its equivalent educations as the minimum educational requirement for anyone to register as an unemployed intellectual. Official programs of training and recruitment had absorbed many with knowledge and skills or college educations into various occupations. Seeing many relatively young people among the registrants, the authorities nonetheless toed the line of the officially promoted cult of youth and indicated that most of the registrants would contribute to China's socialist development after receiving training from the state.

More disturbing to the registration authorities was their no-less-inescapable discovery of the disagreeable political backgrounds and orientations of the registrants. Six months into its registration drive, the SCHUI issued an installment of what would become a consistently scathing official assessment of unemployed intellectuals during the 1950s. There were, the report stated, "many sons and younger brothers of landlords and rich peasants, members of reactionary parties and youth corps, former judicial personnel, bureaucrats, public school teachers, and former military officers and so on, and the family members of these people." These kinds of registrants generally had "very poor understanding [of the revolution led by the CCP], very backward thinking [about class exploitation inside or outside China], and very insufficient appreciation of the serve-the-people viewpoint [of Chairman Mao]." The commission practically restated the outcomes of the recent purges conducted by the party in government offices, the judiciaries, and other sites in or near Shanghai. But the SCHUI downplayed the institutional sources of the unemployment by highlighting the joblessness as a symptom of the inferior class-based character of the registrants. The latter allegedly exhibited a "strong desire to lead a life of pleasure and enjoyment and hence an aversion to taking jobs outside Shanghai."[59] As we shall see, although jobs were available elsewhere, it was not easy for registrants to obtain any of these positions, even if they were ready to leave their families behind or move with them to the new locations of employment. To the authorities, however, the inability of unemployed intellectuals to get work outside the city was yet another indication that they were refusing to confront their "petty-bourgeois" or "bourgeois" habits and dispositions acquired from families, schools, and workplaces in a city known for its commercialism and consumerism.

The SCHUI's unease about the registrants also reflected disruptions of the registration drive during early 1952, when the Three Anti Campaign, which attacked malfeasance in government, and the Five Anti Campaign were in their early phases. District cadres who worked in the registration offices were reassigned to assist in the investigative and punitive campaigns for roughly two months, when thousands of people signed up as unemployed intellectuals. The SCHUI discovered afterward that "the mental condition of the office staff had slipped into a state of extreme disorder." Worrying about their own prospects and the well-being of friends and relatives, staff members became listless and confused as well as divided and disgruntled. Consequently, the registration drive was tainted by irresponsible and illicit behavior. Zhabei district was an undistinguished working-class area. The registration office there was cited by the commission as an egregious example. Someone who knew little about the registration drive had assumed leadership. The staff "did whatever they felt like doing." They came to work late and left early together, played chess in the office, and used field trips and investigations as excuses to go home or to cinemas or billiard halls. Conventional and emerging social divisions surfaced and produced a fractured workplace at other sites. Staff members from government offices and from state-sponsored associations quarreled with one another, and so did male and female cadres, young and old personnel, and Communist Youth Leaguers and the rest of the staff. In Fenglai district, office staff reportedly dreaded coming to work and hoped the registration would end immediately. Elsewhere, some of the operating funds were stolen, staff members suddenly quit, and even the office sign was not hung properly.[60]

Registration work was predictably compromised. The SCHUI had expected registration office staff to assist in verifying information provided by applicants. Ideally, staff members would visit the establishments (e.g., colleges and companies) and locations (such as previous home addresses) mentioned by the applicants to gather evidence and determine in an "objective" and "systematic" manner whether they had been truthful. Lacking training and supervision, the commission noted, even those who had conducted such investigations performed poorly. Some had asked questions of little value and submitted "crude and careless" reports. In Yimiao district, for example, the registration office failed to catch someone who had lied about a friendship with a CCP member to increase his own chances of placement, and another person who had covered up involvement in the intelligence service of another political regime. In some cases, female relatives of "counterrevolutionaries" had passed as "general representatives of women" of the neighborhood and were recommended for job assignment. In other cases, individuals known locally as fraudsters or bullies were logged as activists who supported CCP policies and personnel. Some staff members, moreover, followed their own belief in "benevolence and gentleness" and compiled grossly simplistic reports about applicants.[61]

The SCHUI uncovered that registration staff had exploited the management vacuum created by the Three Anti and Five Anti Campaigns to help friends, relatives, and others. Some staff members used the official seal fraudulently to approve otherwise unqualified applications and even recommended ineligible candidates to recruiting establishments. For example, a cadre in Laozha district had taken money from applicants. He was prepared to sign up ineligible people as unemployed intellectuals and process their placements. In Xincheng district, a staff member insisted on sending a colleague's sister-in-law to a teacher-training program organized by Shanghai Normal College, even though she did not meet the publicized political requirements. Another staff member had fallen in love with an applicant and sought to use his position to find her a position.[62] The illicit behavior reflected, to a good extent, the challenges that some unemployed persons confronted in acquiring a livelihood, as the state increasingly controlled the labor market and administered opportunities based on principles of class struggle. Other kinds of improper behavior noted by the commission—for example, the registration offices repeatedly sanctioned counterfeit diplomas and letters of employment—were mainly an outcome of the large volume of applications processed by the staff and the lack of training and supervision provided by the SCHUI authorities.[63] From the latter's perspective, however, the registration of unemployed intellectuals was tainted twice: by the selfish, class-based conduct of the applicants *and* by that of the registration staff.

By May 1953, only 31 percent, or 10,500, of the 34,100 unemployed intellectuals represented in Table 2 had found jobs through state assistance. Another 2,300 found work themselves, and 253 saw their registration disqualified after official investigation. A higher proportion of male registrants (34 percent) than of female registrants (29 percent) were assisted in paid positions or traineeships. Educational achievement mattered. Among those who had attended college, 39 percent acquired a position, compared with 36 and 25 percent of the senior high and junior high school graduates. Almost 30 percent of the placements were outside Shanghai. Most of those who received appointment (39 percent) were hired for general office work or as some kind of trainee, 24 percent for finance or accounting work, and another 22 percent as cultural workers or schoolteachers. Only a small number were placed in highly technical fields such as engineering, medicine, or factory management.[64] The relatively low percentage of registrants who received an official assignment did not indicate a lack of interest from recruiting establishments, which were mainly government departments and state-owned enterprises expanding rapidly under CCP rule. Within the first twelve months of the registration of unemployed intellectuals, almost 140 establishments contacted the SCHUI.[65] Some submitted plans to hire hundreds or more of these people. For example, the East China Department of Education had 3,000 vacancies.[66] The low rates of success reflected a mismatch between what many of these establishments wanted—technicians and technical personnel (*jishu renyuan*)—and the registrants' knowledge and skills.[67]

Equally important, the poor placement rates were results of political vigilance on the part of the recruiting establishments, or their efforts to avoid acquiring individuals portrayed or implicated as political undesirables by the state, such as former Guomindang personnel, former landlords, and people who had received official punishment. The general approach of the establishments, the SCHUI observed, was "rather be understaffed than indiscriminately taking on new employees" (*ningque wulan*) and preferential treatment of "the youngest possible candidates."[68] The collective outcome was reflected in the rates of placement of the cohorts represented in Table 2. Thirty-five percent of the youngest cohort of registrants, or those with the least work experience, received assignments, compared to 31, 26, 13, and 1 percent of registrants in the successive cohorts. It is true that young people tended to be single or childless and hence open to relocation. Positions outside Shanghai, while plentiful, usually paid less (because the state calculated salaries on the basis of regional living standards), and therefore were not attractive to many who had a family to support in the city. However, the rates of placement suggest that discrimination against older registrants was in play. For the recruiting establishments, the backgrounds reported by young registrants in their applications and autobiographical narratives, however misleading, were easily verifiable compared with the long lists of appointments, connections, and activities or, worse, the lack of such information furnished by older candidates. The political vigilance of the establishments reflected and reinforced the cult of youth spreading within the state sector.

What happened to Yu Jielin's job search, which the SCHUI cited as not uncommon, is instructive. Yu was a struggling 36-year-old with two years of senior high education and a family of three to feed. Before the registration of unemployed intellectuals began, he had received two months of training from the Shanghai branch of the People's Insurance Company of China but was not given a position there. To make ends meet, he performed various kinds of lowly physical work. After successfully registering as an unemployed intellectual, Yu was recommended to the Shanghai Medical Equipment Manufacturing Company and passed its written and physical exams. Still, the company did not offer him anything. Quite puzzled, SCHUI officials contacted the company and learned that he was rejected because of his "complicated political background." According to the registration information provided by Yu, he was no more than a former low-level supporter of Guomindang rule who had served as a village chief and attended an officially sponsored political training course.[69] Other establishments, the commission noted, took caution to a similar extreme when considering unemployed intellectuals for positions. The East China Bureau of Mining Management declined to accept any candidates unless the Shanghai Public Security Bureau investigated their backgrounds and guaranteed that the candidates had not been members of Guomindang organizations. Some establishments wanted to know that the candidates were "politically reliable" or had a "clean history," and refused to accept qualified police statements such as "up to now no political problem has been found with this candidate." According to SCHUI, the Provincial Government of Rehe evaluated 134 candidates for 100 positions in finance and economics and hired only 12 (a 9 percent rate of acceptance). The East China Bureau of Geology was apparently more risk-tolerant. Management looked at 611 candidates for 500 trainee vacancies and took 167 (a 27 percent rate of acceptance).[70]

Once detected by those seeking to register as unemployed intellectuals, the recruiting establishments' vigilance compounded these persons' tendency to withhold information from the authorities. Some of them inverted a well-known official slogan to express what they believed would give them the best chance of rejoining the workforce. They stated that the state practiced "ruthlessness for those who confess [their wrongful pasts], and leniency for those who cover up [such background]" (*tanbai congyan yinman congkuan*), instead of the other way around as promised. The SCHUI indicated that there were registrants who had chosen not to reveal some of their connections, activities, or appointments until after starting the new position.[71] To be sure, recruiting governments and enterprises understood that among unemployed factory and other manual workers were people who had been dishonest about their backgrounds and activities. However, since the state had no plan to place such workers in professional or administrative positions in large numbers, such establishments did not have to worry about their impact on everyday operation.

In brief, a self-fulfilling prophecy emerged. The Mao regime wanted to exploit the knowledge and skills of "unemployed intellectuals" for purposes of socialist development, even though it considered these persons politically unreliable. The way in which the emerging state conducted appointments and dismissals as well as the registration drives predetermined the kinds of people who came forward as unemployed intellectuals and asked for assistance. Few of them possessed professional training or experience. Many had worked for Guomindang or had other background disapproved by the state. Furthermore, neither the state nor recruiting establishments could quickly verify personal information provided by those who claimed to be unemployed intellectuals. In the end, the Mao regime obtained what it had anticipated—a pool of intellectuals who could fill various kinds of position but who it feared would wreak havoc on socialist development.

THE DEEPENING OF THE SURVEILLANCE STATE

In April 1952, after five months of registering unemployed intellectuals, the SCHUI responded to lingering questions from higher authorities and recruiting establishments about the registrants' backgrounds. The commission's leaders gathered staff members from every district and explained to them a "mass-line" (*qunzhong luxian*) approach to investigation, borrowing the term from the famous method of revolution articulated by Mao during the Yan'an phase of Chinese Communism. The investigations would henceforth involve local branches of state-sponsored associations and local residents' committees; local officials, CCP activists, and homemakers; and the relatives, friends, neighbors, and former colleagues of the applicants. With each application, registration staff would approach the local associations and the local residents' committee to confirm claims about educational attainment, work experience, family background, and so on. Additional care would be needed for applicants whose "situations are relatively complicated," or with whom hints existed that they had worked for the Guomindang or other political regimes, served the exploiting classes beyond the role of an ordinary white-collar worker, or lied in their applications. Staff members were instructed to interview as many people as necessary in the local neighborhood, contact the applicant for further information, and visit or write to the mentioned workplaces to clarify what positions the applicant had held, the quality of performance, and the reasons for termination. Staff members were asked to hold "investigative group meetings" with people who knew the applicant well to obtain further information. If doubts persisted as to whether the person had committed serious crimes, assistance from the Public Security Bureau or the local police station would be warranted. The goal was to have everyone contacted "candidly disclose every piece of information" they had on the applicant. The staff could then assess the credibility of the informants and the evidence and therefore the true identity of the applicant.[72]

This mass-line approach of the SCHUI to investigating unemployed intellectuals was fanciful thinking. The commission and its staff constituted but an extremely thin layer of the municipal bureaucracy, which was simultaneously managing other official campaigns across the city. The frontline registration personnel lacked opportunities to execute the ambitious investigation, not to mention appropriate training or support to accomplish the task. Nonetheless, the approach revealed that the official view of the intellectual as a usable but unreliable subject informed surveillance practice in urban society. The registration authorities feared that some unemployed intellectuals might be resentful of CCP rule or even plotting against it. At the very least, these intellectuals shared habits and dispositions harmful to socialist development. In the authorities' minds, who these persons were, what they believed, and what they had done thus had to be clarified. As we have seen, two of the investigative procedures mentioned by the commission were actually deployed during the subsequent Unified Unemployment Registration: extensive neighborhood participation and public discussion.

As official surveillance on the unemployed intensified across Shanghai, recruiting establishments that could neither wait for the SCHUI to complete its investigation nor exclude unemployed intellectuals from hiring plans took matters into their own hands. What happened at the New Education College of Shanghai (*Shanghai xinjiaoyu xueyuan*) offers a window on the tactics and strategies of such establishments, few of which had resources to pursue comprehensive personnel investigation during the early 1950s. The college was originally set up to train instructors in primary, secondary, vocational, and factory-run schools to become CCP activists. Due to the rapid expansion of the Shanghai school system, the college quickly switched to preparing displaced schoolteachers to return to work. A few months into the registration of unemployed intellectuals, the college's mission was extended to the training of such persons for school positions. During the summer of 1952, the college enrolled almost 3,000 unemployed intellectuals, of whom over two-thirds were women, in a six-week residential course. The training involved little instruction in pedagogical skills or academic subjects. The course was modeled after the ideological reeducation program that the CCP had developed in Yan'an, which was then deployed widely across Shanghai as part of Thought Reform of Intellectuals. The trainees were required to learn about the policies of the Mao regime, its interpretation of politics, society, and history, and what it regarded as the correct approach to work. Most important for our purposes, mandatory "confessions" (*tanbai*) were an integral part of the training.[73]

The college authorities were most interested in learning the political backgrounds and activities of the unemployed intellectuals. The details obtained through confessions would not only reveal how each of these persons had approached the 1949 revolution, but also serve as the bases for determining job assignment and other kinds of action. The authorities apparently guided the trainees in a particular manner to elicit their cooperation.

> Depending on the ideological state of the trainees, we repeatedly explained the official policy [of educating, reforming, winning over, and uniting with intellectuals] to dispel misgivings, and we patiently and sincerely taught and helped the trainees to attain self-awareness. We did not push or force them. We let them move from ordinary issues in their political life to past involvement in significant political activities, from their thinking to their participation in organizations and activities, from helping them to identify friends [of the revolution among people whom they know] to recognizing its enemies, from fragmented self-examinations [of ideological missteps and mistakes] to holistic confessions [of background and activities] as their awareness improved . . . At every stage, we selected successful examples as guides, played instructional films, and showed what the trainees had accomplished with the confessions to educate the trainees themselves. Finally, we helped the trainees further to reveal their backgrounds in a lucid and concrete manner through their writing of autobiographical narratives and open discussions of the content of the narratives.[74]

From the confessions, the authorities identified 952 of the trainees (33 percent) as having "problems" in their backgrounds. Among the serious cases, which numbered above 200, 49 people had reportedly held leadership positions at the district or higher level of the Guomindang or other "reactionary" political organizations. Forty-eight were former special agents of Guomindang intelligence or para-intelligence agencies or had served the collaborationist regime in similar capacities during the Anti-Japanese War. Thirty-eight had occupied the post of section chief or higher offices in the Guomindang government. Seven had attained the rank of brigade commander or above in the Guomindang military. Ten were former landlords; 51 were "CCP renegades." A few were former drug traffickers and convicted criminals.[75] It is unclear how these results compared with what the trainees had stated when they registered as unemployed intellectuals. The state recognized that, in general, some thought reform participants exaggerated their past activities and wrongdoings because of pressures to conform to official expectations as well as to show cooperation and remorse in front of peers and superiors.[76] One thing, however, is incontrovertible. The college expended material, symbolic, and intellectual resources to investigate every trainee in response to direct instructions, with the underlying belief that unemployed intellectuals were usable but unreliable.

Official surveillance at the college did not stop with the backgrounds, beliefs, and behavior of the trainees. The authorities monitored, evaluated, and documented the "ideological state" (*sixiang qingkuang*) of everyone and any changes therein, or what these men and women were prone to feel, think, and do as class subjects.[77] The official discourse on intellectuals became the analytical foundation on which the trainees were apprehended. Instruction, conversations, symposiums, and other campus activities became occasions for observation, examination, and documentation; the speeches and comportments of the trainees and their inter-action with the authorities and one another were sources of information. The authorities were especially interested in two things: first, the extent to which the trainees supported the socialist project, the official policy on intellectuals, and the state's plan to reeducate these people; and second, the trainees' effort to overcome their own self-centeredness, indiscipline, and other undesirable traits that they had allegedly acquired since childhood and in roles such as official, firm manager, and schoolteacher. Like the confessions, the assessments were used to determine appointments, or punishment if necessary.

When the training began, the college authorities reported that self-interest was a major reason behind the enrollments. Some trainees had no desire to work in a school, but needed a job. Some joined the class so they could show their families that they were making efforts at finding employment. Some women stated that having a regular income would free them from the bullying of in-laws. Diagnosed, too, was a lack of understanding of the training and its intentions, as manifested in allegations such as "training classes organized by the CCP are identical to con-centration camps [*jizhong ying*]; labor reform is inevitable," and in rumors that "those who performed poorly will be sent to Subei [the northern part of Jiangsu Province] or northeast China to help open up remote areas and perform farm labor." The authorities documented cynicism toward ideological reeducation from expressions such as "individualism is part of human nature and can't be altered" and "bring on thought reform if that's what I need to get a job."[78] As comments and conduct were entered into official records, every trainee became "a describable, analyzable object"[79] or, in the authorities' eyes, a class subject with specific ideo-logical, moral, and behavioral inclinations.

The next chapter explores, among other things, how postrevolutionary surveil-lance inside the workplace intensified the objectification of the intellectual with an "ever more subtle partitioning of individual behavior."[80] Suffice it to mention here that the college authorities adopted a quasi-official system of notation, a set of recurring vocabulary based on the official discourse on intellectuals, to sum up their observations. The vocabulary facilitated not only concise communication of the trainees' attributes as class subjects and comparison between trainees, but also their evaluation in relation to the ideological, moral, and behavioral expectations of the state. Desirable attributes identified by the authorities included, among oth-ers, "sincere about learning" (*xuexi renzhen*) the material furnished by the state, "aspiring to make progress" (*yaoqiu jinbu*) to meet official standards, "upright in their ways" (*zuofeng zhengpai*), and "relatively honest" (*jiao laoshi*) given the corruptive commercial and moneymaking culture of Shanghai. Examples of negative attributes were "backward thinking" (*sixiang luohou*) on political, eco-nomic, and social issues; fear of hardship, challenges, and extra work (*pa chiku*); tendency toward being "rash and irritable" (*xingqing jizao*); and "rather strong petty-bourgeois proclivities" (*xiao zichan jieji qingtiao jiaonong*) in terms of speech, attire, and lifestyle.[81]

In the end, almost all of the 3,000 trainees were assigned to a position in a school. This does not mean that the college authorities were confident about their knowledge of these people or pleased with the latter's performance during the six weeks of ideological reeducation. The high placement rate reflected, instead, increasing demand for schoolteachers and other school personnel across Shanghai.[82] In fact, the appointments were only for six months initially. The receiving campuses were expected to examine and further reeducate the appointees to determine whether they deserved permanent employment. In other words, state surveillance of the trainees migrated into their newfound workplaces. Roughly 60 trainees (2 percent) did not receive any assignment. One category of rejects included former Guomindang personnel who were uncooperative and others who had reportedly committed violent crimes or were suspected of having been sabotaging CCP rule. The Public Security Bureau was notified about these people; with its consent, however, they still could be considered for positions at schools. Members of a second category were not considered for any school position. These were mainly men and women who had signed up as unemployed intellectuals fraudulently or fugitives or criminals required to be processed by the court or the police.[83]

In their notable study of social classification, Bowker and Star suggest that if "a category did not exist contemporaneously, it should not be retroactively applied."[84] The alternative, they argue, is to lose sight of dynamics related to how systems of classification emerged and evolved, or a unique window on politics, society, and history. On the eve of the 1949 revolution, ordinary Chinese had little reason to talk or think about "intellectuals," let alone consider whether they personally belonged to this social category. Not long after the revolution, embodied subjects referred to as intellectuals were locatable across China. The registration drive described above captures the impact of the Yan'an approach to the intellectual on its ontological transformation. The triumphant Mao regime wanted nationwide cooperation from usable but unreliable "intellectuals." Before long, the Shanghai government began to use its symbolic power and administrative capability to locate jobless intellectuals. Looking to improve their lives or those of their families, many evaluated whether they were intellectuals eligible for official assistance and nudged others to do the same. The web of texts, conversations, and interactions that spread across the city during the registration drive turned it into a collective learning exercise, one that involved the intellectual as a classification of people. When the drive ended, every neighborhood had a new category of people—intellectuals—albeit with the boundaries of this population remaining ambiguous.

At the same time, governance in Shanghai took on specific features because of the official view that some of the unemployed were usable but unreliable intellectuals. For one thing, the municipal government spread its tentacles deep into neighborhoods and performed propaganda, liaison, training, and other tasks that served to strengthen its presence. Second, the government deployed large amounts of resources on surveillance because of worries that some unemployed intellectuals were saboteurs, criminals, or others who would wreak havoc in the workplace. Third, the government expanded ideological reeducation as means to transform as many unemployed intellectuals as possible into assets of socialist development. In a nutshell, as the registration drive objectified otherwise perfectly ordinary people into intellectuals, official deployment of mass surveillance, ideological reeducation, and workplace management by party cadres intensified under Chinese Communism.

Classification and Organization in a School System

For a while after [the 1949 War of] Liberation . . . even those intellectuals like ourselves from old liberated areas [in northern China] were able to shake off the [kinds of political] discrimination that we had long endured [within the Chinese Communist movement] and became "veteran cadres" . . . going from being persecuted to becoming persecutors.

—WEI JUNYI, CA. 1991

During the mid-1930s, Wei Junyi (1917–2002) was a philosophy major and political activist at the prestigious Tsinghua University in Beijing. She was so inspired by what she learned in her spare time about the CCP and its resistance to the ongoing Japanese invasion of China that she joined the party in 1936 and went to Yan'an three years later. Like many young people in the remote town during this period, she specialized in literary and educational work, traveled with Red Army troops, and performed subsistence agricultural labor. That is, she became an "intellectual" under the Mao regime. When the Rectification Campaign sponsored by the regime descended during the 1940s into the Rescue Campaign (*Qiangjiu yundong*), a ferocious hunt for spies and traitors in the ranks of revolutionaries within the Shaan-Gan-Ning base area, Wei was working in a town near Yan'an.[1] She initially believed the extraordinary tales of conspiracy and betrayal reported by the local party leaders, including their discovery of female students using sex and romance as bait to gather intelligence for the Guomindang and of enemy agents as young as six years of age. As close friends and eventually her husband were detained and identified as spies by the authorities, she realized that false accusations had been widespread. To avoid further punishment, her husband concocted self-incriminating stories with her support and, like many others, confessed publicly to trumped-up charges. With her trust in the local leadership shaken, Wei wrote to Chairman Mao to seek justice. Her husband even went to Yan'an to try to clear his name, only to find out that the abuses there had been still worse. Shortly afterward, Mao and his deputies issued public apologies for maltreating revolutionaries, which was small consolation to Wei and her husband, who had lost their child to illness partly because of the strain and isolation suffered by the family when it was under attack.[2]

Anyone who expects that Wei's loss and trauma as a Yan'an revolutionary would have hardened her into a noble woman daring to stand up against injustices under Chinese Communism will be disappointed. When she and her husband returned to Beijing during the late 1940s to assist in the CCP takeover, what they saw was a bizarre and depraved city, a far cry from how they had experienced the place before joining others in Yan'an. Filled with joy and confidence, they considered themselves part of the righteous forces that would remake Beijing from top to bottom. As successive punitive campaigns swept across the city during the first years of CCP rule, Wei, who worked in propaganda and literature, responded almost exactly as she had during her Yan'an years. At first, she believed the charges brought against others by the authorities. When the latter denounced her friends and colleagues, she recognized the baselessness, injustice, and even absurdity of the accusations. Nonetheless, she participated in and even led the persecution of colleagues of whose innocence she was certain. When she or her husband became a target of attack, they exploited their connections to higher officials to shield themselves from or minimize the resulting humiliation and punishment. In her own words, she "carried on the abominable practice of political persecution that the Mao regime deemed to be appropriate and beneficial to CCP rule."[3]

In this chapter, we move our investigation of the mutual constitution of the intellectual and Chinese Communism into the postrevolutionary workplace. A Marxist-Leninist dictatorship, the Mao regime was determined to industrialize China. The regime appointed large numbers of CCP cadres officially classifiable as intellectuals, especially those who had joined the party before 1949, to colleges, newspapers, factories, and other establishments to oversee those whom it labeled intellectuals, while the state media unceasingly criticized the politics, knowledge, and character of such subjects. Management by party cadres, ideological reeducation, and mass surveillance became features of such establishments and led to an unending flow of texts, signs, and cues that reproduced the official discourse of class. Ordinary professional workers (e.g., journalists, accountants, engineers) not only were objectified into usable but unreliable intellectuals for all to see; they were divided further into various subtypes for purposes of political control. To deflect their own stigmatization by the state, the cadres distanced themselves from the professional workers through various means. As Wei Junyi hinted in the epigraph, many represented themselves in words or deeds as "veteran cadres" (lao ganbu) by drawing attention to their loyalty to, sacrifices for, and knowledge of Chinese Communism. As the professional workers coped with official criticisms of selfishness, indiscipline, and other failings and the often callous behavior of the cadres, professional life became infected with fear and anger, shame and resentment, pretension and deception as well as antagonism, withdrawal, and humiliation. The domination, division, and demoralization impeded the

official goal of rallying party cadres and professional workers to build a successful socialist polity together.

To use the terminology of the late sociologist Erving Goffman, the CCP takeover of industry, education, and other sectors based on the official discourse of
intellectuals created two vulnerable populations. The *discredited* comprised ordinary professional workers, or those who fit precisely into the Marxian definition
of intellectuals of the party. They were subjects of state disparagement and objects
of political control. The *discreditable* included party cadres who were relatively
educated and thus susceptible to being categorized as intellectuals by superiors
and others. As members of the two populations engaged in *stigma management,*
or efforts to reduce the damage that the classification would do to them, a culture
of anxiety, distrust, and resentment grew increasingly to mar the workplace. This
outcome could not but harm the prospect of Chinese Communism.[4]

To clarify these aspects of the intellectual and Chinese Communism under
the early PRC, I discuss conditions within Shanghai secondary education as well
as professional life in the city, especially during Thought Reform of Intellectuals.
Twelve years ago, I published a book on the school system. The book illustrates
the bureaucratic quagmire that developed in the workplace because of state conduct and the resulting challenges to official governance.[5] As I turned my attention
again to the postrevolutionary workplace with themes of this book in mind, I kept
noticing dynamics similar to those obtaining in the school system in documents
on higher education, industry, and other sectors that I came across in the municipal archives of Shanghai and Beijing. I realized that with the wealth of material
I had gathered on the school system over an eight-year period, I could offer a
rich yet succinct example of how the workplace figured in the mutual constitution of the intellectual and Chinese Communism, while reminding the reader that
any similar survey of another sector must take into consideration its institutional
characteristics (such as division of labor, control mechanisms, and management
decisions). The following account contains primarily data that did not appear in
my previous book.

More specifically, I suggest that two interrelated bundles of administrative
conduct saturated the urban workplace, served to objectify the intellectual, and
shaped social relations and individual calculus. First, I use *textual corroboration*
to refer to the multiple layers of documentation that party cadres maintained on
the staff on the basis of the official discourse of class. The records appeared in
many genres of text (e.g., staff registration, autobiographical narrative, performance appraisal, police report, penalty statement), each corresponding to specific
investigative efforts of the state. The records covered, to varying extents, the family
background, occupational history, work performance, social connections, political activities, and outlook and habits of the individual. The documents consistently
described most professional workers as petty-bourgeois intellectuals and ascribed
to these workers preconceived habits and dispositions from the official discourse.

They also identified a minority of such workers virtually as enemies of the state. Second, I use *everyday signification* to refer to the deluge of signs and cues initiated by the party cadres that reinforced the official representation of ordinary professional workers as petty-bourgeois intellectuals. Some of these signs and cues went together with mandated organizational reform; others arose as the cadres signaled that they were politically and morally superior to ordinary professional workers. Work arrangement, staff meetings, everyday interaction, and other workplace activities were impregnated with terms, meanings, and values from the official discourse of intellectuals, sometimes in a dramatic fashion.

CLASSIFICATION IMPACT OF TEXTUAL CORROBORATON

Sociologist Dorothy Smith argues that "textual reality" is integral to systemic domination. States and other organized powers create their own written accounts of people, things, and events. Built upon "the discourse of ruling" of these powers, or their political and administrative visions, the accounts produce "objectified forms of knowledge." Issues are formulated, studied, and recorded "because they are administratively relevant, not because they are significant first in the experience of those who live them."[6] When the PLA entered Shanghai in mid-1949, the CCP had more than 700 underground agents serving as faculty or staff members across primary and secondary schools.[7] These agents organized teacher associations, set up student groups, promoted street demonstrations, and conducted other activities on behalf of Chinese Communism.[8] Some of these agents had prepared reports on the character, performance, and politics of colleagues in anticipation of campus takeovers by the party. Composed under secrecy, such reports lacked substance and accuracy compared with material assembled later by party cadres through various means of official surveillance. The reports, nonetheless, marked the introduction of textual corroboration into the school systems, or the textual reality of the party based on its discourse of class.

Wuben Girls Secondary School (*Wuben nüzi zhongxue*), which was founded in 1902, had the distinction of being China's first secondary school for girls. The campus was quickly taken over by the CCP authorities after they seized control of the Shanghai Municipal Bureau of Education (hereafter SBE) (*Shanghaishi jiaoyuju*) in June 1949 and tasked it with reorganizing primary and secondary education and instructional programs of various kinds. A few weeks later, an underground agent who had taught at Wuben for two years delivered to the bureau a nine-page report on the faculty and staff. This handwritten report, which was about 7,000 characters long, focused on management personnel and whether they were fit to keep their jobs. School principal Yang Minghui, who had allegedly fled to Taiwan after purchasing an exquisite apartment there with embezzled money, was depicted as a villain and virtually part of the exploiting classes. She was a "typical dirty party politician" of the Guomindang who had sat on its legislative and governing bodies and had obtained her campus position through ties to powerful officials. She traveled ostentatiously by car or rickshaw, smoked heavily, wore expensive clothing and heavy makeup, and indulged herself in playing mahjong and other activities unbecoming of educators. Had Yang stayed on campus, the SBE would have removed her from her position and very possibly worked with other emerging state agencies to have her arrested. Forty other faculty or staff members appear in the report as usable but unreliable intellectuals, but also to different extents. Three components loom large in these brief assessments. First, appraisals of work performance, or the functional value of the individual to the institution of education, range from "well-learned" and "dedicated to students" to "indifferent" to their duties and "incompetent." Second, descriptors of personal character, or the likelihood that the individual would heed the socialist message of the state, include, for example, kind-hearted, even-tempered, timid, and despicable. Third, political judgments were constant, and sometimes expressed in stock phrases (such as "progressive in thinking" and "emphasizing personal safety first") to signal how the person had reacted to public protests against the Japanese invasion of China or Guomindang rule. Overall, the assessments hinted at how likely it was that the individual would support CCP rule. For example, physics teacher Yuan Chengming was presented as someone who could be trusted, because she was "open-minded" as well as "straightforward and kind" and did not exhibit the materialistic "styles typical of Shanghai people," besides being an instructor well received by students. In contrast, part-time instructor of Chinese literature Zheng Yimei (1895–1992), though well respected in the local literary and art scenes, was depicted as an obstacle to revolutionary change, because he was arrogant, stubborn, self-absorbed, and irresponsible, in addition to clinging to "outmoded ways of thinking" about gender, labor, and other issues.[9]

Within Shanghai secondary education, no event of the early 1950s was as influential as Thought Reform of Intellectuals in supplying a textual reality for objectifying faculty and staff members into "petty-bourgeois intellectuals." The well-documented national campaign, which also targeted professors, writers, and other professional workers, was partly an outcome of textual material gathered about these people by party cadres through investigations and mandated self-reports. The SBE had used pertinent records to identify supporters, remove others from their posts, and implement mechanisms of control on campuses. Thought Reform enabled the bureau to collect material on virtually every faculty and staff member. More than 7,000 of them participated in the campaign in three successive groups between July 1952 and March 1953.[10] There is no need to detail the activities that defined the campaign, that is, mutual criticism and self-criticism of the political, moral, and professional wrongdoing of the participants, their writing and rewriting of autobiographical narratives, publication of select compositions on site and in newspapers for instructional purposes, and study of state policies and other preassigned topics. The activities were informed by the discourse of intellectuals and the practice of ideological reeducation that the party had developed before taking power. The activities led to countless mentions of the intellectual by individuals and organizations, along with descriptions of what the state expected from such subjects and their supposedly undesirable and even objectionable traits.[11]

The surge of textual material during Thought Reform enabled the SBE to characterize and compare faculty and staff members as class subjects and to highlight the overall distribution of attributes of these "intellectuals." Notwithstanding the presence of false and inaccurate information, the records furnished details of the political, occupational, and family backgrounds of the individuals and their habits and dispositions, social networks, political activities, and responses to CCP rule. Let us look at the main findings of the bureau, or what it most wanted to know about the faculty and staff. Virtually half had allegedly had ties to Guomindang organizations; at least 20 percent were former government officials, military officers, special agents, or political organizers. The SBE singled out some of these people as potentially serious threats to its control of the campuses. These individuals had reportedly served in ranking positions, acted as undercover agents in schools, or participated directly in thwarting student movements against the Guomindang government. The SBE discovered others whom it regarded as former local bullies, landlords, bandits, or religious sect leaders, or people who had used force or other means to take advantage of and even physically hurt others.[12] On top of this picture of unacceptable political allegiances, outright criminality, and class-enemy backgrounds, the SBE reported large numbers of comparatively minor offenses and transgressions, some of which had occurred shortly before and even during Thought Reform. For example, at Yuedong Secondary School, which had twenty-five faculty and staff members, eight confessed to corruption or other economic wrongdoing and twenty-three to illegal gambling or lending. Fourteen said that they had womanized or patronized dance halls, and ten reported that they had "abominable workstyles" that sometimes involved severe physical punishment of students. Prostitution and syphilis, drug addiction and trafficking, and tax evasion and theft were documented on other campuses.[13]

What happened to physics teacher Cao Qingjun demonstrates further how the textual reality of the SBE turned faculty and staff members into usable but unreliable intellectuals. Using material gathered during Thought Reform and other occasions, the bureau put together a portrait of Cao when seeking to impose punishment on those who had committed wrongdoing recently. First, Cao turned out to be a former Guomindang official. He had served as a military interpreter during the Anti-Japanese War and received Song Meiling (1897–2003) when she visited the town where he worked. Song was the wife of Chiang Kai-shek, the leader of the Guomindang. Second, Cao was greedy, undisciplined, and untrustworthy. He had engaged in economic speculation before and after 1949. He owed money to restaurants where he wined and dined, had taken money from students and colleagues, and had stolen from the schools where he worked. Third, Cao was as an unscrupulous instructor. He failed to grade students properly and made improper advances to female students, so much so that he had stolen examination papers and used them as bait to get close to teenagers whom he liked. Despite these findings, the SBE merely issued Cao a formal warning (*jinggao*) for his behavior, which was one of the lightest sanctions that the bureau could administer.[14] An almost twofold expansion of student enrollment within the school system between 1949 and 1953 made the bureau reluctant to dismiss any instructors except those considered incorrigible.[15] Moreover, Cao's punishment, or the lack of it, suggests that he had been cooperative with the authorities during the investigations. In short, he remained usable from the bureau's perspective.

As textual material on the faculty and staff accumulated because of state surveillance, the SBE performed *paidui,* an official approach to control that was becoming increasingly common. *Paidui* literally means lining up people or things in order. Administrative documents use the term to refer to the division of a population into a sequence of political subcategories supplied by the higher authorities. The procedure enabled the state to experiment with various schemes of classification and accordingly formulate measures of supervision, punishment, encouragement, and so on. Within the school system, party cadres used gathered documentation and their observations to combine and recombine faculty and staff members into lineups of political subtypes—and therefore produced even more written records on these "intellectuals." What happened at the reputed Nanyang Model Secondary School is instructive. It shows that while the state saw most schoolteachers as petty-bourgeois intellectuals, the use of *paidui* placed a small minority on the edge of the category of class enemies and even squarely inside it. In the spring of 1952, Nanyang's faculty and staff took part in a pilot run of Thought Reform. After weeks of investigation and ideological reeducation, the cadres had collected sufficient material to place twenty-four of the fifty people into literally five subcategories according to the political activities of the individuals and their cooperation with the authorities, or how much of a threat they posed to the school system and the state. "The first category" included those who had in their backgrounds minor "historical problems" of aiding enemy regimes. A former diplomat and a former director of a Christian church were two of the five people assigned to this subcategory. The authorities assigned another five people to "the third category," which was reserved for individuals who had "serious problems in [their] political history" but "no current activities" against the state. Placed in this subcategory was a woman who had disclosed two decades of service to the Guomindang and ties to former key members of the collaborationist regime during the Anti-Japanese War. A former Guomindang official who reportedly had placed CCP cadres under arrest, engaged in criminal activities, and indirectly caused suicides among his victims was the single member of "the fifth category," or people who had "a debt of blood" or were involved in "existing activities" against the state and who had been evasive about such wrongdoing.[16]

After Thought Reform formally began within Shanghai secondary educa-tion, faculty and staff members were separated into analytical and administrative subtypes by school party cadres, sometimes repeatedly, to facilitate reorganiza-tion and management of the campuses. The principal lineup divided the faculty and staff into five segments—that is, "progressive," "intermediate," "backward," "reactionary," and "counterrevolutionary elements"—according to the political experience of the individuals and their willingness to support or submit to CCP instructions and standards, especially those publicized within the school system. The SBE made recommendations as to the proportion of the faculty and staff to be placed in each segments (for example, approximately 25 and 15 percent were to be designated as progressive and reactionary elements, respectively).[17] Other political lineups and schemas of subcategories appeared. On the one hand, these instruments reflected official vigilance, or the view that intellectuals constituted a threat to Chinese Communism. On the other hand, they helped to justify the deployment of penal and other administrative measures within the school sys-tem, especially the appointment of party cadres to management positions. For the state, the classification further captured the political and class character of some of the faculty and staff members. For instance, by September 1952, after roughly half of the faculty and staff had undergone Thought Reform, the SBE instructed the cadres in charge of the campaign to designate some as "key targets [of attention]" based on evidence or clues of involvement in counterrevolutionary activities or serious crimes. The targets were to be separated into "first," "second," and "third" types according to wrongdoing and willingness to cooperate with the authorities, before the administration of criminal punishment or administrative sanction, of which the bureau included immediate arrest, continual subjection to ideologi-cal reeducation, deprivation of political rights, and other measures.[18] The cadres were instructed to identify another four types of people for removal from cam-pus, demotion, formal reprimand, or warning based on wrongdoing, poor work performance, insufficient remorsefulness, and other factors. Put differently, as Thought Reform proceeded, the bureau used gathered records to establish that some faculty and staff members were objectionable or incompetent, and yet some of them could still be used by the school system.[19]

After Thought Reform, textual material continued to build up within the school system, leaving none of the faculty or staff members an unchanging "intellectual." As official investigation continued, previously unknown details of the political, professional, or other activities of these persons came to light. The state's shift-ing emphasis on the relations of intellectuals to socialist development affected how the SBE interpreted professional conduct and past activities. The state, fur-thermore, introduced new schemes of political classification, for example, dur-ing the mid-1950s Campaign to Wipe Out Hidden Counterrevolutionaries. As a result, the bureau reassessed and reclassified faculty and staff members regularly, even though it continued to regard most of them as petty-bourgeois intellectuals. The vicissitudes of Zhu Shouzhong (1920–1970) illustrate how dramatically the CCP's endless documentation of the background, thought, and behavior of so-called intellectuals altered some of these people's class and political identities— sometimes with life-and-death consequences. When the PLA entered Shanghai, Zhu was already a well-documented supporter of the socialist revolution. When he was a secondary student in the late 1930s, he participated in public protests against Guomindang policies and practices. He subsequently graduated from the Economics Department of the famous Fudan University, but chose to become a schoolteacher. During the civil war, he became an influential member of the Shanghai Secondary School Teachers Association, a front organization established by the CCP to rally support for the revolution. After the takeover, Zhu was one of the first Shanghai schoolteachers recruited into the CCP. His education, hard work, and service to the profession earned him the posts of school inspector and then deputy director of teacher-training programs at the SBE. In 1954, the bureau made him the deputy principal of a teachers' college. If Zhu's success exemplified from the official perspective what a supportive petty-bourgeois intellectual could achieve under CCP rule during the early 1950s, he discovered shortly afterward how other facets of his life, once documented officially, would destroy the career and lifestyle that he had worked for. When Land Reform reached his native place after the 1949 revolution, the authorities categorized Zhu as an absentee landlord because of land he had received from his father. We do not know how Zhu had handled the land prior to the campaign. But he did tell some colleagues about the worrisome classification. Nothing disturbing happened to him until the Campaign to Wipe Out Hidden Counterrevolutionaries swept across education and other sectors. The record that he was an absentee landlord became the basis on which his CCP membership was revoked. During the Antirightist Movement roughly a year later, his landlord classification was brought up again at his expense. The SBE accused Zhu of having lied about his class background and sentenced him as "a class adversary who had infiltrated the party" (*jieji yizi fenzi*). He was reassigned with 500 other people from Shanghai's cultural and educational sectors to the forbidding Ningxia Hui Autonomous Region in northern China, where he was repeatedly denounced and finally executed in 1970.[20] Once a trustworthy intellectual to the state based on official documentation, Zhu became a class enemy from the official perspective, equally because of textual corroboration.

DYNAMICS OF EVERYDAY SIGNIFICATION

Following Lenin, the CCP leadership believed that if intellectuals were not placed under the supervision of the party after the socialist revolution, they would continue to use their knowledge and authority to serve the interests of the exploiting classes. Using well-trained party cadres to take over banks, newspapers, universities, and other places where intellectuals normally work is vital to advancing socialist development, not to mention defeating any of their attempts at counterrevolution. As soon as the PLA seized Shanghai, party cadres began to move into Shanghai secondary education. Their work engendered an abundance of signs and cues that reinforced the official representation as well as textual corroboration of faculty and staff members as usable but unreliable intellectuals. More concretely, the cadres turned the official understanding of intellectuals into distinct patterns of work, opportunity, and social association within the school system, or social boundaries saturated with the political meanings and moral values used by the party to define the subjects since the Yan'an phase of Chinese Communism. Three types of activity of the cadres were especially influential in this regard: their reassignment of roles and responsibilities, their enforcement of curriculum and other institutional changes, and their interaction with faculty and staff members.

The CCP takeover of the SBE during the summer of 1949 involved objectifying significations that would spread across the school system. The cadres assigned to the bureau were former underground agents of the party within the city or members of the PLA contingent.[21] Although the crumbling Guomindang government left behind 383 employees in the bureau, the cadres retained the service of only 54 for accounting, mimeograph, and other technical tasks.[22] The dismissal of the rest of the staff, which included educational program directors, campus inspectors, and other kinds of officers, cast the dismissed immediately as unfit for guiding socialist reform of the primary or secondary school system or other programs directed by the bureau. The latter's treatment of the dismissed suggested further to these persons that, based on the Marxian thinking of the party, they were a variety of inferior class subjects. Reflecting the Mao regime's concerns for social stability and political control with regard to the takeover of the city, the cadres arranged retraining and financial subsidies for almost three hundred people. This group underwent self-criticism, political study, and other ideological reeducation activities that targeted self-centeredness, materialism, and other habits and dispositions which the Mao regime alleged to be widely shared among intellectuals. After several weeks, the SBE provided eighty-four people with placement assistance, half of them for positions outside Shanghai. In particular, nine were recommended for Russian-language training or enrollment in a "revolutionary university" established by the party. These individuals were given exceptional assistance that probably allowed them to envision themselves serving the state again soon in some respectable capacity. By contrast, the SBE handed over the information of eight "reactionary elements" to the police for further investigation and even arrest, because "irrefutable evidence of repulsive activities" existed against these people. Based on their performance during retraining and other factors, the rest received dismissal subsidies (*qiansan fe*) or return-home subsidies (*huixiang fe*), or were put on a waiting list for job assignment.[23]

Across the secondary schools, official reorganization of roles and responsibilities signaled to faculty and staff members that the emerging state considered them heretofore allies of the exploiting classes. The SBE introduced management by CCP cadres through removing school principals from office or hollowing out their work and authority. The bureau's plan was to have every campus led by at least one experienced party cadre with support from a score of junior cadres. By 1954, almost 430 party cadres served across the schools.[24] Two years later, 73 percent of the 200 campuses had a party cadre serving as principal or deputy principal.[25] Ordinary faculty or staff members rarely enjoyed upward mobility during this period, even though the expansion of the school system created many managerial positions. Even the small number of faculty and staff selected by the SBE for career development purposes because of their favorable background and quality of work, or those regarded by the bureau as most desirable among "progressive elements," did not escape everyday stigmatization as usable but unreliable intellectuals. Despite assumption of significant responsibilities after receiving official training and even recruitment into the party, few of these faculty or staff members gained top campus positions, as they were usually reserved for party cadres assigned from elsewhere.[26]

On the campuses, other mandated changes embodied and expressed official criticism of the faculty and staff as previous partners of the exploiting classes and functionaries in their ruling apparatus. Swiftly abolished were curriculum items required, sponsored, or controlled by the Guomindang regime based on its political, cultural, and moral visions, including the system of "character-development education" (*xunyu zhidu*) in public schools as well as scouting, military training, and civic instruction and their related classes, rituals, and events.[27] As Robert Culp has noted, these programs and activities were introduced into the school system at various junctures of the Republican era (1912–1949). They were influenced by Continental European, Anglo-American, and traditional Chinese models of education and "could variously be characterized as liberal, Confucian, authoritarian, or fascist."[28] Their elimination had symbolic impact inside and outside the school system, as did the official abolition of the teaching of Christianity, takeover of missionary schools, and reduction of English instruction as well as the mandated tuition cuts in the large numbers of private schools. The changes suggested that the ruling classes and even the imperialist powers had exploited the campuses and their workforces to propagate values and practices at the expense of Chinese society. Likewise, the rapid expansion of student enrollment orchestrated by the SBE to include "children from peasant and worker families," by relaxing age restrictions and academic standards, reinforced the official criticism that the faculty and staff had mostly organized the campuses to serve landlord, capitalist, and petty-bourgeois families. Within three years after the CCP takeover of Shanghai, the proportion of secondary students from underprivileged backgrounds had reportedly increased from 12 to 26 percent, or roughly from 9,000 to over 33,000.[29]

Inside the schoolhouse, everyday interaction between CCP cadres and the faculty and staff signaled to these ordinary professional workers that they were at best petty-bourgeois intellectuals as described in official discourse. Let us briefly look at the backgrounds of the cadres, which was a main reason why they acted the way they did. The cadres did not take over campus management because of any of their conventionally acceptable qualifications (e.g., college education and teaching experience), even when they had such qualifications; they were appointed by the state without consultation with the faculty and staff. In fact, the cadres generally lacked professional experience and academic credentials compared with the displaced school principals and administrators, an achievement gap exacerbated by the dearth of CCP cadres in the wake of the revolution as well as competition for their service across sectors.[30] Equally significant, many of the campus cadres shared family and occupational backgrounds similar to those of faculty and staff members. The 39 cadres who took over the SBE were former schoolteachers, office workers, or secondary students.[31] By 1958, even after efforts to improve the class composition of campus leaderships, the bureau noted, only 27 of 73 full-time party secretaries in secondary schools were from worker or poor-peasant families; the rest were raised in petty-bourgeois, bourgeois, or landlord families. Among 356 school principals, over 70 percent of whom were party members, only 76 were from the "exploited" classes.[32]

To secure their newfound but problematic authority, the cadres often resorted to what Bourdieu identified as *elementary forms of domination,* or pointed, coarse, and even brutal tactics of management that commonly follow a dramatic change in the authority structure.[33] The tactics allow rulers to reproduce *conditions of domination* (e.g., fear and retreat among the ruled) when *objective mechanisms* (such as law, convention, or consent) have yet to mature to the extent of normalizing the hierarchy. From early on, the SBE reported, the campus cadres tended to adopt a hostile approach toward the faculty and staff. They wanted to expose wrongdoers of all kinds and see them officially punished together with those who continued to promote the interests and ideas of the exploiting classes.[34] The hostility served to produce *symbolic profit*[35] for the cadres, or recognition on and even off campus that they were different from as well as superior to other faculty or staff members. Thought Reform and other state campaigns that targeted "intellectuals" and exposed their alleged wrongdoing and undesirable habits and dispositions apparently emboldened the cadres, even as the SBE repeatedly instructed them to act firm but collegial inside the schoolhouse. After Thought Reform, the bureau conducted a study of private secondary schools, which still accounted for roughly half of the campuses in the school system. It discovered that instances of party cadres violating the official policy of "uniting, educating, and reforming intellectuals" were "rather common as well as extremely serious." Some cadres were full of "sentiments of arrogance and self-content." They verbally abused faculty and staff members, labeling them "shameless" and "backward," and even questioning their presence in the teaching profession.[36] Roughly a year later, the SBE reported that "the relations between the party and the masses [i.e., between school cadres and the ordinary faculty and staff] are generally not good." The case of principal Ji Bin at Yangjing Secondary School suggests the extent to which some cadres would go to distinguish themselves from their colleagues. Ji's "brutal" (*cubao*) treatment of faculty and staff members had been so unacceptable that both the district-level and the city-level commission set up by the party to investigate the conduct of its members had already forced him to undergo self-criticism and other educational activities. His behavior on campus changed little afterward, as he continued to "discriminate" and lashed out against "backward instructors."[37]

Social distancing, which can be interpreted as "a kind of informal ostracism,"[38] was another common approach adopted by school party cadres toward the ordinary faculty and staff. Like public condemnation, the conduct supported the image that the cadres were officials overseeing intellectuals. The primary tactic of social distancing was apparently refusal to participate in instructional matters, or the central function of a profession which the state described as filled with petty-bourgeois subjects. During the early 1950s, the SBE observed that "primary and secondary school principals [who were CCP members] generally do not take care of matters directly related to classroom instruction."[39] They concentrated on handling official campaigns, financial and construction issues, and hiring, discipline, and other personnel matters.[40] To be sure, many of the national campaigns that penetrated Shanghai secondary education led to multiple levels of investigation and cases of punishment. Appointment, budgeting, space, and other issues surged forth because of unprecedented increases in student enrollment. School principals justifiably complained to the SBE that there were "too many assignments with too little explanation, too-tight deadlines, and too numerous changes."[41] Meanwhile, lack of teaching experience could not but prompt some principals to avoid instructional matters. However, refusing to act in the role of schoolteacher was also another creative way for the cadres to enact social boundaries, or present themselves as different from other faculty or staff members. To the dismay of the SBE authorities, a follow-up survey of nine secondary schools conducted in the mid-1950s indicated that the school principals still failed "to go deep into classrooms or grade levels" to give lessons, advice, or study directions.[42] These party cadres, instead, let other party members take over instructional matters, with some of them exhibiting similar disaffection toward the responsibilities. Consequently, some of the schools used instructors who were not favored by the bureau to provide pedagogical leadership. Even when the bureau asked leading campus cadres to take charge of the instruction of socialist politics and values for students' benefits, a task that these party members were seemingly most qualified to perform, some cadres ignored that responsibility, too. At China Secondary School, for example, the cadres did not give any lectures on the topic. They employed, instead, "unreflective campaign-like approaches," which included bringing visitors to the campus to speak to students, as many as eleven times during one recent semester.[43]

Other forms of social distancing orchestrated by school party cadres also served to objectify ordinary faculty and staff members into usable but unreliable intellectuals. Even though the party cadres had access to policy information and state resources through the SBE, some offered little advice or assistance to their colleagues, while the latter faced unfamiliar political and economic challenges as a result of the revolution. What reportedly occurred at Yan'an Secondary School during the mid-1950s is instructive. Six party cadres were present on this relatively large campus, a number comparable to other schools of similar size. The cadres served as school principals, personnel executives, or instructors on socialist politics and held other influential posts. In political terms, the campus was hardly an extremely challenging place for management. Only 10 of the 73 people on the faculty and staff were "reactionary" or "backward elements." Nonetheless, the bureau remarked, the cadres lacked "compassion, regard, and patience," or proper sentiments deemed to be necessary for "assisting, educating, or nurturing" their colleagues in officially recommended ways. None of the 20 "progressive elements" on campus received training, support, or opportunities from management that would help them to become party members. The cadres, instead, "exploited" (*shiying*) the enthusiasm and energy of these people to help themselves run the campus.[44]

Using Yan'an Secondary School further as an example, the SBE emphasized two other areas in which the conduct of school party cadres was unsatisfactory. Faculty and staff members sometimes turned to the cadres for assistance when confronted with housing, subsistence, and other livelihood issues, since the state increasingly controlled job assignment as well as salaries and benefits within the school system,. Regardless of merits of a given request, the bureau discovered, the cadres at Yan'an responded poorly. They withheld subsidies and other forms of assistance established by the bureau, labeled the applicants "backward," and accused them of having a "purely economic perspective on life" (*chun jingji guandian*), which was a refrain used by the state to describe the petty bourgeoisie. A vice principal even stated that the campus had been "wasting money" by supporting an ill instructor with 60 percent of his salary. The other issue raised by the SBE had to do with ideological reeducation of the faculty and staff, which the state considered extremely important given that they interacted with students on a daily basis. The cadres at Yan'an, like those on other campuses, received official training periodically on how to help the faculty and staff to improve their political thinking and understanding of Chinese Communism. The bureau found out that the cadres did virtually nothing after returning to the campus from the training sessions. They passed on official directives during meetings with faculty and staff members without providing any guidance on understanding the content, let alone practicing the recommendations. They did not organize on-campus activities or take advantage of off-campus events for instructional purposes. When faculty or staff members asked for advice, the school principal told them to work harder to comprehend the material themselves. The bureau noted that some faculty, furthermore, had quite unpleasant interaction with the cadres. "[The cadres] cannot bear the sight of aged (*laonian*) teachers; they always highlight the backwardness of these teachers and fail to recognize their strengths. Even when they see the strengths, they do not offer any praise. With the teachers who are classified backward, the cadres cannot hide their disgust. They give up educating these people and set them adrift."[45] Some of the cadres on the campus continued to tell others that punishment was needed for the faculty or staff members who had cooperated with the Guomindang or other regimes.

In effect, the cadres who headed the campuses extended the class difference that CCP leaders had long constructed between themselves and other educated people—that is, proletarian revolutionaries versus petty-bourgeois intellectuals—to their own everyday interaction with faculty and staff members. Like those of the party leaders, the efforts of the cadres to consecrate themselves as such revolutionaries at the expense of colleagues were not always successful. The educational achievement of the cadres and their professional responsibilities in the school system made them vulnerable to attacks, especially from superiors who were engaged in their own self-consecration. These party officials attacked some of the campus cadres, similar to how the latter turned ordinary faculty and staff members into targets. What happened to deputy principal Pan Lengyun of Dunhua Primary and Secondary School is an excellent example. In March 1955, together with two other commissions, the district-level CCP commission of disciplinary inspection that supervised her work issued a report after a "preliminary investigation." The commissions criticized Pan for using the tactics of punishment, insult, and distancing mentioned above. Although the report did not label Pan a petty-bourgeois intellectual, it included many complaints used by the party to describe such subjects since the Yan'an period of Chinese Communism, and therefore left little doubt with regard to how the authorities thought of her. After being transferred to the campus, Pan gradually became "very arrogant and complacent" as well as "subjective, inflexible, and irascible." Above all, she displayed "the syndrome of a self-styled hero." On the one hand, the commissions observed, Pan did not "rely on [the advice of] the party or its organizations." She refused to study or implement official instructions on how to work with intellectuals. On the other hand, she was "divorced from the masses." She brushed off even "well-grounded ideas and assessments" from faculty and staff members. What she wanted were "grandiose achievements to make herself noticeable" by peers and superiors. To rectify the situation, the commissions recommended "severe criticism" of Pan and the transfer of a few "capable" party cadres to the campus to restore proper control.[46] In other words, the commissions regarded Pan as a flawed but usable intellectual.

STRATEGIES OF STIGMA MANAGEMENT

As a classification of people under the early PRC, the intellectual marked the classified with what the state pronounced as class traits, or an assortment of so-called petty-bourgeois and bourgeois habits and dispositions deemed to be harmful to Chinese Communism. We have seen that the CCP cadres assigned to Shanghai secondary education were aware of their vulnerability to being treated by superiors and colleagues as petty-bourgeois intellectuals. Some exploited their official positions and authority to set themselves apart from the ordinary faculty and staff. Here we look at how the faculty and staff and other professional workers negotiated the stigma associated with their official classification as intellectuals. Compared with the cadres, these persons did not have symbolic resources based on active political participation in Chinese Communism or access to administrative means to fend off the dubious classification. Nevertheless, stigma management flourished within this discredited population of "intellectuals" due to their attempts to resist or test CCP rule or to benefit or protect themselves from it.

Let us return to the aftermath of the immediate dismissal of more than 300 SBE employees when the PLA seized Shanghai in 1949. Though shocked and dismayed, the majority of the dismissed enrolled in the retraining program offered by the bureau in hopes of receiving financial and employment assistance. They encountered for the first time ideological reeducation organized by the CCP, learning in a formal setting its interpretation of class and the latter's relations to Chinese society and global history. In addition, they participated in self-criticism and other activities built upon the critical view of intellectuals of the party. The SBE's analysis of how these former employees behaved during the retraining provides an otherwise unavailable glimpse at their initial reactions to stigmatization as usable but unreliable intellectuals. Former ranking officials turned out to be most defiant toward the denigration of their knowledge and experience. They took advantage of ongoing uncertainty involving the CCP takeover of Shanghai and the mainland as well as their former professional status and understanding of the bureau to fight off stigmatization in general and ideological reeducation in particular. According to the bureau:

> [The former ranking officials] assumed airs of superiority, considered themselves always in the right, and refused our [ideological] reform. They turned up at events to see whether there were opportunities [to rebuild their careers] . . . and listened to reports only when they did not reject the speakers. They indulged in high-sounding but meaningless talks, nitpicked at the words and phrases of others, and declared their own view to be "objective" and "above politics." They [disputed what they were taught and] claimed that the Soviet Union is as imperialistic as the United States, and that [all] political parties and factions are tools of people who seek power and money. They pretended to be exploring political thought and doctrines and insulted and rejected our [teaching based on Marxist-Leninist] theory.[47]

Other former SBE employees who underwent the retraining apparently submitted to official stigmatization without accepting its claims. The overwhelming majority, the bureau stated, went along with the program but saw it merely as a path to return to work. A few used "every means" to present themselves as "progressive" to get the authorities' attention. Some tried to "poison" the cadres' minds with agreeable words and deeds in attempts to conceal "evil acts" of exploitation or counter-revolution that they had committed. Only a small number genuinely wanted to "reform" and "strengthen" their political thinking. Outnumbered by others, they "did not have the courage to debate or defend the truths [that they noticed in Marxist thought]."[48]

Within primary and secondary schools, similar defiance, manipulation, and acceptance of official stigmatization arose. Roughly a week after the PLA seized Shanghai, SBE officials met with some faculty and staff members about placing their campuses under the bureau's control or direct supervision, thus signaling distrust of existing personnel. Some of those approached sided with the officials and even demanded in front of them the firing of public school principals, seizure of private schools controlled by "reactionary elements," and "exposure and condemnation of diploma mills." These persons acted in what they considered a cooperative manner. While some continued to support the emerging state, others changed their minds or remained defiant after realizing that the official attack on intellectuals could harm their own careers and professional authority. Some even started to work with "backward elements" to resist mandated campus reforms.[49] As the bureau removed school principals, seized some campuses, and forced the closure of others, some continued to defy official instructions of reform. In March 1950, the SBE formally launched political study classes within primary and secondary schools after months of sponsoring related instructional activities. The bureau's goal was to gather faculty and staff members regularly on campus to study official material on class, politics, and history and learn about state policies and activities. Over thirty "study committees" staffed by 470 faculty and staff members were shortly formed across the city for supervisory and administrative purposes.[50] The bureau discovered that the faculty and staff on some campuses refused to meet with visiting members of the committees, while those on other campuses deliberately appointed persons with no instructional responsibilities to receive the representatives or disregarded their instructions and advice altogether. The representatives had to return to some of the schools up to five or six times before seeing genuine efforts to set up political study properly. Elsewhere, the bureau observed, faculty and staff members approached political study with a "perfunctory attitude." They did not read the assigned texts or attend small-group meetings. They used instructional or administrative work as excuses for their absence, and even preferred to "waste their time on chitchats and watching [lewd] American 'thigh' movies."[51] Others attended the meetings but did not utter a single word. The SBE reported that reactions to political study in missionary schools were especially offensive. During discussion sessions, "backward" instructors received applause for their "oppositional views" from colleagues who had otherwise remained silent. Some school principals and directors of instruction "adopted a hostile attitude" toward the Resist-America-Aid-Korea Campaign organized by the state after the Korean War broke out, and even declared that they had views about the war different from that of the state.[52]

When Thought Reform of Intellectuals started to spread across Shanghai's cultural and educational sectors in 1952, open defiance against official policies and measures by ordinary professional workers and against their stigmatization by the state as petty-bourgeois intellectuals was no longer a safe course of action. State violence during the Campaign to Suppress Counterrevolutionaries had resulted in hundreds of execution and thousands of imprisonment in Shanghai.[53] Across rural schools alone, the SBE reported in July 1951, ninety-nine people had been arrested and three sentenced to capital punishment.[54] What Goffman termed as "covering" emerged as a major strategy of Thought Reform participants to cope with the stigma forced further upon them. While the participants did not dispute or deny the selfishness, indiscipline, or other shortcomings alleged by the state, many sought to keep these attributes from "looming large,"[55] that is, spotlighted by others to the extent of endangering their own careers, livelihoods, or safety. One common tactic of covering was *redirection* during self-criticism, or the steering away of negative attention from the self. Some participants reportedly brought up multiple problems in their personal outlook, lifestyle, and political thinking, but indicated that these were consequences of broader patterns of belief and practice, or conditions in their family, workplace, social networks, and even Chinese society.[56] Some "dwelt on minor flaws" in their personality, sometimes in colorful terms, as means "to hide major wrongdoing" or their support of the exploiting classes.[57] Some "mechanically repeated" phrases and ideas from self-criticisms published in newspapers and avoided talking about their own background, activities, or thoughts.[58] Some even changed their appearance to highlight their agreement with official ideology. Some schoolteachers, for example, "shaved their heads" and started wearing "running shoes" to project "the appearance of a veteran worker."[59] Like what revolutionaries had done in Yan'an, especially after the Rectification Campaign, these individuals covered up their previous appearance. Others worked together to prevent political or moral issues uncovered by the state from hurting one another, a method that the authorities derided as the "pursuit of collective harmony" (*yituan heqi*).[60] The following exchange illustrated in *Wenhui Daily* was apparently common when college instructors were asked to read one another's writings and identify and criticize ideological mistakes.

A: Professor X, did you not slander the Soviet Union in your work Y?
B: Where? Where? That's not true.
C: From what I know, it's perhaps an overstatement to call it a slander. However, it's completely obvious that it's a criticism of the Soviet Union.
D: Hmm, yes.[61]

Concealment of personal details, which often coexisted with redirection, was another tactic of covering used by professional workers to reduce stigma. Here the individuals sought to hide backgrounds in politics or other areas that they believed to be objectionable by official standards. They wanted to be recognized at worst as petty-bourgeois intellectuals. Zhu Shouzhong was an example. He was the CCP cadre who did not disclose to the higher authorities his official classification as an absentee landlord. While Thought Reform was underway, the Shanghai authorities found out that some participants "who are clearly from the landlord class by family background insist nevertheless that their class status is at worst middle-peasant; others who obviously belong to the bureaucratic-capital class portray themselves blithely as members of the petty bourgeoisie."[62] Covering of personal details took other forms, too. Some Thought Reform participants reportedly glossed over various aspects of their background (e.g., political activities, friendships, hobbies) during self-criticism by offering vague or empty accounts.[63] Some underreported their age in order to hide things they had done in the past. Some talked about their hardships, honesty, and charitable deeds to imply that they had not supported class exploitation. Some pinned "severe [ideological] labels" (da maozi) on themselves, such as extreme indiscipline or hedonism, to draw attention away from other conduct or activities of theirs.[64] The SBE reported that when the last group of secondary school faculty and staff members took part in Thought Reform, comprising some 1,500 people, many arrived with prewritten autobiographical narratives and self-criticism, wanting to ride out the campaign without fully disclosing their backgrounds, activities, or thoughts.[65]

During Thought Reform, "self-exposure" was another strategy used by professional workers to negotiate their officially imposed stigma. Rather than bury details that would confirm shortcomings alleged by the state, some broadcast their mistakes and misdeeds with little prodding from party cadres. They wanted to convey comprehension of official ideology as well as cooperation and contrition, or be seen as working to turn over a new leaf. Although suitable for those who did not work closely with the Guomindang or other political regimes, self-exposure, like covering, was a difficult balancing act. The confessors had little control over how their cooperation was interpreted. The authorities sometimes saw the confession as yet another routine in the self-serving repertoire of petty-bourgeois intellectuals. It was believed that some participants disclosed offensive beliefs and behavior, not because they wanted to reform themselves politically, but because they wanted to show everyone else how "courageous" and "honest" they were.[66] The authorities were unimpressed with others who allegedly resorted to histrionics, through "crying their heart out" and declaring that "they deserved a thousand deaths for their crimes." Other participants reportedly submitted themselves to criticism by choosing wrongly not to contest any complaints and even false accusations leveled against them by colleagues.[67]

While use of covering or self-exposure by ordinary professional workers to cope with official stigmatization reflected fear, anxiety, shame, confusion, or other emotions that they experienced, another strategy, "going on the attack," not only involved some of these reactions; its deployment deepened conflict and resentment within the workplace. With this approach, one played an aggressive role during mutual criticism or other activities to demonstrate cooperation with the state. Some Thought Reform participants reportedly adopted a "severe" and "leftist" attitude from early on. They loudly accused colleagues of multiple crimes and mistakes, "banged on the table and kicked the bench" to express their indignation, and used "severe labels" indiscriminately against the targets. The authorities were critical of such viciousness apparently as much as what they dismissed as insincere ready admission of wrongdoing. Some attackers, it was noted, "put on a show to deceive people" about who they really were, besides confounding facts with fiction in their complaints against others. For the state, even when the complaints were accurate and the attackers were forthcoming about their own wrongdoing, they still violated the intents and purposes of thought reform, which was "an endless and self-conscious process of discovery" of the truths in Marxist theory, working-class experience, and the Chinese socialist revolution. The state had multiple mechanisms in place to ensure that the reeducational activities introduced in the campaign would become "an integral part of the everyday life" of intellectuals, "much like eating, washing one's face, and sleeping."[68] To the attacked, the experience was harrowing, even for those who had tried self-exposure. The attacked were "often flushed with shame and anger and were unhappy and dejected." They felt that the badgering and embarrassment was unnecessary. Many "promptly despised" the attackers, believing that they were "too backward" and "too confused" to understand thought reform and the consequences of their actions. Some confronted their attackers afterward. Some waited for their turn and took revenge. They hit the attacker with "a head-on blow," "randomly reprimanded him," and labeled him "reactionary."[69] To salvage their own reputation, some exaggerated the wrongdoing of the attackers and even gathered "trumped-up charges" to discredit these people.[70]

As Thought Reform proceeded, the authorities discovered another unpleasant trend. Ridicules, innuendos, and gossiping flourished, occurring regularly "over a cup of tea or after a few glasses of spirits" as the participants congregated during recesses or after work. The participants mocked colleagues openly or behind their backs on the basis of the revelations about desire, dalliance, or deviance, for example, yearnings to be rich, affairs with neighbors, and acts of embezzlement. Some "added inflammatory details" to what they had heard or "stitched together fragments" of material to spread rumors about colleagues.[71] We have seen this kind of finger-pointing behavior among veteran revolutionaries in Yan'an and school party cadres in Shanghai. When the subjects found themselves vulnerable to stigmatization as petty-bourgeois intellectuals, they combined official values with those of their own to belittle colleagues as means of elevating themselves within their own minds, among their peers, and inside their profession.

Regardless of how Shanghai schoolteachers or other professional workers reacted to official stigmatization, the state's interpretations of their conduct, as we have seen, reinforced their assigned status as usable but unreliable intellectuals—because of what Dorothy Smith identifies as "the circularity of the ideological process" commonly associated with hierarchical forms of administration. After publicizing widely the CCP discourse of class, the Shanghai authorities used this "predetermined conceptual framework" to illustrate in newspapers, internal reports, and other channels how professional workers responded or failed to respond to the requirements of Thought Reform and other ideological reeducation activities, or addressed self-centeredness, materialism, and other personal shortcomings. "Issues, questions, and experiences" that did not fit how the party understood class were simply left out of the official analyses.[72] Rendered illegible in these innumerable accounts were, especially, profound changes in work and governance because of the revolution and their impact on how the workers reacted to official stigmatization, not to mention personal, familial, and other factors.

Research has examined the urban workplace under the early PRC for good reasons.[73] The site was central to the CCP pursuit of socialist development. The accounts describe key mechanisms of official domination such as central planning, management by party cadres, and ideological reeducation. They illustrate major patterns of conflict, cooperation, and inequality (for example, those related to party cadres and between party cadres and the ordinary staff) as well as individual and collective responses to official governance (e.g., pride, criticism, protest). The scholarship, however, does not explain how classes portrayed in the official discourse became everyday recognizable populations inside the workplace, or how jobholders assumed legible class identities. In comparison, studies of the countryside have spotlighted how land reform produced "landlords," "poor peasants," and other Marxian categories of people paradoxically as the party abolished conventional and capitalist economic relations. These studies underscore the role of official classification and pertinent institutional mediums (such as mandated self-reporting, investigation, and mass assemblies orchestrated by the party) as well as ambiguities and manipulations involved in the process.[74]

With a focus on the creation of petty-bourgeois intellectuals in a postrevolutionary school system, this chapter has suggested that the urban workplace occupied the center of the production and reproduction of the social classes envisioned by the Mao regime. To borrow a metaphor from Foucault, the school system became "a sort of artificial and coercive theater," one in which tens of thousands of ordinary people eventually assumed the character of the intellectual based on the Marxian view of the state.[75] Scripts, designs, props, and dramas, as it were, inundated the school system. The CCP discourse of intellectuals (the primary script) permeated the system because of a variety of organizational rearrangements (or designs) mandated by the state, such as a new division of labor, thought reform, political lineups, and mass surveillance. The official use of multiple administrative tools (or props)—for example, official directives, personnel reports, statistical summaries, confessional statements, and autobiographical narratives—reproduced the discourse. An unending array of dramas with classification effects appeared: official accusations, self-consecrations, mutual antagonisms, judicial prosecutions, self-deprecations, withdrawals, and so on. Everyone within the school system doubled as a cast member as well as an audience member in a thickening plot of class struggle prepared by the state, the punitive authority of which guaranteed the production. Relearning about the self, colleagues, and Chinese society took place as the performance unfolded. Like official classification in the countryside, ambiguities and manipulations with regard to class identity arose.

Equally important, we have seen that because the Mao regime pictured usable but unreliable intellectuals as an integral part of the workplace, management by CCP cadres, ideological reeducation, and mass surveillance flourished. The institutions became the official means to protect Chinese Communism from these subjects as much as to cultivate it with their knowledge and skills. Within the school system, the institutions made possible the revision of academic curricula, the expansion of student enrollment, the reassignment of responsibilities, and, more generally, experimentations with socialist education. At the same time, the institutions enabled the official condemnation and increasing suppression of the alternative political and moral views of the faculty and staff. In short, the institutions served to extend both the symbolic and the administrative capacity of the state.

What happened with the school system reveals that the objectification of the intellectual had seriously negative implications for Chinese Communism—by turning workplaces with professional workers into perpetual sites of official concern as well as internally divided organizations. The practice of textual corroboration engendered an unceasing flow of what the authorities regarded as evidence of work deficiencies, moral transgressions, criminal conduct, and political wrongdoing of professional workers, especially because the state repeatedly launched investigative and punitive campaigns. The practice of everyday signification produced and reproduced schisms, distrust, and resentment that undercut the potential of professional workers to cooperate with the state as well as with one another. Viewed in retrospect, the dynamics could not but lead to further turmoil.

6

An Open Struggle of Redefinition

On May 1, 1957, the CCP launched another rectification campaign under Chairman Mao's direction. Unlike the one that had engulfed Yan'an during the early 1940s, which turned those whom he referred to as intellectuals into the targets of attack, the new campaign sought criticism of the party's governing performance from this category of people. Mao believed that the airing of criticism by intellectuals in the manner of "gentle breeze and mild rain" would help strengthen state-society relations and that the exercise was necessary to prevent political unrest such as those that had recently shaken socialist Poland and Hungary, in which students, workers, and others staged public protests, clashed with police, and demanded the removal of the government established by the communist parties. The new campaign followed eighteen months of high-level pronouncements and state measures aimed at improving relations with intellectuals, after they had been subjected to official disparagement and surveillance as well as reeducation and punishment since the 1949 revolution. Exclusive meetings with and encouragement from Mao and other party leaders gradually emboldened renowned writers, scientists, and other social notables to take the lead in providing critical evaluations of official policies, practices, and personnel. Professional workers, college students, and even factory hands, including some who were party members, then joined a growing protest at once condoned, encouraged, and to a large extent coordinated by the state.[1] Dismayed by the hostility exhibited in some of the complaints and suggestions, the Mao leadership ended the campaign abruptly in early June and started to orchestrate counterattacks. The state launched the Antirightist Movement (*Fanyou yundong*) shortly afterward with the aim of punishing those who had spoken out or supported unacceptable views. The population of intellectuals suffered further loss of prestige and autonomy, while CCP rule slid further down the path of coercion, violence, and abuse.[2]

This chapter examines the 1957 Rectification Campaign and its aftermath in a new light—as an open struggle to redefine the intellectual as well as Chinese Communism. During those restive months, observations on challenges confronting the revolutionary project blossomed, and so did recommendations for

change. Inside and outside the state, the crux of the debate was arguably the relations between the intellectual and Chinese Communism. Since 1949, economic
nationalization and land reform had eroded the power of the urban and the rural
economic elites. Mandated changes in the political, occupational, and educational
systems had benefited industrial workers and other laborers, even though some of
them were still dissatisfied, and for good reasons. Large numbers of scientists, writers, and other professional workers, however, had remained lukewarm toward CCP
rule, especially after the Campaign to Wipe Out Hidden Counterrevolutionaries
penetrated education, journalism, and other sectors and led to interrogations,
demotions, imprisonments, and suicides.[3] However fuzzy were the boundaries of
the category of intellectuals, its members used the Rectification Campaign not
only to air their criticisms of Chinese Communism and articulate alternative
socialist visions; they tried to reconstruct their social identity to improve their
status and influence and therefore what an intellectual was in Chinese society. The
regime reacted to these challenges by expressing further its vision of the socialist
project and the corresponding role of the intellectual.

Three major reinterpretations of the intellectual and Chinese Communism
appeared. Championed by distinguished scholars and other social notables during the Rectification Campaign, the first reinterpretation was built upon the
Confucian literati tradition as much as the official acknowledgment of widespread
problems of competence in socialist governance. The scholars and notables portrayed intellectuals as experts and professionals outside the party who had the
vital knowledge and experience to be its governing partner. They called for an
expanded involvement of intellectuals in politics, production, and administration
to save Chinese Communism from potential ruin. Another major reinterpretation
was promoted mainly by college students. The proponents demanded that intellectuals redefine the socialist project in its totality. They combined contemporary
ideas of democracy and equality with their reading of Marxism and Leninism to
challenge how the revolutionary project had been formulated and executed by
the Mao regime and the prerogative of the party to monopolize those tasks. In
effect, the students and their allies redefined intellectuals as "legislators" of major
social and political issues (to borrow an idea from Zygmunt Bauman) and architects of a different socialist China.[4] When the Mao regime hit back, it drew on
the Yan'an understanding of intellectuals and emphasized more than ever before
the professional and political value of these people to Chinese Communism. The
state introduced proposals to support the work and learning of professional workers and college students as well as to strengthen their ideological reeducation.
Also stressed was the nurturing of industrial workers and others of underprivileged background into capable professional workers. The Mao regime pictured
a surge of "red-and-expert" intellectuals who were dedicated to pushing Chinese
Communism to new heights.

The dominance of these perspectives not only indicates that the intellectual was quite objectified by the mid-1950s; it reveals that the intellectual had become the fulcrum with which the state and other forces organized their political visions and sought support. With each of the perspectives, symbolic boundaries were redrawn around the classification based on a specific set of experiences under the PRC. The scholars and notables who wanted to become partners in official governance had watched their influence and authority be eroded by CCP rule in general and workplace management by party cadres in particular. They represented themselves and other professional workers as intellectuals who were eager to serve the state and capable of improving Chinese Communism. The college students who advocated a complete overhaul of the socialist project combined political theories and ideas available in the university with the contemporary tradition of student protest. In their eyes, intellectuals were "spokesmen for enlightenment"[5] with obligations to expose systemic injustice and steer China onto a superior socialist path. Drawing on its experience of revolution and governance, the Mao regime persisted in portraying professional workers and college students inside and outside the party as intellectuals as well as added workers with professional training to the social category. The regime's intention was to produce as many usable and *reliable* intellectuals as possible on behalf of Chinese Communism.

To be sure, the three perspectives on the intellectual and Chinese Communism—intellectuals as state partners, as legislators, and as red-and-expert personnel—are analytical constructs. During the Rectification Campaign, analyses of political and social problems under the PRC and proposals to tackle the challenges were commonplace. Even more abundant were ritual affirmations of CCP rule, praises of Mao and other party leaders, highly emotional complaints, and self-deprecating remarks, or repertoires found in the innumerable ideological reeducation classes sponsored by the state since the 1949 revolution. As the campaign proceeded, individuals doubled down on, retreated from, and even altered their positions. When the Mao regime reasserted political control, elements of its arguments were reinterpreted at various levels of the state. Each of the constructs, however, captures political interests, beliefs, and imaginations that tended to coalesce together under the young PRC: the influence, respectively, of the Confucian, May Fourth, and Yan'an traditions of political thinking. Although the traditions support incompatible models of governance, they each envisage an important role for the educated. In addition, each construct reflects the location of its proponents in the socialist political economy. The college students who promoted the most radical approach to change were much farther from the center of power than were either the scholars and notables who wanted an improved part in governance and management or, closer still, the official and quasi-official spokesmen of the red-and-expert ideal.

INTELLECTUALS AS STATE PARTNERS

I've only been exerting sixty percent of my strength and energy [when at work]. It's not that I'm unwilling to do my best; there is no opportunity to do so, to become a soul mate of the party,

—FU YING, PROFESSOR OF CHEMISTRY AT PEKING UNIVERSITY, APRIL 27, 1957[6]

During the 1957 Rectification Campaign, leaders of various minor political parties approved by the state and scholars officially designated as higher (*gaoji*) intellectuals were chief proponents of the view that intellectuals and the state should work closely together to advance Chinese Communism. These scholars and notables generally had privileged access to CCP leaders and state assemblies as well as enviable positions and benefits approved by the state, because of its united front policy designed to secure cooperation and support from the elites outside the party.[7] Before the campaign began nationwide, party leaders, including Mao, had invited these scholars and notables to forums to discuss official governance.[8] During the campaign, the scholars and notables attended "airing-view" (*mingfang*) meetings sponsored by a variety of agencies, including central ministries, high-level CCP commissions, regional government offices, college party committees, and state-approved professional associations. They published their views on Chinese Communism in major newspapers and specialized journals. Because of their superior access to state affairs, the scholars and notables framed their criticism around "the most authoritative sources,"[9] all of which were based on Mao's speeches delivered on the campaign's behalf. There is no need to repeat his famously positive assessment of class struggle or its declining significance under the PRC, other than his concern with the continual maltreatment of intellectuals by party cadres, or what he denounced as "the three evils of bureaucratism, subjectivism, and sectarianism" harming the development of the socialist project.[10] His criticism of the cadres became the foundation on which the scholars and notables pushed for involvement of intellectuals at all levels of governance and management, with the belief that this would strengthen fairness, justice, democracy, and efficiency nationwide. In other words, the proposal of the scholars and notables reflected the schism that had opened up between party cadres and other professional workers in the postrevolutionary workplace. If many cadres had escaped stigma by representing themselves as dependable revolutionaries overseeing petty-bourgeois intellectuals, the stigmatized now tried to redefine the meaning of the intellectual to reclaim their lost status and authority.

The scholars and notables invoked to different extents the Confucian tradition of literati in using their learning and wisdom to serve the state. Although the maneuvers signaled support of CCP rule, they involved critical disagreement with the official understanding of intellectuals. The Mao regime had attacked intellectuals for their alleged selfishness, apathy, and other "petty-bourgeois" and even "bourgeois" shortcomings, and considered these persons usable but unreliable when it came to developing Chinese Communism. For the regime, the Rectification Campaign of 1957 was merely another exercise that the state organized to tackle the undesirable values, ideas, and habits shared by intellectuals. The campaign offered intellectuals who were outside the party an opportunity to help its cadres, a good number of whom were deemed to be intellectuals, improve their work. The scholars and notables downplayed the regime's criticism of intellectuals, emphasizing instead their preparedness to serve the state as well as their untapped potential as a result of its unwise governing approaches. Huang Yaomian (1903–1987), a professor of Chinese language and literature at Beijing Normal University, was among those who recited this popular theme. In an essay published in *People's Daily* (*Renmin ribao*), the official organ, he stated that intellectuals were "bearers of the literati-official (*shidafu*) tradition" with "precious knowledge" acquired through "many years of labor" (*laodong*). The last phrase hinted at the discipline exhibited by intellectuals and their lack of connection to class exploitation, and therefore contradicted the official evaluation of such subjects. For Huang, intellectuals wanted badly to serve "the state and the country" and deserved respect, assistance, and direction from the authorities.[11] Gong Canguang was the vice chancellor of Chongqing Teacher Training School as well as a member of the Sichuan Provincial Committee of the China Democratic League (CDL), a political party established during the Anti-Japanese War and operated under CCP auspices after 1949. He published a forceful defense of the political value of intellectuals for the Mao regime. He agreed with the official claim that a mutually expedient "employer-employee" relationship had been the primary dynamics between rulers and intellectuals before 1949. But he rejected the official view that intellectuals had been uninterested in politics, noting, instead, that they were knowledgeable and concerned about this dimension of social life through the ages. Even when they were "ruthlessly attacked" by the state and party cadres after 1949, they had been "perfectly happy" to study Marxist thought. He wanted the regime to adopt policies and practices that would help intellectuals recognize that they were "masters of their country" who could propose ideas to improve socialist development "without any future worries" of attacks and punishment.[12] Feng Kexi (1922–2004) was another CDL member and an official in the Chongqing municipal government. He complained about the Mao regime's distrust of intellectuals and their abuse by party cadres. Unlike Huang and Gong, he argued that existing intellectuals were different from past generations of literati, who were derided by the regime as self-serving and corrupt. Intellectuals had made "substantial [political] improvements" before and more so after 1949, to the extent of parting with their wealth and risking their safety to "serve the people rather than the ruling classes." Nonetheless, he invoked the tradition of literati serving the state to counsel the cultivation of "friendship and contact" between intellectuals and party cadres, workers, and peasants as means to improve the involvement of imperfect and timid and yet loyal, talented, and dedicated intellectuals in the socialist project.[13]

The proposal that the state and intellectuals build a partnership to advance Chinese Communism was daring on another level: it undercut the official ideology of class struggle and decades of CCP denunciations of the complicity of intellectuals in this drama. For the Mao regime, the appointment of party cadres to authority positions after the 1949 revolution was as vital to the liquidation of the exploiting classes as land reform and nationalization of industry had been. Everyday management by veteran revolutionaries and other party cadres was the only means to bring the dictatorship of the proletariat to the local level. The setup was essential to keeping expropriated landlords and capitalists from regaining power through collusion with intellectuals, or to preventing the reproduction of the political and economic relations that these populations had shared before the revolution. The scholars and notables ignored and even challenged this official premise. They built upon Mao's recent observations on the diminishing significance of class struggle and his criticism of party cadres to argue against reliance on this population in governance and management. To the vice chancellor of Beijing Normal University, Fu Zhongsun, intellectuals were useful and reliable subjects. He stated that the official policy on intellectuals was "one of the CCP's biggest misjudgments in recent years." Attacking professors and other experts and professional workers as old-fashioned (*jiu*), bourgeois, or petty-bourgeois intellectuals led to widespread abuse against such persons and their distrust of the state, when "the era of class struggle" had already ended with the demise of landlords and capitalists and "the majority of intellectuals" had been supportive of the "goals of socialism and communism" of the state.[14] Xu Zhongnian (1904–1981), a professor of French at the Shanghai Foreign Language Academy, took a comparatively subtle approach when criticizing the theory and practice of class struggle. He agreed with the official assessment that most intellectuals had "a dual character" (*liangmian xing*) under Chinese Communism—that is, they sometimes acted for and sometimes acted against the revolutionary project. However, this was also true with party cadres, because they, too, had come of age in "the old society" and had been influenced by its characteristic thoughts and habits. Even worse, Xu continued, many of the cadres had joined the CCP for self-serving purposes. Permitting the cadres to lord over and abuse intellectuals, especially those who deliberately stayed behind in China to contribute to Chinese Communism, would only harm its prospect.[15] In short, Xu questioned whether party cadres were any more politically reliable than intellectuals as the Mao leadership assumed.

After the high tide of the Rectification Campaign subsided in June 1957, Minister of Food and Grain Zhang Naiqi (1897–1977) continued to promote his sanguine interpretation of class struggle under the PRC, until pressured by the state to repudiate what he had said. Zhang was a founder of the China National Democratic Construction Association (*Zhongguo minzhu jianguohui*), another political party that operated under CCP guidance after 1949, and a former busi-nessman and college professor. While he acknowledged that class struggle is vital to any socialist revolution, he proclaimed that "no one [in China] wavers over the socialist path" anymore, not even the remnants of the capitalist class, who "cannot and will not rebel" against the CCP, still less return to power. Even when the state was gearing up to punish its critics, he defended critical viewpoints from airing-view meetings and newspapers that had been labeled "counterrevolutionary" as mere "grumblings" from a few about their personal difficulties. Zhang continued to borrow from Mao when the Chairman had already changed his mind about the Rectification Campaign as a result of the avalanche of complaints against the state. Zhang noted that class struggle in general and ideological reeducation in particular had produced "tremendous results" for CCP rule since 1949, notwith-standing some "negative consequences" among party cadres, intellectuals, and others, such as frictions and mistrust and feelings of superiority and inferiority. Furthering "class cooperation" under CCP leadership, or the inclusion of margin-alized intellectuals in official governance, would improve state-society relations and economic development as well as extend and deepen socialist consciousness across classes.[16]

Research has shown that the measures of political reform promoted by the scholars and notables were consistent with their recommendation of expanding the role of intellectuals in politics, production, and administration. The schol-ars and notables pressed for participation, voice, and authority under the exist-ing framework of government. An important proposal was the strengthening of the political, legislative, and advisory functions of the National People's Progress (NPC) and the Chinese People's Political Consultative Conference (CPPCC), the high-level official bodies which had strong representations of scholars and other educated people outside the party but little practical influence over state affairs. Other important measures included the incorporation of members of these bod-ies into the investigation of wrongful convictions in previous political campaigns and the reduction of CCP involvement in everyday governance.[17] A main vehicle with which the scholars and notables sought to realize these and other long-term changes was *fazhi,* which can be translated as rule of law. A negligible idea in the official discourse of the Rectification Campaign, *fazhi* has received little attention in research.[18] The notion of rule of law, however, seemed no more nor less contro-versial to the scholars or notables compared to their other proposed reforms. That this was the case indicates further the unbridgeable ideological gap between the Mao leadership and the scholars and notables as well as the extent to which these people sought to redefine the intellectual and Chinese Communism.

The scholars and notables, especially those with legal training, wanted to use law to establish structural constraints on the behavior of the CCP and the state. They wanted to realign governance away from management by party cadres, from campaign-style violence and justice, and from institutionalized discrimination on the basis of class, politics, or other factors of personal background, especially against intellectuals. After 1949, the institution of law encountered dramatic reorganization but not standardization in terms of rules, procedures, or staff competence.[19] Huang Shaohong (1895–1966), a former Guomindang high official, was one of those who complained about the low "cultural level" and poor knowledge of the party cadres in the legal field and the lack of oversight in areas from legislation, prosecution, and policing to verdicts, sentencing, and administration of penalties. He pressed for institutionalization of penal and civil codes, disciplinary codes for civil servants, economic laws, and regulations on organizations, among other instruments, to improve uniformity and transparency in the delivery of justice.[20] His proposal, like others mentioned below, would work only when the legal field involved specialists and other educated people who had been excluded from it. The jurist Yang Zhaolong (1904–1979), who had been a prosecutor-general in the Guomindang government, similarly wanted promulgation of formal codes without further delay: "In many circumstances, ordinary people cannot tell what is legal from illegal, what a criminal offense is and the appropriate punishment and so on; even those involved in investigation, prosecution, and trials do not have a clear and uniform set of standards that they follow." He criticized the state's emphasis on the individual's acquiring the correct proletarian "standpoint, perspective, and work style," seeing this push based on official ideology as an impediment to using law broadly to advance democracy, stability, citizenship, and justice under CCP rule.[21] Wu Jialin (1926–), who headed the teaching-research team on Chinese constitutional law at People's University of China, stated that a lack of legal knowledge permeated even the highest CCP organs and resulted in widespread infringements against the 1954 Chinese constitution at all levels. He listed examples that included "black palaces and government offices" where officeholders had not gone through any proper appointment procedures. His recommendations to the leadership—strengthen the work of legislation and of legal education and research, act as a law-abiding model, and reorganize and clarify the roles of the party and the state—captured the legal reforms desired by the scholars and notables.[22]

The scholars and notables seldom promoted multiparty competition, direct election, or other sweeping changes to the existing political system. Instead, they wanted the CCP to adopt serious political, legal, administrative, and personnel reforms that would elevate first and foremost their participation in governance and management. Such a position reflected the close but unequal relations that the scholars and notables had shared with the party leaders under the PRC, as well as the intense official mobilization of these people to set examples in evaluating and criticizing official governance. The ideas and ideals of the scholars and notables betrayed their dismissiveness toward the official discourse of class and their disapproval of official denigration of intellectuals. In practice, the scholars and notables built upon Mao's dissatisfaction with party cadres to improve their own positions and those of the professional workers outside the party. The proposal from Minister of Transportation Zhang Bojun (1895–1969), a leader of two officially approved political parties, is a perfect example. He suggested that national issues be discussed and advised by such parties as well as by higher intellectuals and pertinent experts. He wanted reforms that would strengthen the advisory function of the NPC Standing Committee, the CPPCC, and the minor parties, all of these being establishments filled with educated people who had yet to acquire influence over state affairs. He did not discuss the role of workers or peasants in national political life, a ringing concern of the CCP since its inception, except to include "state-sponsored mass organizations" (*renmin tuanti*) together with the NPC, CPPCC, and minor political parties as a primary component in his proposed "political design department," a forum that would advise the leadership on all important matters.[23] His recommendations were aimed at curbing rather than protecting the political participation of underprivileged populations.

In sum, the scholars and notables redefined intellectuals as experts and professional workers outside the CCP. This revision of the official view was borne out of a sense of frustration and concern about governance and management under the party, a material-cum-symbolic division between party cadres and ordinary educated people inside the workplace, as well as a protean tradition of Confucian thought. The scholars and notables emphasized the goodness of education for the individual and society and wanted the educated to be part of the governing elites effecting changes from within the state. The scholars and notables did not question the right of the CCP to rule, but disagreed with its disruption of the conventional order of prestige and influence. They did not oppose China's pursuit of a modern socialist society, but rejected the official endorsement of class interest and class struggle as, respectively, the basis of societal divisions and means of their unification. The future of Chinese Communism, they believed, hinged on the incorporation of intellectuals in political debates and deliberations as well as in governance and management. Their proposals embodied the Confucian preoccupation with hierarchy and harmony.[24] Had the CCP leadership adopted the reforms proposed by the scholars and notables, Chinese Communism would involve patterns of value and authority quite familiar to the general population.

INTELLECTUALS AS LEGISLATORS

Peking University is the birthplace of the May Fourth movement. . . . We need to learn from our May Fourth elders the spirit of asking bold questions and forging daring creations, and to strive for truly socialist democracy and culture.

—A STATEMENT FROM THE INAUGURAL ISSUE OF *THE SQUARE*, A STUDENT PUBLICATION AT PEKING UNIVERSITY, MAY 21, 1957[25]

In his 1987 book on intellectuals, Bauman describes the legislator as an enduring role that "men of letters" in Europe have played since the Age of Enlightenment. Here individuals claim intellectual authority on the basis of their expert knowledge and its alleged objectivity, arbitrate controversies related to the social order in highly public manners, and provide aesthetic, moral, and political judgments. They see themselves as having "a right (and a duty) to address the nation on behalf of Reason, standing above partisan divisions and earth-bound sectarian interests."[26] During the 1957 Rectification Campaign, the role of the legislator was filled not so much by renowned scientists, writers, or artists as by college students. The leaders of these students were often from the distinguished Peking University (colloquially known as Beida). For decades, the campus had been a center of political protest and intellectual innovation and, by mid-century, one of the "most recognizable symbols of opposition to autocracy."[27] Like the scholars and social notables discussed above, the students supported the building of a modern socialist China. But they challenged the philosophical, epistemological, and political justifications of CCP rule supplied by the Mao leadership. The protesters publicized their views in forms of posters, essays, poems, open letters, and speeches. Their idealized self-image was that of an advocate of reason, equality, democracy, and justice, a bearer of the critical spirit of the May Fourth movement of the early twentieth century.[28] For this reason, some students consecrated their political protest by naming it the May Nineteenth movement, after the date when the first protest poster appeared in Beida.[29] In the weeks that followed, the protesters framed their criticism of the state and proposals for change around the intellectual generally in tangential ways. Given the exclusive education the students were receiving and, as we shall see, their erudition, it was hard for their peers and instructors, as well as for party cadres and state leaders, not to see that the students were redefining the intellectual with Chinese Communism through their protest.

Some student protesters presented themselves as authoritative interpreters of Marxist thought. They took aim at what they regarded as inaccurate CCP interpretations as well as at the people and organizations supporting those views, including Chairman Mao and *People's Daily*. One such protester was Beida student Tan Tianrong, a physics major who shot to fame during the Rectification Campaign. He produced a series of provocative and sometimes rambling essays, boldly titling them "poisonous weeds," a metaphor that Mao had employed to denigrate political ideas unacceptable to the party leadership. What Tan considered poisonous, however, was the extent to which Lenin and Stalin—and the CCP—had misinterpreted Marxism and hence stifled its emancipatory potential. Drawing on the work of a professor at Nankai University, Tan contended that since Engels's death in 1895, the "revisionism" and "dogmatism" of Lenin and Stalin had "absolutely dominated" Marxist political philosophy, leading to single-party rule, systemic political discrimination, cults of personality, individualized attacks, and other forms of state abuse under the cover of the pursuit of communism.[30] Tan criticized "More on the Historical Experience of the Dictatorship of the Proletariat," the influential essay published by the CCP in *People's Daily* in December 1956. The essay was the party's international response to the unexpected criticism of the recently deceased Stalin by Nikita Khrushchev, the head of state of the Soviet Union, as well as to the unrest in Poland and Hungary.[31] The Mao leadership affirmed communist party rule as essential for maintaining working-class control in socialist countries, and indicated that official abuses, including the types of murder perpetrated by Stalin's regime, were preventable through the implementation of correct policies and methods of governance and the teaching and learning of appropriate work styles by officials.[32] The leadership used the essay to support the launching of the Rectification Campaign. Tan criticized the essay for its "idealist" and "metaphysical" thinking and its incompatibility with dialectical materialism.[33] The latter school of thought, which stresses the impact of material conditions on social consciousness, had been extolled by the Mao leadership as the epistemological basis of CCP rule, Marxism, and valid knowledge. In effect, Tan accused the leadership, the self-proclaimed arbiter of Marxist thought, of lacking understanding of its underlying philosophy. He attacked the leadership with terms that it had long used to discredit its ideological competitors (that is, revisionism, dogmatism, and idealism). He even predicted the failure of the campaign to improve state-society relations. Yan Zhongqiang, another physics major at Beida, went further in his critical interpretation of Marxism and Chinese Communism. Using a combination of Kantian and Lockean emphasis on human sensibility, experience, and understanding, he argued that the "theory of materialism" underlying Marxism had been proven useless for and unscientific in the natural sciences: the theory is but a form of "religious belief" imbued with "class interests," like Christian, Buddhist, or other religious thoughts. While Yan applauded the use of the "sharp knife" of materialism by the proletariat in class struggle, he suggested that ruling communist parties had been exploiting this "entirely disposable" weapon, using it "to deceive and lord over the people." He expected that the people would rise up someday and teach the regimes a lesson.[34]

Other protesters combined their knowledge of Marxist thought and lived experience under CCP rule to dispute the official account of the class structure of the PRC and its alleged elimination of exploiting classes. No evidence suggests that the protesters had read Yugoslav dissident Milovan Djilas's 1957 treatise on the rise of a ruling class of party officials under communist political rule.[35] Their understanding of the emergence of such a ruling class in China was probably inspired by Leon Trotsky's famous indictment against the Soviet system in *The Revolution Betrayed*, a Chinese translation of which was available by the early 1940s.[36] Zhou Dajue, a lecturer at the Beijing Aviation Academy, brought up Lenin's and Engels's definitions of social class to contest Mao's recent observation that "non-antagonistic contradictions among the people" had replaced class struggle as the major form of political conflict on the Mainland.[37] Zhou observed that a new class of "important personages in the party, government, and military" who wielded redistributive power had appeared. These people, he said, enjoyed unwarranted compensation and had committed brutally repressive acts, by which he probably meant unjust sentences meted out to critics of CCP rule. Furthermore, an organized circle (*jituan*) of party officials had begun to take shape with the aim of gaining economic, political, and other advantages over the rest of the population.[38] For Zhou, class struggle was well and alive under the PRC, but the exploiters had changed. A history student at Beida, Pang Zhuoheng advanced his own class analysis which took into account "direct and indirect relations to the means of production" and "locations in production and distribution." He contended that CCP rule had produced six classes with different collective interests. Party officials and members formed the core of the "leadership class," and other classes, which included a class of intellectuals, were supportive of this leadership. However, even party leaders, like any members of the other classes, constantly struggled between following and transcending their self-serving habits and values. Pang's rejection of the claim that the CCP leadership represents the interests of the working class led him to conclude that the party could become counterrevolutionary, especially when it uses violence to suppress the socialist demands of the rest of the classes.[39]

An important outcome of their theoretical and analytical challenges against the official discourse of class, party, and revolution was that the protesters disputed whether China had established socialism based on the vision of Marx and Engels. Such skepticism was compounded by national publication of complaints about governing practices, including lack of due process, invasive surveillance, physical punishment, workplace abuses, wrongful convictions, and widespread discrimination in appointments and allocation of benefits and opportunities.[40] Zhou Dajue articulated a popular view held by the protesters: the "three evils" of workstyles that the state identified as common among party cadres, as well as the cult of Mao and the appearance of new types of economic and political inequality, revealed the "strong feudal color" (*nonghou de fengjian zhuyi secai*) of the existing political system.[41] Like "revisionism," "dogmatism," and "idealism," *fengjian zhuyi* (feudal thoughts) was a term that the CCP leadership had employed to attack its opponents and, especially, what it considered to be the obsolete and oppressive character of their ideas and conduct. Zhou deployed the term, instead, to indicate that the constitution of Chinese Communism was more traditional than revolutionary, and its governing practices were exploitative rather than emancipatory. In a similar vein, Beida mathematics student Qian Ruping suggested that Marxism-Leninism, public ownership, and collective ownership were misleading "shop signs" erected by the state, behind which economic exploitation persisted, as "some had taken control of the labor of others."[42] Lin Xiling (1935–2009), who studied law at People's University of China, became another leader of student protesters. She questioned whether the Soviet Union, from which the Mao regime borrowed its approach to socialist development, had actually become a Marxist-type socialist society.[43] In her opinion, the Soviet Union, not to mention China, was at best in a "transitional period" toward socialism.[44] The protesters' complaints against Chinese Communism, especially its philosophical basis, are not always comprehensible because of the speed with which the views were assembled during the protest as well as the competition for intellectual sophistication on college campuses. Yet there is little doubt that some students and instructors saw sweeping change as indispensable for building a genuinely socialist China.

The young protesters demanded institutional reforms to expand political participation, curb official abuses, and prevent the rise of a new exploiting class. Central to their demands were competitive elections. While the Mao regime feared that such elections would lead to the reintroduction of capitalist and other forms of exploitation and ultimately destroy Chinese Communism, the protesters held the opposite view. They believed that the postrevolutionary elimination of the capitalist and landowning classes as well as grave disparities in earnings from the political economy had created conditions for deepening working-class rule through competitive elections—and that such elections were vital to thwarting officials becoming unaccountable to the laboring masses.[45] Despite limited official news coverage of political reforms in Yugoslavia,[46] the introduction there of self-government to replace centralization of political and economic management was widely hailed by the protesters as an example of socialist democracy.[47] In a letter to a worker at Beida's printing house, Long Yinghua, a philosophy major at the university, captured the depth of political participation that some protesters wanted to achieve through competitive elections. Among other things, this blueprint, which echoed the concept of socialist democracy in Lenin's famous 1917 essay *The State and Revolution,* recommended that the factory choose its managers and other leaders through direct elections. The elected would be subject to recall and would be responsible for implementing collective decisions.[48] Reacting against the existing official control of elections, others demanded that candidates should explain their principles and policies publicly before the elections, and that the elected report their work regularly to the workforce.[49] A general belief was that direct election should be extended to the political realm, including the selection of provincial heads and members of all levels of the people's congresses.[50] Some even suggested that voting should be included in the process of recruitment and expulsion of CCP members to permit popular control of the membership.[51] This last suggestion implies that the protesters wanted competitive elections to be implemented broadly in the countryside, too, although their views rarely mentioned conditions in rural areas.[52]

If adopted, the reforms proposed by the protesters would reduce the CCP's role in governance and management dramatically. Ma Yunfeng, who studied at the Beijing Aviation Academy, envisioned that the party's domination of state and society through multiple layers of party cells would give way to "a system of decision by the majority." Within workplace management, party cadres and non-party personnel would have equal status and authority. If no cadre occupied management positions, nonvoting delegates would be assigned to enable the party to publicize, explain, and provide leadership on policies and directions.[53] A biology student at Beida, Jiang Xingren, saw the CCP becoming one of the political parties competing for management posts in the self-governing workplace.[54] No one seems to have commented directly on the future role of Mao, but with the popularity of the notion of competitive elections and the criticism of cults of personality, it was evident that the protesters did not want him to wield supreme authority. Beida law student Li Shaolin, who supported electoral democracy at all levels, suggested what appears to have been the desired change when he proposed that the National People's Congress become the highest ruling body through which "the people supervise and monitor the state apparatus and its personnel," an arrangement that had been legally but not actually in effect.[55]

Unlike the scholars and notables introduced earlier in the chapter, the young protesters did not redraw the boundaries of the category of intellectuals explicitly. Nonetheless, they redefined what it meant to be an intellectual as much as the scholars and notables did, especially for their own generation of college students. The protesters did not see themselves as heirs of Confucian literati, still less a cog in the state machine of socialist development. They placed critical reason above the political and class hierarchy enforced by the party and its demand for political submission and ideological reeducation. The protesters promoted personal autonomy, social equality, popular participation, and competitive election as preconditions for a truly socialist China—and considered CCP rule its main obstacle. They were inspired by those who had led the May Fourth movement decades before. When we consider content and context together, it is clear that the protesters also borrowed from the critical political analyses of the intervening years and demonstrated exceptional political courage. As Edmund Fung has noted in his study of Chinese political thought, non-Marxist scholars continued to "rethink, reevaluate, and reformulate the Chinese past and articulate visions of Chinese modernity" before 1949.[56] During the Rectification Campaign, the protestors reintroduced into the public realm key political issues debated between the May Fourth movement and the CCP takeover of China, including the role of the state and political parties, law and constitutionalism, and individual rights and liberties. Their goal was to promote democratic values and institutions as means to prevent socialist development from being ravaged by what they saw as political despotism and state violence under the PRC. Unlike May Fourth or other political activists of the Republican era, these protesters confronted not ineffective ruling regimes with limited capacity to police and punish, but an unprecedentedly powerful state which had penetrated the workplace, controlled livelihoods, exacted conformity, and even executed large numbers of "counterrevolutionaries." Even taking into account relentless official appeals for criticism of the state during the campaign, it is clear that the protesters stood up against a proven dictatorship and pointed toward another alternative path of socialist development.

INTELLECTUALS AS RED-AND-EXPERT PERSONNEL

In order to establish a fine socialist society, the party and the state have issued a call to intellectuals. Within ten years, the working class will have its own vast army of intellectuals. Let us work hard to reform ourselves, study and learn, and become working-class intellectuals.
—AN EDITORIAL STATEMENT, *WENHUI DAILY,* OCTOBER 28, 1957

After abruptly ending the Rectification Campaign, the Mao regime orchestrated the Antirightist Movement to attack and punish critics of the CCP and the state, an episode that has been well documented.[57] Here I focus on the official understanding of intellectuals expressed between July 1957 and January 1958, before the gravely anti-intellectual and ultimately disastrous Great Leap Forward engulfed China.[58] Succinctly captured by the phrase "red and expert" (*you hong you zhuan*) and its variants, which began to saturate the media nationally during the last months of 1957, the official understanding reflected how the party leadership had conceptualized the intellectual since the Yan'an days of Chinese Communism—with a newfound but short-lived optimism.[59] We have seen the Yan'an approach to intellectuals in action in the last three chapters. On the one hand, the Mao regime sought to harness knowledge and skills for the revolutionary project as well as to protect it from any "petty-bourgeois" and "bourgeois" influence, or the agenda and behavior of writers, journalists, professors, and other educated people. On the other hand, the regime was determined to provide professional and educational opportunities to members of the underprivileged to enable them to become proficient in political, technical, and administrative work. After the Rectification Campaign, the regime reaffirmed commitment to this approach, even though it had produced deep tensions and divisions within Chinese society. The regime proposed that a refinement of the approach would deliver to Chinese Communism large numbers of useful and reliable intellectuals.

On a theoretical level, the red-and-expert extension of the Yan'an approach to intellectuals shares some strong similarities with the writings of the Italian Marxist Antonio Gramsci (1891–1937). He believed that the communist party must play the leading role in the transition to socialism. Large numbers of "organic intellectuals" must serve as conduits of socialist values and builders of the state and other robust socialist institutions. The development of such intellectuals, however, presents many challenges, because unbecoming values, beliefs, and habits from the prerevolutionary society will continue to loom large after the socialist revolution. On one level, Gramsci argued, the state must assimilate "existing categories of intellectuals" into the socialist project, because their knowledge and reputations are valuable assets for governance and development. The targets include what he called traditional intellectuals (e.g., writers, artists, clergies) and what Lenin referred to as "bourgeois experts" (such as industrial managers, research scientists, and urban planners). On another level, the state must provide training to "indigenous representatives of the proletariat," people who have been deprived of educational and other opportunities. These individuals must be taught to combine Marxist thought with personal experience of labor and poverty to help "transform the contradictory consciousness of the working class," or the tendency of its members to sometimes support and sometimes resist change, into "revolutionary self-awareness."[60] After the Rectification Campaign, the Mao regime invested further in the political and technical education of party cadres, professional workers, college students, and labor and peasant representatives. Of the three perspectives on the intellectual discussed in this chapter, the red-and-expert ideal was the only one pursued by the regime—and that, only for a very short while.

During the Antirightist Movement, the Mao leadership promoted further rationales and methods to intensify the ideological reeducation of professional workers and college students. Because members of these groups had complained about CCP rule and received wide support from their peers, the state now derided these populations in the media as "bourgeois intellectuals" (*zichan jieji zhishifenzi*), that is, intellectuals who wanted to restore class exploitation across China.[61] As the state punished those whom it singled out as "rightists," it also advanced proposals to rectify how professional workers and college students related to "the laboring masses." The official goal was to turn such workers and students into "intellectuals of the working class" (*gongren jieji zhishifenzi*). Like before, the state argued that this would be a long and arduous process. Although thought reform, mass campaigns, and other forms of ideological reeducation had helped intellectuals improve their appreciation of Chinese Communism, "the overwhelming majority" still did not understand the "thoughts and sentiments" of workers or poor peasants, let alone embrace their class interest as the interest of all. Among intellectuals, including those who had joined the party, residual belief in bourgeois ideology, property, and individualism was commonplace, and manifested as self-centeredness, careerism, condescension toward workers and peasants, and other undesirable habits and dispositions.[62]

For the Mao regime, most important for the future success of the ideological reeducation of intellectuals was their self-determination. "Intellectuals must make up their minds, even if it is painful, to unite with the laboring masses, starting with becoming one with the masses and integrating the individual into the collective. They must draw a clear distinction between labor and exploitation and between who and what to love and hate. They must establish a correct understanding between the collective and the individual and work hard to overcome and guard against individualism."[63] Repeated abundantly in the media, this kind of demand on scientists, writers, and others epitomizes what Timothy Cheek observes as the twin premises of governance under Mao. *Epistemological elitism* held that "legitimate answers" to ethics, politics, history, and development could only be provided by the CCP leadership; *attitudinal fundamentalism* put forth "attitudes as the prime mover of behavior" of all kinds.[64] The Mao regime was confident with its existing approach to intellectuals. As class subjects, journalists, engineers, college students, and other educated people were politically unreliable, but not irredeemable.

Because the Mao regime used Marxist philosophy to argue that political consciousness is intimately connected to practical activity, a host of organizational measures that would supposedly assist intellectuals to turn over a new leaf was quickly affirmed. The measures, some of which were already familiar to the general public, included the deepening of self-criticism and mutual criticism among professional workers, the use of peasants and workers and their firsthand experiences to help with the ideological reeducation of schoolteachers and students, and sending writers to "the midst of the masses" and assigning college graduates to stints of labor training to help these intellectuals understand the difficult lives of workers and peasants and their hopes and perseverance.[65] Within six months after the Rectification Campaign's conclusion, tens of thousands of writers, editors, schoolteachers, and officials from Beijing, Shanghai, and other places had traveled to various provinces to live and work with workers and peasants.[66]

For the Mao leadership, equally important was to rectify the relationship between intellectuals and science, or how to support the enterprise further on behalf of Chinese Communism. A major complaint from professors and others had been the state's heavy-handedness and, especially, the vesting of management authority in ill-trained party cadres. A Yan'an revolutionary with a degree from Tsinghua University, Yu Guangyuan (1915–2015), worked at the CCP Department of Propaganda during the 1950s. Shortly after the Rectification Campaign, in an article in *People's Daily,* he explained official thinking in a socialist country "like ours in which the development of science has been comparatively backward." Yu reaffirmed that central planning and organization of research were necessary to thwart localized decision-making based on self-serving reasons. But he also pledged state support of universities and research institutes and mentioned the development of industrial zones and the introduction of science and industry to ethnic minority areas. He emphasized the limited role that the party foresaw for itself in the realm of science. The CCP wanted neither "to take up scientific research" nor "to arrange work [in such detail] as scientists do with their [research] assistants." The party, instead, would provide leadership in three areas: putting forward principles, policies, and plans to facilitate research and setting up the necessary systems of work; winning scientists over and giving them education in Marxism and Leninism; and mobilizing personnel and institutional support to improve working conditions. To foster scientific development, he remarked, the state would sometimes need to reassign scientists in ways requiring some to apply their expertise in related intellectual areas, move to other geographical regions, and even temporarily endure taxing working and living conditions.[67] To support scientific progress, the State Council soon approved four proposals related to the purchase of library books, reference works, equipment, and chemical reagents, partly because "the absolute majority" of suggestions recently voiced by scientists during the Rectification Campaign "should be affirmed." Overall, the state noted that improving scientific performance would be a "complex and painstaking" task, but essential for the future.[68]

Jiang Nanxiang (1913–1988), a veteran CCP member, was the chancellor of Tsinghua University, which specialized in science and engineering education. His opening address to a campus symposium on science and his commencement speech to the graduating class of 1957 suggest that the "red-and-expert" ideal was stressed across colleges. During the symposium, he strongly criticized "rightists" and intellectuals similar to what other authorities did, before addressing "bourgeois" habits and thinking in his workplace: "Quite a few [faculty still] emphasize scientific research in slanted and disconnected manners, seeing it as the only noble work above everything else." Some faculty used science for personal advancement and belittled production and the laboring masses; others sneered at student instruction, administrative work, and thought reform for diverting their time and energy away from research. However, Jiang did not want research on his or other campuses to be downgraded, because it was of "utmost importance" to higher education. Rather, he wanted research to be strengthened to the extent that all instructors who had mastered teaching content and techniques would place scientific research on their "daily agendas." Moreover, he wanted research to be redirected to serve public goals, of which he named two: producing "a national army of scientific and technical personnel" and contributing to "national construction." The first would require faculty to improve their research and teaching "in a complementary way." The second would mean developing theory, not for its own sake, but to connect it to the practical needs of the country.[69]

In his commencement speech, Jiang warned Tsinghua graduates against their "individualism." He complained that 503 graduates had requested to be assigned to a university, a research institute, a design department, or other comfortable professional establishments, while only 83 had listed factories, mines, or other demanding sites as their choices. Over half of the graduates wanted to stay in Beijing; a total of 296 had asked for special consideration based on health or family reasons; only 16 were open to all assignments; and merely 2 had volunteered to work in the underdeveloped and formidable northeast region. Jiang chided the graduates for their selfish calculus and insisted that they "happily accept any assignment from the state."[70] He supported the assignment of college graduates to labor training to help them understand the socialist spirit. By the fall of 1957, Tsinghua faculty and students had begun to travel to nearby communes to assist in harvesting crops.[71] All the while, Jiang did not doubt that colleges should continue to improve "living and learning conditions" and help to turn as many students as possible into scientific and other experts.[72]

Based on its red-and-expert ideal, the state continued to promote professional education for former workers and peasants, as well as for party cadres of such backgrounds. As before, it was assumed that these individuals had a high potential to comprehend class struggle and the purpose of Chinese Communism. With appropriate training, they would combine their professional knowledge and life experience to serve the socialist project, becoming what the state called "worker-peasant intellectuals" (gongnong zhishifenzi). Their professional and intellectual elevation would help to alleviate the entrenched separation and inequality between mental and manual labor in Chinese society. In practice, the state kept on expanding literacy training, unconventional enrollments in schools and colleges, and part-time education and other skill-based classes. Tsinghua University admitted hundreds of young soldiers and other atypical students to its regular academic programs in 1958.[73] The enrollment of cadres and students of underprivileged backgrounds in Shanghai's higher education was projected to increase from 28 percent in 1957 to at least 40 percent in 1962 and 60 percent in 1967.[74] In Sichuan Province, leaders of colleges and universities wanted to expand all sorts of programs through increasing the enrollment of such students and using "minimum admission standards" to replace preferential enrollment for those who had achieved the same score as other candidates.[75]

At the national level, proposals were available on how to tackle challenges confronting the training of CCP cadres and others of underprivileged background within higher education. Lu Ge (1913–1988), a veteran party member and official at the Ministry of Education, insisted that proper procedures be established to enroll those of genuinely underprivileged background, because others had misused the opportunities. Preference in admission should be given to underprivileged candidates once they had achieved the required academic standards. To smooth their transition from work and address their academic underpreparedness, additional attention would be needed to place these persons in appropriate classes, including use of separate training programs, and to ensure proper financial and academic assistance. Family circumstances should be considered when assigning graduating students to new positions. The abruptly ended Rectification Campaign had revealed that existing students and professors resented the admission of unconventional candidates to colleges and, especially, elite universities.[76] Lu wanted the state to refute opinions that unconventional enrollees should be educated outside existing campuses. He wanted colleges and universities to tackle everyday discrimination against such enrollees.[77]

During its short-lived prominence, the red-and-expert ideal of the intellectual was an auspicious as well as ominous sign for Chinese Communism. It was auspicious because the Mao regime, though confronted and embarrassed by unprecedented complaints from those whom it considered intellectuals, planned and implemented policies and measures not only to change the minds of these people, but also to turn out others with knowledge and skills to advance the revolutionary project. The official pursuit of an educated, industrialized, and socialist China continued. But it was also ominous, because what was proposed or implemented to achieve the ideal involved little philosophical, political, and hence institutional innovation compared with what had already been done. The Mao regime simply reaffirmed its Yan'an approach to intellectuals, which had helped the CCP seize state power but was recently proven to be politically incendiary and socially divisive under the PRC.

On a theoretical level, the proposed and implemented measures exposed key differences between the CCP's Marxism and Gramsci's Marxism. The divergence provides a valuable window on why the Mao regime would turn against the category of intellectuals shortly afterward by denigrating the value of formal education during the Great Leap Forward and then launching a wholesale attack on such people during the Cultural Revolution. The Mao leadership saw the development of what Gramsci called *organic intellectuals* as vital to furthering Chinese Communism. Unlike Gramsci, however, the regime never once imagined using these persons to build "egalitarian social relations and democratic political forms" to support the socialist project.[78] Instead, the leaders continued to consecrate themselves as proletarian revolutionaries, define most educated people as unreliable intellectuals, and rely on state tutelage to attain a unifying governing structure and culture with the CCP on top. Gramsci was aware that top-down cultivation of organic intellectuals may empower the latter to the extent that they would pursue their own political agendas. But he "was clearly willing to live with such risks" rather than embrace the attempt "to impose socialism from above."[79] The imposition, he believed, would breed bureaucracy or tyranny or both at the expense of democracy. Not only did the Mao regime share no such reservations; even as it promoted the red-and-expert ideal, the state continued to vilify and dominate those whom it labeled intellectuals and even singled out some of these people for prosecution, labor reform, and other kinds of punishment. In retrospect, the ideal was the last gasp of the Yan'an approach to intellectuals under the PRC.

The 1957 debate on the intellectual and Chinese Communism reveals the full extent of their impact on each other under the early PRC. What the socialist project had become was inseparable from how it had defined the intellectual and from the institutional and political consequences that followed. Where the project would go depended on its redefinition of the intellectual and the roles and responsibilities assigned to this subject. With each of the perspectives delineated above, important questions about China's transition to a supposedly improved socialist society were unanswered. The young protesters who wanted to reinvent the socialist project, for example, failed to address why competitive elections based on the ideas and qualifications of the individual would serve to overcome the entrenched divide between mental and manual labor, let alone prevent the emergence of new types of social inequality. The protesters also did not explain why CCP leaders and cadres would accept a greatly reduced role in governance and management or facilitate the expansion of political participation in all areas. Did the protesters want a violent revolution against CCP rule? How would official violence be used in the new society? Likewise, the scholars and notables who sought to be state partners did not clarify why elevating or returning scientists, lawyers, and other experts to positions of authority would improve the political or economic prospect of traditionally underprivileged populations. What did these experts share in their backgrounds that made them fit to promote socialist values and habits? What was the place of workers and other laborers in such a socialist society? The issues that the state elided in its counterargument are equally obvious. How would the intensification of ideological reeducation improve the socialist consciousness of professors, writers, or others, given the deep dissatisfaction that they had already shown with CCP rule? How would the professional education and empowerment of select members of the underprivileged affect their loyalty to the latter population? And what role in governance would the party play after creating an abundance of red-and-expert personnel?

Notwithstanding their incompleteness, the three perspectives on the intellectual and Chinese Communism are evidence that alternative directions of socialist development continued to exist after 1949. The perspectives were each based on a critique of existing political and social conditions. They addressed important concerns such as freedom, justice, equality, democracy, education, science, and productivity under the PRC. They received support from different sections of the general population, which indicate that they were not products of blithe utopianism, but of burgeoning movements for social change. We will never know how China would have fared had any of the perspectives become the foundation of a national agenda of socialist development. Even had such a journey taken off, it would have been filled with challenges, complications, and setbacks. However, it is difficult to imagine that the collective experience of the alternative would have been as traumatic and deadly as that which unfolded afterward with the Great Leap Forward and the Cultural Revolution sponsored by the Mao regime. After all, each of the perspectives embraced as political and moral principles some combination of critical reason, personal autonomy, technical competence, and collectivism as well as shared governance, class cooperation, rule of law, and scientific development. In contrast, what the state promoted in the following decade was the disparagement of science and education, the cult of Mao, class struggle, and a search for class enemies. These official principles would lead to false imprisonment and torture on a mass scale as well as starvation, murders, mob rule, collective killings, and tens of millions of fatalities.[80] The next chapter will look at reinterpretations of the intellectual between the late 1950s and the early 1960s and the central role that they played in the devastating atrocities.

Ugly Intellectuals Everywhere

During the early 1960s, the musical drama *Third Sister Liu* (*Liu Sanjie*) took China's cultural scene by storm. The musical was created in Guangxi Province, far removed from the PRC capital at Beijing. It drew on the folklore of Third Sister Liu, whose legend has permeated South China since the Tang dynasty (618–907). The performance features a peasant heroine of Zhuang minority origin using her ingenuity in singing and improvising mountain folksongs (*shan'ge*) to help poor villagers fight against predatory landlords and their hangers-on. The musical was staged in Beijing between July and September 1960, including four times inside the official compound of Zhongnanhai, where Chairman Mao and other CCP leaders worked and lived. After receiving praise from the leaders, the troupe toured no fewer than thirteen provinces and regions and some twenty cities, many of which staged their own productions of the play.[1] By January 1961, radio and television stations nationwide were playing excerpts of the musical to ring in the Western and the Chinese New Year; gramophone recordings of the musical were available for sale and distribution. Later that year, Changchun Film Studio (*Changchun dianying zhipian chang*), one of the biggest in China, released *Third Sister Liu* as a musical feature film set along the banks of the Li River in spectacular Guilin in Guangxi. With an impressive score, witty lines, memorable characters, and superior cinematography, the movie was an instant hit. Productions of colored pictures of the actresses and actors as well as sheet music and artwork related to the movie followed, just in time for another New Year celebration. By the fall of 1962, the New China Bookstore, which was founded by the CCP when it was headquartered in Yan'an, had begun national sale of a ninety-page illustrated storybook on Third Sister Liu, an ideal keepsake for the family.[2]

Any mature audience member who watched *Third Sister Liu* then would recognize that it contained a severe rebuke of intellectuals by the state, thanks to the musical's most famous and entertaining scene—the singing competition (*duige*). In the movie, the scene lasts for twenty minutes. It shows Liu, a talented, adorable young woman with an angelic voice, in a contest of improvised singing on the river bank. The narrative tension of the contest is intensified by Liu's pledge to cease singing should she be beaten in her art. Her rival, the wicked local landlord, has hired three Confucian literati from nearby areas to handle the competition. These self-proclaimed "highly regarded scholars" arrive at the showdown with a boatful of songbooks and the intent of crushing a lowly woman. They are joined by two dozen sycophantic literati, some of whom are mostly attracted to the food and drink served by the landlord. On the other side, hundreds of villagers, including some from distant places, show up to support Liu. They are heartily amused by the literati's failure to match her quick wit and artistry. They sing with her to expose the scholars' ignorance of the simplest of agricultural labors. When the literati feel pressured during the competition, they state that they are followers of "ancient sages and virtuous men" and experts in Chinese classics, and try to abuse their opponents for lacking education. But Liu hits back every time when they boast of their achievements, criticizing further the uselessness of their learning, to the peasants' delight. The singing competition is magnificent theater.

In this chapter I use theater and cinema as a window on the mutual constitution of the intellectual and Chinese Communism during the late 1950s and the early 1960s. Since the revolutionary project entered its Yan'an phase, the CCP leadership had portrayed "intellectuals" mainly as petty-bourgeois but usable subjects. Ideological reeducation was considered essential to helping these otherwise self-serving persons recognize the virtues of Chinese Communism and overcome their shortcomings. A champion of this view, Mao began to question it after the party encountered a deluge of complaints against its policies, practices, and personnel during the 1957 Rectification Campaign. The official representation of the intellectual as a former accomplice in class oppression and an enduring threat to Chinese Communism gathered strength afterward, epitomized by Mao's revised claim that all intellectuals were "bourgeois intellectuals,"[3] and by official punishment of critics with demotion, labor reform, and other measures during the Antirightist Movement. The state promoted further negative assessments of intellectuals during the Great Leap Forward (1958–1960) to spark "the enthusiasm and creativity of the masses" on behalf of the national production campaign.[4] Sciences and other academic disciplines were neglected. Party cadres, professors, journalists, and others were sent to the countryside to be taught "proletarian virtues" by peasants.[5] *Third Sister Liu* turned this heightened official disparagement of the intellectual, or the redrawing of the symbolic boundaries involving the subject, into popular entertainment. The musical reinforced the descent of Chinese Communism into what Andrew Walder calls "a centrally planned depression"[6] that cost tens of millions of lives.

I use the production of *Third Sister Liu* to illustrate how the Mao regime mobilized local populations to create, circulate, and consume degrading ideas, images, and idioms about intellectuals. Well before the Leap, the state had gained control over theater and cinema. To put socialist development on an anti-intellectual path, the state, ironically, relied on educated CCP cadres, scriptwriters, and other professional workers, or those classified or classifiable as intellectuals, to organize the performances, because these kinds of persons had the literary, artistic, technical, and organizational skills to deliver impactful works. Meanwhile, top-down mobilization of society to support the Leap absorbed many others into the productions. As state and society partook in denouncing intellectuals, tensions and resentment between party cadres and ordinary professional workers deepened. To escape the growing stigma attached to the intellectual marker, cadres who oversaw the productions presented themselves as superior to the professional workers who wrote, adapted, or staged the musical. To cope with their amplified humiliation by the state, some artists, critics, and even cadres contested in subtle fashions the official condemnation of intellectuals. In other words, as Chinese Communism featured the intellectual as a dangerous subject with limited use value during the Leap, the rift between educated party cadres and ordinary educated people, or the discreditable and the discredited, widened.

I then turn to *Early Spring in February* (*Zaochun eryue*) to illustrate the increasingly strident struggle to redefine the intellectual and Chinese Communism before murder, corporal punishment, and other forms of abuse descended upon many identified as intellectuals during the Cultural Revolution. A star-studded film produced in 1963 under tight official control, *Early Spring* epitomized the post-Leap efforts of some of the CCP leaders to reemphasize the importance of intellectuals to socialist development. The movie features an educated couple in a small town during the 1920s coping with local poverty and parochialism amid their budding romance. They appear thoughtful and progressive compared with other educated people in their lives; they are willing to make sacrifices to help the poor and potentially for revolutionary struggles to improve Chinese society. The film is the ideological antithesis of *Third Sister Liu*. It challenged the Leap's denigration of intellectuals and even the Yan'an depiction of the subjects as selfish and untrustworthy. Even before *Early Spring* was released, it became a target of official attacks. Mao and his supporters were regaining control over the direction of Chinese Communism. They stressed vigilance against capitalist restoration, especially efforts waged by "bourgeois intellectuals" within state and society. The film was spotlighted as a "poisonous weed" which glorified "bourgeois thinking" and "bourgeois intellectuals." Another layer of virulent ideas, idioms, and imageries about the intellectual saturated the nation as the Cultural Revolution approached. Many movie audiences in Shanghai, however, rejected the official interpretation of the film, which prompted the state to reach deep into society, again, to propagate official denunciations of the intellectual.

STAGING *THIRD SISTER LIU* NATIONALLY

In the scene of the "singing competition," the literati each wore an operatic makeup of an animal: one was a pig, another a dog, and the last one a fox. These men of letters had retractable necks [like turtles]; they bent and twisted their bodies and sang and spoke in a pretentious manner, behaving disgustingly on stage.
—AN OBSERVATION ON A LOCAL PERFORMANCE OF *THIRD SISTER LIU*[7]

In 1958, as CCP officials across China began to prepare for the tenth anniversary celebration of the PRC, the proposal to stage the folktale of Third Sister Liu surfaced in the city of Liuzhou in Guangxi Province in a meeting between party cadres and artists arranged by the local CCP department of propaganda.[8] Although theater scripts and performances about Liu had been available, much work would be needed before a socialist rendition of her legend would emerge.[9] In retrospect, the proposal was an ingenious idea. It suggests the cadres' and artists' astute understanding of art policy under the Great Leap Forward and capacity to bring together tradition, art, and politics to serve the state. For one thing, the state had initiated a mass campaign to collect and publicize folksongs, folktales, and folk poetry to extol the hard work, creativity, and artistry of peasants and workers on behalf of the Leap's anti-intellectual approach to production.[10] Liu's legend as a "singing immortal" of folksongs was a potentially rich resource for such propaganda. Second, the plan to use stories and songs related to Liu, many of them passed down from imperial times, fit perfectly with another decision of the Mao regime to rehabilitate theatrical and literary heritage to help popularize official ideas.[11] Third, the state had been seeking to showcase the national minorities in the performing arts for political and educational purposes—and Liu's legend was strongly rooted in the Zhuang population in Guangxi.[12] Most important for our purposes, Liu's legend features literati as central figures. These characters or, from the state's perspective, models of intellectuals of the bygone era could be rewritten to lend support to the Leap's anti-intellectualism.

After the musical drama was proposed, Liuzhou's authorities organized artists, workers, and others to travel across the province to speak with peasants and folksingers as well as hold forums to collect stories about Third Sister Liu and her songs. The travelers brought back some 20,000 folksongs, more than 200 folktales, and many types of folk tunes.[13] According to S. H. Chen, the gathering of folk poetry and songs during the Leap often went beyond existing material, or those rooted in the local population. The collectors included local schoolteachers, college graduates, and others whose education impressed villagers and was vital to documenting their mostly oral testimonials. Channeling the lofty goals and rhetoric of the state, the collectors lauded the CCP's revolutionary vision and achievements, paid homage to "labor heroes" and "model workers," and praised activities in the locality, before rousing villagers into "a festive mood" of singing and improvisation. New songs and poetry were invented and old ones collected or altered to suit the Leap's purposes.[14] Still, the stories, songs, and poetry about Third Sister Liu gathered from peasants and other sources reflected a central characteristic of folklore. The content as a whole was full of inconsistencies and contradictions, or diverse meanings and values from the contexts in which the legend was remembered, retold, or reinvented.[15]

The material places Liu in different dynasties, but mainly in Tang times. Some have her from a well-to-do family and well-versed in the classics and history from a young age. Some indicate that she was a loafer with many romantic affairs. Some see her as a poor village laborer. Some suggest that she was murdered by her brother. There are even debates about her ethnicity and provincial origin. Many accounts are essentially love stories or fairy tales.[16] A principal aspect of the accounts is that Liu is involved in singing competitions with literati. In one well-known version, the contender is her admirer, a young and handsome scholar, and they sing for seven days and nights without producing a winner, before both turning into stone. In another version, they finally sing with one heart and voice and rise to heaven as immortals. In other versions, literati come from different places to challenge Liu but are all beaten by her majestic singing.[17] None of the well-known versions depicts literati colluding with landlords to stop Liu from stirring up local peasants. The version closest to this soon-to-appear revolutionary theme has a powerful magistrate hiring four scholars to take on Liu in a singing contest. They arrive with a boatload of books, and she is obliged to marry him if she loses the competition. The accounts show Liu as bantering with her opponents and asserting her independence as a woman. She is polite, addressing the scholars as "gentlemen" (*xiansheng*) and "elder brothers" (*a'ge*).[18]

Under official supervision and "repeated discussion and informal deliberation,"[19] Liuzhou's scriptwriters and art workers produced a socialist rendition of the legend of Third Sister Liu. Liu appears as a feisty, sharp-witted peasant woman who fights with her musical talent against depraved landlords and slavish scholars. The work was staged as a *caidiao* opera in a province-wide theater event in April 1959. The authorities were so pleased with the performance that they sponsored further research on the folklore and revisions of the musical drama. The authoritative script appeared a few months later. The singing competition scene was excerpted in the nationwide journal *Scripts* (*Juben*) in September 1959. Meanwhile, two companies performed the musical under official auspices at various locations across Guangxi and received praise and support from local party leaders.[20] By year-end, more than sixty professional and amateur companies had staged the performance across the province. The success prompted the Guangxi government to sponsor a festival of *Third Sister Liu* performances at the capital of Nanning, the location where Mao had first pressured his colleagues to accept the Leap as a national development project.[21] During the festival, more than 1,400 people from all over the province performed the drama in eleven genres of traditional Chinese theater.

By then, some 1,200 "cultural work units" and almost 60,000 performers, some of whom were peasants and workers, had reportedly staged the play for 12 million people, or 60 percent of Guangxi's population.[22] After the festival, the scriptwriters and artists deliberated about the variations that they had seen across performances and polished the script further under official instructions and guidance, especially from the Guangxi Bureau of Culture and the Guangxi CCP Department of Culture and Education.[23] A complete script was printed in *Scripts* in mid-1960 and later by the Chinese Theater Press. The Guangxi Folk Song and Dance Theater was officially established to take the play to Beijing and around the country.[24]

While *Third Sister Liu* was staged in Beijing, Wu Jinnan (1909–1999), the CCP secretary of Guangxi Province, stated in a *People's Daily* article that tight official supervision had led to the production's success.

> The [Guangxi section of the] party not only supported this production; it provided frequent, detailed, and strong guidance on creative thinking, staffing, and material resources as well as on the script, music, and stage design and on the performances. The comrades in charge of the Guangxi Party Commission and other county, city, and district party commissions watched the performances repeatedly and offered ideas for improvement. Some district commissions organized special discussions of the script and the performances, to the extent of going over every song, every line of the lyrics, and every costume. Some members of the commissions even performed on stage and directed the production. The party commissions assumed leadership in tackling many problems of the performances. Under the uniform leadership of the commissions, various districts and departments as well as cultural and art organizations implemented mutual cooperation that guaranteed the smooth progress of the [Third Sister Liu artistic] movement and the ceaselessly improving quality of the performances.[25]

Wu was undoubtedly blowing his own trumpet, or that of the Guangxi's party cadres for how well they had served the state during the Leap. Nonetheless, the cadres did combine organization and representation successfully to produce and promote the musical drama, which Mao declared "a revolutionary play" after watching it.[26] The success of *Third Sister Liu* in Beijing and the publicity garnered by the performance prompted authorities elsewhere to remount the production and organize related events to demonstrate local support of the Leap and its anti-intellectualism.

Table 3 is a schedule of theater performances, television screenings, and radio broadcasts of *Third Sister Liu* in Shanghai between late 1960 and mid-1962, based on announcements from two major local newspapers. As the right-hand column shows, the singing competition was the first scene to be showcased on television. Unlike radio, television was not a common household possession. Only the privileged, which included party and state officials, had access to a family television. The early broadcast of the scene to this population suggests that the Shanghai authorities supported the Leap's denigration of intellectuals. The schedule of theater productions confirms the intensity with which the play was promoted. By February 1961, seven months after *Third Sister Liu* debuted in Beijing, at least eight Shanghai companies had staged the musical in six genres of traditional theater. We do not know how many performances the companies put on altogether. What the Shanghai Academy of Experimental Opera went through before staging *Third Sister Liu* suggests that the companies performed the play numerous times in a wide range of venues. Since the Antirightist Movement, the academy had been pressured by the government to perform more than usual. Its performances had jumped from an average of 170 per year to 1,100 in 1958. Many of these performances were staged inside factories or military compounds or before village crowds.[27]

Information on the role of CCP cadres in organizing or supervising the Shanghai productions is not available, but the productions' timing and the timeliness of related events suggest strong official intervention. The height of the 1961 productions coincided with New Year celebrations in both the Western and the Chinese calendar, excellent occasions for state propaganda. The musical was promoted in newspapers as actively as other cultural events sponsored by the local authorities, such as movies and exhibitions. The performances were staged in main theaters and local playhouses and in the city center as well as in workers' neighborhoods. In other words, Shanghai virtually hosted its own *Third Sister Liu* performance festival. The climax of the events was the performance by the touring Guangxi Folk Song and Dance Theater. The company debuted in Shanghai on January 27, 1961. The same day, China's preeminent Peking Opera singer Mei Lanfang (1894–1961) published a cheerful poem about Third Sister Liu in a major local newspaper, lauding her artistry, courage, and class consciousness—as well as the Leap.[28] The following night, the performance was aired on prime time television.[29]

In Shanghai, a host of cultural activities supporting the musical appeared and spread its images of dimwitted, shameless, and sycophantic literati, language of class struggle, and ideological support of the Leap. The most obvious of such activities were newspaper articles that introduced the play and the performing troupes. Once the performance began, congratulatory commentaries flourished, pictures and drawings of the characters were published, and actors and actresses wrote in the newspapers about the play and their participation in it. The Shanghai branch of the China Record Company produced gramophone records of *Third Sister Liu* to coincide with the productions. The album quickly became a bestseller, with the songs being played in bookstores.[30] Images from the performances were included in photograph exhibitions. At Tongji University, students apparently performed scenes from *Third Sister Liu,* paradoxically enough, as part of the 1961 commemoration of the May Fourth movement as well as created art works based on the newly minted socialist legend of the female singer.[31]

After three months of intense programming, the productions and broadcasts of *Third Sister Liu* began to peter out. This was not because the play had run its

TABLE 3 *Third Sister Liu* Performances in Shanghai, 1960–1962

Date	Activities	Performing Organizations	Remarks
1. *The Western and Chinese New Year period, 1961*			
November–December 1960	Theater	1. Shanghai Academy of Experimental Opera 2. Jiading *Xi* Theater Company	
December 20, 1960	Television broadcast	Jiading *Xi* Theater Company	"Singing competition"
December 31, 1960	Television broadcast	People's *Hu* Theater Company	"Singing competition"
January 1961	Theater	1. Chuxin *Yue* Theater Company 2. Qunyi *Hu* Theater Company 3. Guangxi Folk Song and Dance Theater Company 4. Shanghai *Yue* Theater Company	
January 1, 1961	Radio Broadcast	Jiading *Xi* Theater Company	Songs from the play
January 28, 1961	Television broadcast	Guangxi Folk Song and Dance Theater Company	
February 1961	Theater	1. Haiyang Comedy Theater Company 2. Fenghuo *Huai* Theater Company 3. Shanghai Academy of Experimental Opera	"Singing competition"
February 13, 1961	Radio broadcast	Singers of *Huangmei* theater	Two days before Chinese New Year's Day; "singing competition"
2. *Mid-1961*			
April 1961	Theater	People's *Hu* Theater Company	
April 1, 1961	Television broadcast	Shanghai Academy of Experimental Opera	
May 4, 1961	Theater	Fudan and other universities	May Fourth commemoration
July 1, 1961	Radio broadcast	Singers of *Hu* Theater	Songs from the play
August 1961	Theater	Jiangsu *Huai* Theater Company	

Date	Activities	Performing Organizations	Remarks
3. The Western and Chinese New Year period, 1962			
January 1962	Theater	Shanghai Academy of Experimental Opera	
January–February 1962	Movie shows in cinemas	Feature film *Third Sister Liu*	
February 7, 1962	Television broadcast	Feature film *Third Sister Liu*	Two days after Chinese New Year's Day
4. Mid-1962			
April 12, 1962	Television broadcast	Unknown	
August 1962	Theater	Ningxia *Yue* Theater Company	

SOURCES: Electronic databases of *Wenhui bao* and *Xinmin wanbao* at Shanghai Municipal Library.

course as popular entertainment. With its size and rich history in the performing arts, the city had a huge audience for theater. Even before the performances began, the Leap was coming to an end. Against Mao and other leaders whose political position had been weakened by the production campaign's failure, Premiers Zhou Enlai (1898–1976) and Chen Yi (1901–1972) and other officials had been pushing for renewal of official cooperation with "intellectuals" to improve national economic performance.[32] Full-fledged support of the anti-intellectual musical by the Shanghai authorities was probably withdrawn as soon as news of top-level policy and attitudinal change was confirmed in the city. Put differently, the Shanghai performances mentioned above revealed that the authorities there, too, had impressive capacity to combine organization and representation to serve the state.

When the movie *Third Sister Liu* was shown in Shanghai in 1962, screening was mainly organized by the municipal government and workplaces. The picture was quickly scheduled for television release, and mobile projection teams brought the film to rural Shanghai for viewing by peasants.[33] Two reasons explain why the authorities continued to promote the musical and hence ideas, images, and idioms disparaging to the educated to an even broader audience. First, as Lydia Liu suggests, the artistic achievement of the production "seemed to lift the work above official propaganda and made it appealing to both children and grownups."[34] Second, there was a soon-to-be-exposed, deep disagreement about the relations between the intellectual and Chinese Communism at the highest level of the state.

REPRESENTING INTELLECTUALS IN CINEMA

In a reflection written some years later on the highly successful movie *Third Sister Liu*, an audience member aptly summarized the appearance of the three literati hired by the wicked landlord to compete with Liu in the singing competition: they look like a thug, a halfwit, and a whoremonger.[35] Shortly after the Mao regime took power, cinema, like theater, became a primary medium of official propaganda. Characters based on the official view of class struggle dominated feature films, some of which featured educated people and their responses to war and revolution and played an important role in the objectification of the intellectual. Compared with the theater performances of *Third Sister Liu* in Guangxi, Shanghai, or elsewhere, the movie version leaves behind an enduring record of the representations of the literati in the musical drama, or how the state used it to inscribe further negative meanings on the intellectual. Let us review some of the noteworthy portrayals of educated persons in postrevolutionary cinema and how the representations reflected and reinforced the development of Chinese Communism, before returning to the characterization of literati in the national hit.

The March of Democratic Youth (*Minzhu qingnian jinxingqu*) (1950), one of the first notable works of the state-controlled Beijing Film Studio, was completed during the beginning of what has been officially termed the New Democracy period (1949–1953). A theme of official governance then was cross-class cooperation under CCP rule to rebuild and reform China. Notable scholars and other educated persons who had supported the 1949 revolution became CPPCC members and were appointed to ministerial positions, while the Mao regime criticized the politics and beliefs of the educated population.[36] The state, as chapters 4 and 5 have suggested, expended large amounts of symbolic and material resources to establish political control mechanisms in workplaces and local neighborhoods, including the assignment of educated party cadres to positions of authority. Under these circumstances, *The March* presented many faces of educated people in its depiction of student protest at Peking University on the eve of the revolution. In it, there are patient and understanding underground CCP members and a mixture of levelheaded, impulsive, muscular, frail, hard-working, and hedonistic students. Some students are economically privileged; others struggle to get by; a few are thuggish Guomindang agents in disguise. The film narrates the transformation of a handsome, stylish man from a diligent but politically indifferent student into a staunch supporter of the protest and then of the new republic. The movie also paid homage to those whom the state regarded as progressive intellectuals. The moral authority on screen is not so much the handful of indefatigable CCP members as an elderly professor, a participant in the May Fourth movement. In an early scene, this hoary, bespectacled scholar energizes student protest with an inspirational speech that attacks the Guomindang and the United States. *The March* captured the optimism-cum-unease that made up the Yan'an approach to intellectuals of the Mao regime as well as its efforts to coopt well-known figures in academic, art, journalism, and other circles.

When the Mao regime launched Thought Reform of Intellectuals and then denounced Yu Pingbo (1900–1990), Liang Shuming (1893–1988), Hu Feng, and other notable writers for their "petty-bourgeois" and "bourgeois" thinking and characters, cinematic criticism of intellectuals intensified.[37] Yet, the Yan'an representation of the subjects as politically improvable and usable to the socialist project remained a staple in films, just as the assumption continued to inform everyday organization under CCP rule. *The Diary of a Nurse* (*Hushi riji*) (1957) is typical in these respects. The timing of the film, however, would earn it condemnations during the Antirightist Movement for exaggerating the significance of intellectuals to Chinese Communism. The movie features a good-looking nursing school graduate in Shanghai, Jian Suhua, who chooses to serve the socialist project by relocating to a remote and barren construction site, while most of her classmates long and fight for choice assignments within the city. Her lover, an ambitious and successful young surgeon, does not understand her selflessness, let alone the construction workers' dedication to their work. Her supervising doctor is disagreeable, too: a womanizer who provides perfunctory care to the workers. In the end, her lover leaves her for his career, but her boss turns over a new leaf. This tripartite statement on intellectuals—the good, the bad, and the improvable—resembles the representation in *The March* with one important exception: none of the educated people featured in *The Diary* have moral authority in their own right. Jian is commendable because she does not act like her peers or other petty-bourgeois intellectuals, but possesses worker-like altruism.[38]

Products of the ill-fated political thaw sanctioned by the state that culminated in the 1957 Rectification Campaign, *The Man Unconcerned with Details* (*Buju xiaojie de ren*) (1956) and *Unfinished Comedy* (*Wei wancheng de xiju*) (1957) are unusual political satires in the history of cinema in the Mao era. Director Lü Ban (1913–1967) did not use his works to repeat the official interpretation of intellectuals as usable but unreliable subjects. Instead, he took aim at CCP policies and authorities in the artistic circles and portrayed ordinary educated people as reasonable and hard-working. In *The Man Unconcerned with Details,* the object of ridicule is an accomplished writer and advocate of satire who tours and lectures on its importance for art and literature. He is extremely self-absorbed and inconsiderate (and probably a party member, from the deference that he is shown to command from his hosts). He litters in public, picks flowers in a park, smokes in a library, and talks loudly during a theater performance. Everyone else behaves properly.[39] In *Unfinished Comedy,* the spoof goes even further. Lü's target is an unkempt middle-aged man with absurdly thick glasses who is described as an authority in literary and art criticism. This is a thinly disguised caricature of CCP cadres from rural areas (or perhaps even Yan'an revolutionaries). The man uses high-sounding political jargon and rhetoric, quotes Mao and Stalin, and speaks condescendingly to the film crew that receives him. He rejects out of hand any experimentation that deviates from the dogma articulated by Mao in the Yan'an Forum on Literature and Art.[40] Both of these films were denounced during the Antirightist Movement. *Unfinished Comedy* was branded as "poisonous weed" and banned from release. Lü was sentenced to labor reform as a rightist.[41] The authorities in charge of cinema, however, did not discard the techniques of caricature and ridicule of educated people along with political satire. Instead, the techniques were redeployed to support CCP rule.[42] Its incorporation in *Third Sister Liu* would take the attack against intellectuals in PRC cinema to a new height.

Singing competitions, the activity in the most memorable scene of *Third Sister Liu*, are a popular pastime in southern, southwest, and northwest China. During such a contest, the participants take turns to ask and answer questions using folk-style singing. Because the subject matter is virtually unlimited, excellent knowledge and improvisational skill are necessary for maintaining superiority.[43] In the movie, the thug, the halfwit and the whoremonger each have physical and intellectual characteristics spotlighted to insinuate the ugliness of intellectuals in the history of class struggle in China. The thug, the leader among the three, is played by a middle-aged, homely man with unusually high cheek bones and a mouthful of crooked and discolored teeth, an actor who specialized in playing dubious characters. He serves as the adviser of the wicked landlord and plots with him to use violence and other means to control Liu and dominate the villagers. The whoremonger, a pale, skinny man with a salacious grin, was cast to stress that literati lived off the labor of others and had decadent lifestyles. He acts condescendingly toward the villagers and disrespects women publicly. The halfwit is a comedic figure. His sincerity toward Liu does not help to conceal his stupidity, which he does not recognize. He stutters and moves awkwardly and depends on songbooks to compete with her. Even the landlord and other literati are embarrassed by his performance (see figure 4).

In the singing competition scene, mutual antagonism between the competing parties in relation to the meaning of knowledge is obvious. Liu mocks the uselessness of the literati's training in Confucian classics; the literati defend their education as morally superior and look down upon their opponents. She derides them as imbeciles and tell them they are confused and deranged; they call her crazy and disrespectful. But there is no doubt who wins the contest. During part of the competition, the literati merely sing against villagers who are there to support Liu. The villagers hold their own against these men and even trip them up with simple riddles about agriculture. The film's attack against the literati and their education reaches a climax when Liu responds after the landlord angrily snatches a songbook from the humiliated scholars and throws it into the river. She sings:

FIGURE 4. The three literati in the film *Third Sister Liu*. From left to right: the "whoremonger" (played by Xu Juntai), the "thug" (played by Ma Biao), and the "halfwit" (played by Li Wancheng).

> This river is pure and clean,
> Your songbook reeks.
> Do not ditch your stinking book here,
> For fear that it will soil the river.

Unable to tame Liu through the contest, the landlord kidnaps her afterward and tries to force her to become his concubine, all the while receiving support and advice from the literati, especially the thug. In the end, the villagers storm the landlord's estate and rescue her so that she and her lover can leave the area.

Compared to the other films mentioned above, in *Third Sister Liu* three representations of educated people have conspicuously vanished. First, the movie does not contain any educated person who is remotely decent: every literati portrayed is reprehensible or dishonorable in one way or another. Second, not one of the literati becomes a better person as the plot unfolds. Third, the value of formal education is not highlighted anywhere. Whereas Liuzhou's and Guangxi's authorities had skillfully staged and reinforced the Leap's devaluation of education and suspicion toward intellectuals by reorganizing Liu's legend into a musical drama, the movie brought to a national audience theatrical images that suggested such people were slavish, scheming, and useless. In the process, the filmmakers had made changes to the musical drama. Specific phrases that Mao used to ridicule intellectuals and popularized during the Leap, such as "lazy bones" and "incapable of telling the five grains apart," were inserted into the singing contest. And Liu's imprisonment by the landlord with support from the literati was added to the movie to highlight their complicity in class oppression.[44]

CADRES' AND ART WORKERS' REACTIONS TO THE MUSICAL

Tight supervision, multilayered organization, skillful storytelling, and ingenious artistic techniques orchestrated by the CCP transformed the folklore of Third Sister Liu into theatrical and cinematic representations that reinforced the anti-intellectualism of the Great Leap Forward. Resistance to the official denigration of the intellectual, however, persisted throughout the creative process as well as the staging and screening of the performances, just as reinterpretations and manipulations of the classification occurred amid its objectification under the CCP. Like their peers in science, education, or industry, the party cadres who oversaw the musical's production in Liuzhou and Guangxi were generally classifiable as intellectuals according to official definition. In fact, some were assigned to the production because of their educational achievements and artistic or literary knowledge. How did such cadres navigate between their classification as intellectuals and the production's anti-intellectualism? The above-mentioned newspaper article by Wu Jinnan suggests that some cadres sought to redefine the official meaning of intellectuals through finger-pointing. The latter, as chapters 3 and 5 have shown, involved party cadres exploiting their political and management authority to portray themselves as dependable revolutionaries and stigmatize other educated people as unreliable intellectuals. Wu's conduct was an excellent example. According to him, the cadres in charge of Third Sister Liu insisted that scriptwriters and artists follow the principles on art and literature articulated by Mao in Yan'an—or "using the past to serve the present" and "politics first, art second"—and highlight class struggle and restore the character of the legendary folksinger to a "spokesperson" against class oppression. The cadres preached the use of "historical materialism" to remove "slanders" and "distortions" against Third Sister Liu based on "feudalist" and "bourgeois" thinking as well as "the large amounts of rubbish" in her folklore. The cadres, Wu reported, found out that the production teams tried to inject into the production "every hue of the thinking of the capitalist class." The scriptwriters and artists focused on aesthetics, splendor, sentimentality, and other stage qualities. They drew on the "backward and conservative" features of the folktales and even argued that popular folksongs "lacked good taste" to be used

in a major performance. Some of the scriptwriters' and artists' ideas were probably attempts to rein in the production's emerging and thinly disguised vilifica-
tions of intellectuals under the PRC. The cadres apparently rejected the ideas one
after another, because their implementation would "water down the educational
effect" of the musical drama.[45] In short, Wu presented the cadres as revolutionaries
who thwarted intellectuals from using Liu's folklore to engage in class struggle on
behalf of former exploiting classes.

This does not mean that the CCP cadres who supervised the production of *Third
Sister Liu* were equally comfortable with its denigration of intellectuals. Although
public condemnation of the production would have invited harsh punishment
under the Leap's severe political climate, tacit criticism remained an option. A
writer and party member, Qiao Yu (1927–), went to Liuzhou in the fall of 1959
with a music composer and a theater director under the auspices of the National
Federation of Playwrights and the Central Academy of Experimental Opera to
assist in the production of the musical drama.[46] Qiao would turn the script into
the movie's screenplay. As the Guangxi Folksong and Dance Theater was touring
the country, he penned a review of *Third Sister Liu* in the authoritative *Literature
and Art Gazette* (*Wenyi bao*). After a ritualistic glowing assessment of the theme of
class struggle and other aspects of the play, he suggested that the singing competition scene had no historical basis and that the contest had been inserted into the
performance to highlight Liu as a peasant heroine.

> Although there are many stories about singing competitions in the folklore, these
> accounts mainly convey Third Sister Liu's wisdom and musical talent, and the fact
> that her opponents were motivated by their unwillingness to admit that they were
> inferior. Compared to these original stories, the singing competition was handled
> very differently in the musical drama, almost a change in essence . . . If we look
> at how life was lived, [we will recognize that] there were actually not that many
> literati who also liked to sing folksongs. Literati and folksongs were parts of two
> different worlds. I met a schoolteacher who has lived in the heart of folk sing-
> ing in Guangxi for sixty to seventy years. When I mentioned folksongs to him,
> he was stunned and speechless, apparently not knowing that there are folksongs
> around . . . In the singing competition scene, the literati unexpectedly sang many
> folksongs. Even though the songs were of laughably inferior quality, they nonethe-
> less did it. This was something almost impossible in reality, but it was made to be
> very believable in art.[47]

Qiao's thinly veiled opposition to *Third Sister Liu*'s denigration of intellectuals was
an exception. Rather than applauding or criticizing the singing competition scene,
which would have respectively endorsed the Leap's anti-intellectualism or put one's
career and safety at risk, other critics focused on the composition of other scenes,
scene transitions, and musical arrangement and lyrics. Liu's character received
profuse attention and approbation and even minor complaints. Yet, a recurring

theme in the laudatory commentaries is their emphasis on the fictional nature of the musical, which can be understood as a form of subtle rejection of the production's vilification of intellectuals. In his review of the performance in *Literary Review* (*Wenxue pinglun*), He Qifang, a writer and party member whom we met in chapter 3, expressed approval of the modifications of Liu's legend by Guangxi's theater crews. But he underlined that the "theme [of class struggle] and the rich and dramatic elements of the plot have required many decisions and deletions as well as much imagination and fabrication." In contrast to Wu Jinnan, who claimed that the production recovered the historically accurate and revolutionary character of Liu, He Qifang stated that *Third Sister Liu* is "an original piece of creation built on the foundation of the folklore."[48] Cai Yi (1906–1992), a literary theorist and another party member, went even further in stressing the production's fictional nature. He argued that *White-Haired Girl* (*Bai mao nü*), which portrays the cruelty of rural landlords, was the first milestone of PRC musical theater, and *Third Sister Liu* was the second one. Neither of the musicals would have made much sense if they were produced in the reverse order. Both productions reflected "the spirit of the time" and fulfilled their "historical missions."[49] In other words, they were timely products of CCP propaganda.

When the feature film *Third Sister Liu* was released in late 1961, the Leap had collapsed for all intents and purposes. The CCP leadership had readopted practical economic measures and checked the virulent anti-intellectualism in official ideology. By April 1962, the state had issued new policies on science, higher education, literature, art, and theater and cinema to promote local cooperation with scholars, teachers, scientists, and artists.[50] This high-level change of heart about the role of intellectuals under Chinese Communism emboldened critics of the musical. They deployed their knowledge of art, literature, and history as well as their argumentative skills further to undermine the revolutionary interpretation of the legend of Third Sister Liu, using in particular the well-known magazine *Popular Cinema* (*Dazhong dianying*) as a channel. The major criticism received by the film, the content of which closely resembled the Guangxi musical drama, was that Liu had been turned inappropriately from a mythical folk figure into an idealized contemporary revolutionary. The playwrights and screenwriters had imposed on the folksinger class consciousness, leadership skills, knowledge of political struggle, and other characteristics typical of someone wanting to lead a proletarian revolution. Such "modernizing" (*xiandaihua*) of Liu, some critics argued, made her look like a member of the Chinese Communist Youth League. The movie thus stripped from her folklore the multifaceted expressions of hope and pain, joy and anger, and ideas and ideals as well as the interlaced practical and magical qualities that were part of the stories. The critics claimed that such sentiments and thoughts not only reflected the past conditions of the laboring masses, but also served to produce and reproduce the legend of Liu and enhance its popularity over time.[51] One critic aptly summarized the complaints about the artistic approach in the production: "In the search for the truth [about Third Sister Liu], what is true [about Chinese history and society] is left out."[52]

Although the critics did not mention any CCP cadres or offices by name, the ultimate targets of the criticism were those who sanctioned and controlled the production of *Third Sister Liu,* and even the underlying Yan'an principles of art and literature promoted by the state. One critic stated that "using the past to serve the present" in the art was necessary, but "under no circumstances should [China's] historical legacies be handled crudely and brutally" (*cubao*) by producers.[53] The use of the term *cubao,* which signals vicious, rude, and even violent behavior, was especially poignant. The term had been used by scholars, schoolteachers, and others during the 1957 Rectification Campaign to criticize the behavior of party cadres toward colleagues outside the party. Here *cubao* conjures up the image of the party authorities violating history. Even Mao's homage to the musical for being an emblem of the Chinese socialist revolution was no longer unassailable. One critic wrote that Liu "was a singing immortal and an idealized creation of the laboring masses—not a leader of peasant revolutions."[54] Another indicated that historical materialism, the approach to knowledge sanctioned by the state for comprehending class struggle, was ignored completely in the production: the movie "confounds the past and present and turns them upside down, and thus possesses no basic historical value."[55] The scathing criticisms of the film put the folktale of Third Sister Liu back on its feet. Their publication was evidence of political change since the musical drama debuted in Beijing two years before.

Despite such intense criticism of *Third Sister Liu,* there is no evidence that any critic confronted the vehement anti-intellectualism of the musical head-on. As before, the singing competition scene and its caricature of the literati occupy a negligible part in the commentaries. Why did critics not dispute the musical's disparagement of intellectuals? Did they not want to speak out for themselves and all those regarded as intellectuals within state and society? The silence suggests that speaking on behalf of these people without official sanction was widely understood to be risky business, given what had happened to those who tried during the Rectification Campaign. As we shall see, when prodded by higher authorities, some writers and artists did seek to represent the category of intellectuals in a favorable light. Before we move on, it is necessary to note that little evidence exists with regard to how ordinary theater or cinema audience members responded to the denigration of intellectuals in the musical drama. If what we discuss below offers any indication, it is that even when the state monopolized representations of the intellectual in theater, cinema, and other media, it had limited control over how ordinary people interpreted the ideas, images, or languages.

PRODUCING AND DENOUNCING
EARLY SPRING IN FEBRUARY

Some leaders running the [state's] film production departments [who are veteran CCP members] nonetheless approved the movie script and even spent much public money and used five-color film to shoot the picture. They artfully repackaged, promoted, and peddled as "artistic" mistaken thoughts and values that ought to be exposed and subjected to criticism. What did they want to achieve by doing so?

—A REVIEW OF *EARLY SPRING IN FEBRUARY* IN *PEOPLE'S DAILY*[56]

Research has described the power struggle within the CCP leadership and important policy changes in the wake of the Great Leap Forward. For our purposes, the accounts show that the intellectual and Chinese Communism continued to constitute each other at multiple levels of Chinese society with twists and turns. On the one hand, President Liu Shaoqi, Premier Zhou Enlai, and other party leaders (and even Chairman Mao to some extent) reaffirmed the importance of the intellectual to socialist development. The state advanced measures to relax political control over the work of scientists, journalists, and other professional workers and to reintroduce rational economic planning. Under this climate, writers and artists close to the leadership produced works that criticized the Leap and even Mao. In art and literature, depictions of various kinds of social experience other than those constantly repeated in the official narrative of class struggle appeared.[57] On the other hand, some party leaders held fast to the notion of class struggle and, before long, Mao reverted to promoting the view that intellectuals were real as well as potential enemies of Chinese Communism. Mao broadened the term "bourgeois intellectuals" popularized during the Antirightist Movement to include scientists, schoolteachers, and others who were trained under the PRC but who purportedly subscribed to values and beliefs promoted by the previous exploiting classes. Newly trained intellectuals, he believed, were often corrupted by the old ones, who continued to dominate education, art, and other sectors and even hold important positions within the party and the state. For Mao and his supporters, it was necessary to redeploy intense labor reeducation, political study, and rectification campaigns against intellectuals to protect and further the revolutionary project.[58]

What happened to the movie *Early Spring in February* captures the dynamics of this volatile phase in the struggle to define the intellectual and Chinese Communism. In the film, Xiao Jianqiu, a teachers' college graduate and a former May Fourth student activist, withdraws to a small town to teach in a friend's school during the mid-1920s. He is a passionate reader of philosophy and literature and he dresses well and plays the piano, all of which are symbols of a privileged upbringing. He meets his friend's educated, elegant, and unorthodox sister Tao Lan and introduces her to all kinds of writings, including the journal *New Youth,* which was then published by the CCP to promote Marxist and Leninist thought. Upon learning that a former classmate has died as a soldier and left behind a widow and two small children in dire poverty, Xiao supports her financially, takes her daughter to school, and helps the poor family in other ways. Led by a teacher who wants to marry Tao, Xiao's colleagues spread rumors that he seeks a romantic relationship with her and at the same time fornicates with the widow behind everyone's back. In a desperate move to save the widow from committing suicide after her son passes away from illness, Xiao offers to marry her even though he is attracted to Tao. The widow hangs herself, leaving behind her daughter, for whom Tao and her family now take responsibility. Fed up with the town's parochialism, tragedies, and inequalities, Xiao apparently decides to devote himself to revolution. The film ends with Tao learning of his departure and dashing out to find Xiao, implying that she might follow his path (see figure 5).

Like *Third Sister Liu, Early Spring* was produced under tight official supervision, this time in Beijing. The production received support from two deputy ministers of culture of the PRC: Xia Yan (1900–1995) and Chen Huangmei (1913–1996). A successful playwright, screenwriter, and essayist, Xia had participated in the May Fourth movement and joined the CCP in 1927. Similarly accomplished, Chen doubled as the chief of the ministry's film bureau. After the Leap, Xia, like Zhou Enlai, proclaimed that there was no need to be suspicious of intellectuals anymore.[59] Chen "carefully read" the novel from which the film was adapted and approved its production. Xia and Chen suggested revisions to the movie script and held "serious discussions" with the film crew. Xia even revised the shot-sequence script "in over one hundred places" to achieve the effects that he wanted.[60] Consequently, the film's portrayal of intellectuals is completely different from the thinly veiled attack on them in *Third Sister Liu.* Xiao Jianqiu and Tao Lan are played by a famous and conventionally good-looking actor and actress. They are kind and thoughtful. They are torn between tradition and ideals and dissatisfied with the status quo. They use their education to teach and nurture schoolchildren and make sacrifices to improve the lives of poor people. They wrestle with quandaries and controversies that have no perfect solutions. The widow and other poor people in the film are significant only to the extent that they are examples of dispiriting poverty in Chinese society and the distance to which Xiao and Tao would go to help the underprivileged. True, Xiao's and Tao's colleagues are less than admirable: these intellectuals mock and sabotage Xiao as well as gossip and spread rumors about his relationship with Tao and his interaction with the widow. However, none of these characters are shown to be using their knowledge or status to help the political or economic elites to exploit, dominate, or terrify the poor.

During the fall of 1964, *Early Spring* was screened nationwide, not as an updated view of what the intellectual meant to Chinese Communism, but as a "poisonous

FIGURE 5. Xiao Jianqiu (played by Sun Daolin) and Tao Lan (played by Xie Fang) in *Early Spring in February*.

weed" denounced by the state. When the film underwent official inspection in the previous November, Minister of Culture Mao Dun and other officials expressed excitement and appreciation after the screening. However, Deputy Minister of Culture Zhou Yang (1907–1989) reacted differently. Zhou, who was also vice director of the CCP's Department of Propaganda, was the "chief guardian and top enforcer of the party's cultural line."[61] He criticized *Early Spring* sternly for promoting "humanitarianism of the petty bourgeoisie and the capitalist class." The film buried the cruel and exploitative conduct of these classes of people by depicting what seemed to be acts of kindness of a few of their members. Zhou's criticism prompted Mao Dun and Chen Huangmei to introduce revisions to the film. By then, Chairman Mao and his high-level supporters had already decided to initiate another round of rectification to address what they saw as extensive political and ideological problems in art and literature circles. The Department of Propaganda suspended proposed changes to *Early Spring* and included it along with other films for public screening and scathing criticism.[62] In June 1964, Mao openly criticized veteran revolutionaries and party cadres in the circles for failing to implement CCP policies, "acting like bureaucrats and overlords" (*zuoguan dang laoye*) and teetering on "the edge of revisionism."[63] Official objections to *Early Spring* became a major vehicle deployed by the state to attack intellectuals.

Between mid-September and mid-November 1964, *People's Daily* published 18 essays that denounced *Early Spring,* while newspapers around the country followed suit. In a nutshell, the criticism stressed that the film, through its positive representations of the values, beliefs, and behavior of Xiao Jianqiu and Tao Lan qua intellectuals, promoted "bourgeois individualism," "bourgeois humanitarianism," "bourgeois doctrine of class harmony," and other objectionable views to life and politics that undercut the importance of class struggle in Chinese society. First, the production pays no attention to the uprisings of workers, peasants, and students against class exploitation and their sacrifices during the 1920s, let alone the resulting ascent of the CCP. Second, while the film depicts economic inequality and poverty, there is no indication that class exploitation is the source of the problem. Third, even though the political choices of Xiao and Tao and their treatment of the poor as well as their romance, joy, and despair reveal self-absorption, indecisiveness, conceitedness, cowardice, and other shortcomings typical of intellectuals then and later, the production highlights kindness, decency, learnedness, and other apparently admirable qualities of the two characters. The mere fact that some playwrights, novelists, directors, and artists are CCP members, the first criticism of *Early Spring* in *People's Daily* stated bluntly, does not mean that they would necessarily produce "proletarian" works; to the contrary, some of the works of these people are imbued with elements of bourgeois ideology.[64] In other words, unreformed intellectuals had been working within the party to undermine Chinese Communism. Within a few months, Xia Yan and Chen Huangmei were removed from their positions. Chen was forced to admit that under his supervision "a complete and systematic anti-Party, antisocialist, and revisionist line" had taken shape in the film industry.[65] The intense attack against *Early Spring* and its sponsors by the state proved that the critics of *Third Sister Liu* had been right about their muted resistance to the official denigration of intellectuals—speaking out for this category of people was dangerous, even for those who held high positions within the party or the state.

While the official denunciation of *Early Spring* signaled to state and society that bourgeois intellectuals had been dominating the film industry and, for that matter, other areas of the socialist political economy, screenings of the film showed that the struggle to define the intellectual and Chinese Communism, like before, reached deep into urban neighborhoods and everyday life, sometimes with results unpredictable to the authorities. In Shanghai, *Early Spring* was released on September 15, 1964, the same day when *People's Daily* published the first of its criticisms of the movie. Few people showed up at any of the six cinemas carrying the film. Thanks to the official condemnation of the movie, things changed completely the following day. Even before the box office opened at Huaihai Cinema at 9 a.m., many people had queued up for tickets. At Grand Shanghai Cinema, 800 people had arrived by 9 a.m. Another 2,000 people, some of whom were scalpers, gathered in front of the cinema the following morning. Determined to control how the film would be understood, the municipal authorities in charge of propaganda quickly decided that tickets would not be sold to individuals, even though the original plan was to allot half of the tickets for such sale. Screening, instead, would be arranged by official agencies working together with workplaces and other organizations. After the cinemas posted the official decision in front of their establishments in the evening, the crowd did not disperse. Some demanded explanations from the staff; others asked that they be allowed to purchase tickets because of lack of official affiliation with any organizations. By the following morning, 400 to 500 people were still in front of Huaihai Cinema. Some stated they would "hold on to the end" and pressured the staff to sell them tickets. At 9 a.m., the crowd increased to more than 1,000 people. No amount of explanation from the staff could calm some of these people down. The cinema called the police for help, who arrived shortly and detained five "unemployed youths" who were allegedly leaders of the agitated crowd.[66]

If unanticipated audience enthusiasm toward *Early Spring* indicated to the Shanghai authorities that many people would not accept the official interpretation of the film, initial reactions to the screenings confirmed that the authorities would need to do more than simply sponsor or publish criticisms of the film. Some audience members who had read the *People's Daily* review stated that the movie was not as objectionable as depicted by the official organ. Some who had queued for hours to obtain tickets were disappointed at how unremarkable the film was. Others noted that there was nothing wrong with the movie.[67] Even CCP cadres had difficulty grasping the denunciations leveled against *Early Spring*. A week after the film's release, the authorities in charge of propaganda organized a screening for party cadres. The event was followed by a meeting during which the cadres worked together to summarize how the film spread bourgeois thought as well as disguised and distorted class struggle. Some cadres reported that the collaboration helped them reflect on their lack of political vigilance, as they had not paid sufficient attention to ideological messages promoted in films, novels, and other works.[68] The Leap and *Third Sister Liu* had put down intellectuals for all to see, but even party cadres needed official explanations before recognizing why the leadership regarded *Early Spring* as dangerous propaganda promoted by bourgeois intellectuals inside and outside the party. Although the Shanghai CCP Department of Propaganda would arrange further screenings for party cadres, it decided that professional workers in art, literature, cinema, and other media as well as college students in art and humanities would be the primary audience of the movie.[69]

Through their work these "intellectuals" had or would have access to their own audiences. They needed to understand the objectionable messages and representations in the film and, more generally, examine their own beliefs, ideas, and works with the perspective set down by the state.

Between September and October 1964, Shanghai cinemas screened *Early Spring* for a total of 364 times to an audience of 420,000 people. At least twelve universities and hospitals and other organizations also showed the movie to staff members and students. As the screenings proceeded, the authorities developed what they called "decontamination" (*xiaodu*) work to help the audience understand the film according to the official interpretation. Before the show, the authorities arranged for the audience to listen to reports from the Department of Propaganda and read official assessments of the movie. After the show, some audience members were required to participate in one or two one-hour sessions of follow-up discussion, or occasions that allowed the authorities to promote official views further and gauge individual responses. Despite the intervention, disagreements with the official interpretation of the film and the condemnation of the main characters as objectionable intellectuals persisted. At Jiaotong University, a Chinese Communist Youth League member reportedly argued that *Early Spring* was not a poisonous weed, because what Xiao and Tao did in the movie was appropriate under the political climate of the 1920s, when the Chinese socialist revolution was merely a budding project and genuine understanding of Marxist thought was rare. At Shanghai People's Number One Hospital, a student contended that the film's director, contrary to the official attack against him, was critical of Xiao's and Tao's bourgeois humanitarianism and actually showed its futility as a means to protect the poor. Others stated that the film opposed China's "feudalist traditions" and was therefore politically progressive. At Shanghai Girls Secondary School Number Six, some students questioned why the denouncement of the behavior of Xiao was so intense even if it was improper. They reasoned that he was not a member of the CCP or its youth league and thus naturally did not have the political training to do the right things. At East China Normal University, some students allegedly focused on the performance of the actress who played Tao and her attractive appearance. At Shongshan Secondary School, even students who had not seen the film began to talk about it, with some wanting to watch the performance of the movie stars and their beautiful costumes.[70] In other words, these young men and women did not believe that people like Xiao and Tao, still less the producers and directors of the film, were bourgeois intellectuals intending to undermine Chinese Communism, as the state indicated—or they simply did not care about the state's interpretation of the movie.

Third Sister Liu and *Early Spring in February* were prominent signposts of the mutual constitution of the intellectual and Chinese Communism under the PRC.

The works each brought to the surface of official discourse disturbing meanings that the state invested in the classification. The propagation of each set of meanings coincided with a severe phase of the revolutionary project. From the mid-1930s to the mid-1950s, the Yan'an understanding of intellectuals dominated CCP thinking of this social category. Intellectuals were mainly usable but unreliable professional workers; they were not intransigent class enemies as some party leaders had implied earlier. During the late 1950s, *Third Sister Liu* suggested that intellectuals had been slavish and even criminal sidekicks of the exploiting classes with knowledge and skills worthless for actual production activities. The view reflected and reinforced the Great Leap Forward's disregard of rational planning and scientific knowledge which ultimately led to widespread famine. A few years later, the official condemnation of *Early Spring* hinted that an assault on intellectuals working within the party, the state, and other establishments would be necessary for saving Chinese Communism from a capitalist counterrevolution. Unreformed intellectuals purportedly had been using their knowledge and authority as well as access to resources and opportunities to promote bourgeois values, beliefs, and behavior. Shortly afterward, Mao and his deputies marched China into the Cultural Revolution. From the production of *Third Sister Liu* to the denunciation of *Early Spring,* the official assessment of intellectuals had gone from class enemies of the past with feeble influence on the present to a powerful and imminent threat to China's socialist development.

This is not to say that the increasingly severe official rebuke of intellectuals caused the abuse of writers, scientists, journalists, and other educated people during the Cultural Revolution, still less the murders of party cadres like Bian Zhongyun, the Beijing school principal who was beaten to death shortly after the campaign began. As we have seen, the official representations of intellectuals in *Third Sister Liu* and *Early Spring* elicited resistance, redirection, skepticism, confusion, and disbelief at various levels of state and society, or multivalent responses that had always accompanied the objectification of the intellectual under Chinese Communism. At the same time, however, the productions, performances, and reviews of *Third Sister Liu* and the screenings, denunciations, and audience workshops tied to *Early Spring* demonstrate that combustible conditions involving the objectification continued to build up between the Great Leap Forward and the eve of the Cultural Revolution. For one thing, state and society participated in the officially orchestrated creation, circulation, and consumption of yet further layers of ideas, images, and idioms that attacked intellectuals. Second, even as educated party leaders and cadres were implicated by the intensifying official attacks, they continued to target others whom they denounced as untrustworthy intellectuals. Third, amid the growing assault, the boundaries of the population of intellectuals were not any clearer than they had been since the inception of Chinese Communism, even though professors, writers, scientists, and others were widely regarded as intellectuals across state and society.

In other words, after four decades of the objectification of the intellectual under Chinese Communism, intellectuals were locatable virtually everywhere under the PRC. To be sure, what they stood for, who they were, and how they should be treated remained debatable. Yet, this objectified population was connected more than ever to a vitriolic rhetoric of blame and betrayal, a multipronged system of official domination, and a variety of tactics and strategies of stigma management. That is to say, repertoires of violence in the forms of political ideas, administrative measures, and internecine struggle were abundantly available to be set ablaze by Mao and his supporters on behalf of their political vision and political gains.

The Intellectual and Chinese Society

From Past to Present

The most profound achievement of the Chinese Communist Party after it took power in the 1949 revolution was the reordering of Chinese society according to the Marxian images of the party leadership, or political thinking based on a foreign system of thought. The success, which required persistent mobilization and organization of symbolic and material resources, reveals at once the intellectual prowess, political skills, and governing capacity of the Mao regime. Within a decade, the state literally reclassified hundreds of millions of people in a complex industrializing society as members of a relatively small number of predefined social classes and categories, such as capitalists, poor peasants, workers, rightists, and counterrevolutionaries. To borrow an insight from Sheila Fitzpatrick, the CCP created entirely new "collective social entities whose members had not previously had a common identity, status, or consciousness but acquired them through their experience" under the socialist state.[1]

This book has offered an account of this CCP invention of Marxian classes and categories—off the beaten path. For the party leadership, intellectuals constitute a major segment of society with critical influence on both the socialist revolution and the transition to socialism. Yet, no previous study has illustrated how the party identified members of this population in practice, let alone with the same rigor as has been mustered to describe the appearance of landlords or other classes or categories of people under CCP rule. To be sure, the existing research on the intellectual and Chinese Communism is highly valuable. The scholarship has illustrated ideas and interests, institutions and organizations, conflict and cooperation, and other social and political experiences before and after 1949. By predefining intellectuals as critical thinkers, professional experts, or other social types, the scholarship nonetheless has obscured one of the most creative, productive, and transformative acts of the party—that is, its deployment of the intellectual as a classification of people.

To put this in broader analytical terms, the existing scholarship involves a double erasure of history. The accounts begin with concepts of intellectuals that first appeared in Western Europe or the United States based on the works of Julien Benda, Karl Mannheim, Talcott Parsons, and other notable scholars.[2] Little consideration is given to the historical conditions that produced or supported the concepts, what Bourdieu would describe as the "classification struggles"[3] that occurred inside as well as outside academia and determined how the intellectual was defined and apprehended. The accounts, instead, recombine the ingredients making up the concepts (that is, the social function, work responsibility, and moral performance of the individual) to grasp the intellectual under Chinese Communism. Reliance on such *a priori* definitions has resulted in the masking of a classification struggle that has no parallel in the history of Western Europe or the United States. From the early 1920s to the mid-1950s, *zhishifenzi* evolved from a little-known term, even within the CCP, to a primary social identity of many across state and society. Under Chinese Communism or, for that matter, in any historical context, the intellectual has no ontological existence prior to being defined by the political or academic elites. It is a classification of people deployed by such elites to organize society on paper or in practice. The existing literature on the intellectual and Chinese Communism obscures as much as illuminates the nature of their relations.

At the dawn of Chinese Communism, few people if any identified themselves or categorized others as intellectuals. The heated debate on the intellectual class and Chinese society during the May Fourth movement was similar to the one on *les intellectuels* and French society during the Dreyfus affair. Writers, college students, and other educated people, including leaders of the budding CCP, used their literary and analytical skills, access to newspapers and magazines, and understanding of different traditions of political thinking to advance their own view of the intellectual class, especially its role in the disorder and the renewal of Chinese society. After embracing Marxism and Leninism as their guiding political thought, the CCP elites redefined the intellectual class as part of the petty bourgeoisie as well as the most formidable ideological enemy of Chinese Communism. Before long, the leaders discontinued their use of the term "the intellectual class." From then on, "intellectuals" became an integral component of the CCP schema of classes.

What happened thereafter with the intellectual and Chinese Communism is nothing short of historic. An apparatus in the Foucauldian sense, or a dispersed structure of programs, measures, and routines linked to the classification, arose and grew with the revolutionary project.[4] The apparatus contained a multiplicity of elements: official announcements, instructions, statistics, and reports; regulations on recruitment, appointment, training, and compensation; revolutionary universities, mass campaigns, and political study classes; offices, meetings, and registration forms; films, plays, and newspaper headlines and articles; surveillance techniques and confessional protocols; and various forms of punishment as well as other discursive and organizational practices promoted, sanctioned, or condoned by the CCP. The apparatus was the cumulative result of "the prevalent influence of a strategic objective"[5] that persisted within the party leadership—or its resolve to exploit the knowledge and skills of intellectuals for Chinese Communism but curb the deleterious impact of their values, beliefs, and habits. Even at the peaks of its denunciation of the intellectual, the leadership did not abandon this objective informed by the Leninist approach to the building of a modern socialist society through class struggle. The leadership, instead, altered the content of its governance to fit its evolving priorities. The elements of the apparatus each played a role in shaping ways of thinking, seeing, feeling, and acting from the most didactic to the least transparent manner. The apparatus ultimately turned a diversity of people into "intellectuals" within local society, or class subjects purportedly possessing knowledge and skills as well as attributes such as vanity, materialism, and indiscipline.

In practice, fuzzy boundaries and unstable meanings were ubiquitous characteristics of the objectified population of intellectuals. The heterogeneous elements of the above apparatus developed unevenly across time and space due to many political, administrative, and pragmatic reasons. The elements shared relations from complementarity and interdependence to conflict and contradiction. Their existence created space for different interpretations of who the intellectuals were and what they represented at all levels of CCP governance. Even the party leadership repeatedly redefined the intellectual and its significance to Chinese Communism. No fewer than twelve types of people that appeared in the previous chapters were regarded as intellectuals within the local context: educated CCP leaders; educated party cadres; former workers or peasants who received formal education; novelists, playwrights, and other writers; scientists, professors, and other experts; schoolteachers, artists, and other professional workers; clerical and other office workers; former state officials, Guomindang organizers, and military and police officers with academic qualifications; college students; senior high school graduates; junior high school graduates; and individuals with some junior high education. The local boundaries of the category of intellectuals and its implications for the revolutionary project were complicated further by a protean culture of informal negotiation of social identity, as individuals identified or identifiable as such subjects adopted various tactics and strategies of self-refashioning to navigate between risks and opportunities.

Three notable events that occurred under the PRC capture the widely different implications for the individual resulting from the CCP's deployment of the intellectual as a classification of people. Shortly before the state launched Thought Reform of Intellectuals in late 1951, Premier Zhou Enlai personally adopted the classification to convince professors and college students to embrace their own ideological reeducation. He stated that he was always striving to learn and embrace "the standpoint of the working class," and that he wanted his audience to follow his example.[6] In Zhou's hands, the classification became a tool for political domination. During the 1957 Rectification Campaign, some professors and writers used the intellectual as a badge of honor in contradistinction to the negative meanings officially inscribed on the marker. They emphasized their professional, political, and moral values to the state and attacked CCP cadres as oppressors of intellectuals and obstacles of socialist development. In her attackers' eyes, Bian Zhongyun, the dedicated educator and party cadre brutally murdered during the Cultural Revolution, was a bourgeois intellectual who had wormed her way into the party to do harm to Chinese Communism. For Bian and others, the classification morphed into a painful death sentence. Under the revolutionary project, the intellectual was a classification of people used for multiple purposes. The intellectual was never any particular type of person.

Once the CCP leadership pronounced "intellectuals" as an integral section of Chinese society, Chinese Communism developed prominently between two poles until its decline. The first pole featured the party seeking to extract and exploit the knowledge and skills of the educated, or efforts to build a modern socialist society. The other pole centered on the party controlling these people politically, or using class struggle as a method. The apparatus that objectified the intellectual thus always contained two clusters of principles and mechanisms, the proportions of which shifted with the leadership's priorities. Around one pole, the party assigned privileges, positions, and responsibilities to educated people and even provided them with social and political authority to induce their cooperation and support. It took over, established, and expanded systems of education to ensure the availability of intellectuals to Chinese Communism. Around the other pole, educated people were subject to criticism and denunciation, supervision and investigation, and ideological training and punishment. The party sought to control every establishment that required professional knowledge and skills to function. The goal was to discipline intellectuals to the extent of rooting out their corruptive impact on the revolutionary project.

The CCP's deployment of the intellectual as a classification of people therefore shaped Chinese Communism as a bureaucratic enterprise as much as the latter turned otherwise perfectly ordinary people into intellectuals to be used and abused in specific ways. The party increasingly exploited channels and resources to attack the values, ideas, and habits of intellectuals. Workplace supervision by party cadres, ideological reeducation, and mass surveillance were deemed necessary for preventing subversion of the revolutionary projects by intellectuals. Systems of classifications and structures of reward and punishment grew as the party leadership sought to handle each intellectual in government, industry, education, art, and other sectors in proper political, professional, and moral terms. In brief, the CCP imperative of controlling and utilizing intellectuals engendered methods of representation, reorganization, reeducation, and repression that eventually spread across the Chinese political economy.

The structure of domination thus emerged could not but influence social relations and individual calculus. Educated persons responded in myriad ways. No

common understanding of moral obligation, occupational responsibility, or political interest informed the reactions. The latter were often based on the discourse
and practice established around the intellectual by the CCP, or how individuals
situated themselves within its schema of classes and the local context of risks and
opportunities. A cacophony of conduct surfaced. We have seen that well-educated
party leaders exploited their revolutionary credentials and command of organizational resources to separate themselves from other educated people. As Mao
rose to the top, he acted exactly like his predecessors and attacked other party
leaders as unreliable intellectuals. At lower levels, party cadres likewise acted out
the role of proletarian revolutionary to distance themselves from educated colleagues. Unemployed persons identified themselves as intellectuals in hopes of
landing a job. Writers and scholars promoted themselves as trustworthy intellectuals when contesting state domination. Playwrights and artists produced or
supported anti-intellectual propaganda that undercut their own prestige and even
denounced favorable portrayals of intellectuals. College and secondary school students objected to the official condemnation of intellectuals, which they regarded
as unreasonable, especially when that label was applied to them. These and other
responses not only served to objectify the intellectual; they intensified the ruptures
within the objectified population. The objectification of the intellectual under
Chinese Communism had structural as well as cultural consequences.

Overall, this book has merely captured a thin slice of the mutual constitution of
the intellectual and Chinese Communism, dynamics that spread across multiple
levels of Chinese society for at least six decades. My intention has been to point
out that seeing the intellectual as a classification of people allows us to delve further into the workings of the revolutionary project, because the classification was
both an outcome and a driver of the project's organization. My analysis has been
arranged to spotlight underexamined discursive and organizational practices of
the CCP, the formation of local populations of intellectuals, and consequences for
individuals, organizations, and Chinese society. Besides the themes and episodes
covered here, many other questions await exploration, as the reader probably
realizes by now. How did the intellectual classification take root and reconsti-
tute authority and social relations in the countryside? How did the classification
extend across industry, the military, and other sectors where professional as well as
manual labor was important for operation? Did ethnic traditions modify how the
classification was deployed in minority regions? How did educated and expropriated capitalists and newly educated workers position themselves in relation to the
classification? How did the classification influence friendship, romance, and marriage? Not least, how did the deployment of the classification affect the Cultural
Revolution and vice versa? If we accept that the intellectual as an embodied subject
does not exist by virtue of any features possessed by the person, a host of original questions on politics and society under Chinese Communism can be raised.
To address the questions, it is important to consider dynamics of representation,

methods of identification, and negotiations of social identity. The results would serve to deepen understanding of central and local governance, conflict and cooperation, and, in general, social life under the CCP, issues that have animated the literature on the intellectual and Chinese Communism in the first place.

The decline of Chinese Communism, especially its emphasis on class struggle, since the early 1980s has led to dramatic changes in Chinese society. The CCP regime has reinterpreted in unorthodox fashions how Marxism applies to China and abandoned, for all intents and purposes, Marxian systems of social classification. Megacities and conspicuous consumption, powerful Chinese multinationals and rapid technological growth, imposing government buildings, world-renowned universities, and global traveling officials, executives, and students have become unmistakable features of twenty-first-century China, as have rising social inequality, rampant official corruption, environmental degradation, urban slums, sex work, and mistreatment of migrants. Meanwhile, the population of educated Chinese continues to grow, thanks to state investment in higher education and professional development. Many of them have careers in the diverse, influential, and expanding private sector, and hence are free from the direct supervision of the state. Does the intellectual as a classification of people still matter in such a globalized China? Any satisfactory answer to this and other puzzles regarding the status and use of the classification and its impact on Chinese society would require a book-length response based on ethnographic, literary, and other kinds of research. In this concluding section of the book, I draw on readily available as well as recent examples to suggest that China's struggle to define the intellectual not only remains alive and well but still differs markedly from those occurring in Western Europe and the United States. The objectification of the intellectual in the last century has left behind a powerful legacy that affects ways of seeing, thinking, feeling, and acting on multiple levels.

Since the demise of Chinese Communism, the CCP leadership has continued to regard intellectuals as a major segment of Chinese society as well as assign a diversity of people to the social category. The leadership still subscribes to the Leninist imperative of utilizing and controlling intellectuals as a principle of official governance, even though the party has long since discarded class struggle as a method of rule. For the leadership, intellectuals are both vital assets and potent threats to China's social stability, economic growth, and international ascension. Official conduct therefore continues to objectify some into subjects widely recognized as intellectuals. In March 2017, for example, President Xi Jinping (1953–) reiterated the first half of the modified Leninist imperative during the meeting of the Chinese People's Political Consultative Conference. He stressed that China "needs the contribution of intellectuals to increase the power and wealth of the nation, to revitalize the Chinese race [*minzu zhenxing*], and to improve the well-being of the Chinese people." He lauded intellectuals as "the elites of society, the pillar of the nation, and the pride of the people."[7] For more than three decades, the state has been revising its incentive structures to reward professional knowledge and expertise, or those whom it considers intellectuals, with status, money, and authority. Shortly after Xi's speech, *People's Daily* added a supposedly inspirational special column titled "The Elegance and Refinement of Intellectuals" (*Zhishifenzi de fengcai*) to promote further to the nation the importance of such people. Within three months, the official organ featured the achievements of forty individuals and their roads to success. Thirty-eight are technical experts in the roles of university chancellors or deans, researchers in fields such as medicine, ecology, astrophysics, and agriculture, or engineers in aerospace, computer science, transportation, or other areas. Some of these people double as entrepreneurs. Featured, too, were the successes of a veteran primary school teacher and a classical music conductor.[8] Moreover, the state continues to elect persons whom it deems to be notable and cooperative intellectuals to serve as CPPCC delegates.[9]

As with public adulation, prestigious appointment, and material rewards, state measures of control targeted at scientists, schoolteachers, and others based on the other half of the modified Leninist imperative also reproduce symbolic and social boundaries that serve to objectify these people as "intellectuals." On one level, the state continues to deploy management by party cadres within research institutes, universities, and schools as well as newspapers, radio stations, and other establishments where intellectuals are said to cluster. An important official goal is to prevent the professional workers from using their status, knowledge, and authority to undermine official governance, especially through organizing and supporting oppositional movements. A few months after Xi Jinping praised intellectuals in the above speech, for example, the state instructed top universities to strengthen supervision of the teaching staff and their ideological education.[10] Professors and instructors are regarded, like before, as usable but unreliable intellectuals. Under the supervision of the CCP Department of Propaganda, "offices for working with intellectuals outside the party" (*dangwai zhishifenzi gongzuochu*) have been established across the country. The offices organize policy- and theory-training classes and other activities for lawyers, engineers, journalists, and others to garner their cooperation with the state and compliance with its decisions. Furthermore, the state is determined to punish those whom it regards as wayward intellectuals with change of work responsibility, demotion, layoff, prosecution, and imprisonment because of their leadership in or support of protests or challenges against the state. Under the Xi regime, official prosecution and imprisonment of human rights lawyers and other political activists who expose official abuse and corruption have been on the rise.[11]

The extent to which the CCP still perceives the intellectual as a serious threat to its rule was on full display during the last days of Liu Xiaobo, the former university lecturer who became the 2010 Nobel Peace Prize laureate because of his leadership in democracy movements. During late spring of 2017, the state disclosed that Liu, who had been imprisoned since the late 2000s, had late-stage liver cancer, but prohibited him from receiving treatment abroad. It kept Liu under guard until he died and then orchestrated his funeral, cremation, and sea burial, all the while censoring news of his illness and death on domestic social media and news outlets.[12] For the Xi regime, it was not enough to silence the dying Liu and even hide his death. The regime has actively tried to remove everything about this intellectual it finds unacceptable from the national political consciousness. Baidu, the largest internet search engine in China, has been censoring news about Liu as well as his pictures and all of his writings even for overseas users. The remaining items about Liu on Baidu portray him as a highly educated man and a political criminal who worked to undermine the Chinese nation and who probably worked with the United States government to do so.[13] For his ideas and activism, Liu is vilified by the state as a traitor who received from it magnanimous treatment at his death.

The CCP's reappropriation of the Leninist imperative of controlling and utilizing intellectuals after the decline of Chinese Communism reproduces the entrenched divide that educated party leaders have forged between themselves and the rest of the educated population. Chen Duxiu, Qu Qiubai, Mao Zedong, and other leaders exploited their positions and authority to consecrate themselves as genuine socialist revolutionaries, even though some of them only had temporary success. Since the 1980s, the party elites have been portraying themselves as architects and defenders of "socialism with Chinese characteristics" and identifying other educated people as intellectuals to be governed. The elites sometimes include party cadres with management authority on their side, precisely the kind of officials who expended much energy during the Mao era to present themselves as politically and morally superior to ordinary professional and white-collar workers. These symbolic boundaries, though as fuzzy and unstable as before, were reaffirmed by President Xi when he explained the appropriate relationship between the CCP and intellectuals. "Leading [party] cadres at various levels," he stated, should learn to "maintain contacts" and "become intimate friends and truthful friends" with "intellectuals." They should learn to "fully trust" these people and seek their "proposals and opinions" on important work and decisions. And they must welcome and adopt their well-intentioned criticism, forgive them for their erroneous views, and help them concentrate on their work.[14]

In other words, although the CCP regime no longer uses class struggle as a political-cum-analytical foundation to define and degrade the intellectual, the leadership still relies on the structural and functional assumptions of Marxism and Leninism as well as the experience of Chinese Communism to handle this subject. A heterogeneous population of educated people—in terms of training, occupation, income, politics, age, and other backgrounds—has thus reappeared in official discourse as a single social category, the intellectuals. These persons, some of whom have joined the party, are considered vital to national development;

their productivity and compliance have been and will be managed through praise, trust, and incentives as well as through assistance, supervision, and punishment. This official treatment of the intellectual is only somewhat different from or, more appropriately, an extension of the Yan'an method.

On the level of society, profound changes have occurred in the use of the intellectual as a classification of people since the 1980s. Thanks to state-sponsored political, market, educational, and other reforms, scholars and writers enjoy unprecedented latitude to invest the classification with moral and other meanings different from those promoted by the state under Chinese Communism and even afterward. During the last two decades, hundreds of books and thousands of articles on intellectuals were published. The enthusiasm of the writers and readers reflects the extent to which the intellectual has been objectified under the Mao regime; it also serves to reproduce the objectification with new symbolic boundaries. Some of the works discuss the origins of the term *zhishifenzi* and explore its connection to the French, Russian, and Confucian intellectual traditions. Some introduce influential Euro-American analyses of intellectuals, such as the work of Antonio Gramsci, Alvin Gouldner, Michel Foucault, Pierre Bourdieu, Zygmunt Bauman, and Russell Jacoby, each of whom promoted a different understanding of the subjects and their role in contemporary society. Some are translations of books written by these scholars or others. Many of the works combine elements from various analytical frameworks, explicitly or implicitly, to examine the lives of scholars and writers in twentieth-century China.[15] In particular, researchers use biographical, statistical, literary, and organizational data to study educated people under CCP rule, including the political courage and ideas of those who stood up to the party, such as Wang Shiwei (1906–1947), who was executed by the Mao regime, and Hu Feng, who was imprisoned for two decades not long after the PRC was established.[16]

The scholarship has not only served to rescue the intellectual from the ignominy incurred under Chinese Communism; some of the works have challenged the ongoing official understanding of the subject. The best example is the notable debate on the public intellectual (*gonggong zhishifenzi*) that occurred during the early 2000s. Maurizio Marinelli has shown that scholars and writers combined ideas from Chinese intellectual traditions and Western accounts of intellectuals to examine how the concept of the public intellectual would apply to contemporary China.[17] The debate reached its height when *Southern Personalities Weekly* (*Nanfang renwu zhoukan*), a popular magazine, selected, published, and celebrated a list of the fifty most influential Chinese public intellectuals. For the magazine, these individuals were not only professional experts who participated actively in public life and public debate; more importantly, they were "idealists" (*lixiang zhe*) with "critical spirits" whose work advanced "the onerous pursuit of social justice" (*daoyi*).[18] Proponents of this and similar politically charged concepts of the public intellectual encountered the wrath of the state. *People's Daily* published a scathing rebuttal that ignored the ideas and analyses the scholars and writers had drawn from Chinese history and philosophy to support their understanding of the public intellectual. The rebuttal, instead, stressed what it noted as the foreign, self-serving, and elitist nature of the notion. The author accused the proponents of seeking to "lure intellectuals on to an evil path" of working against the party and the Chinese people.[19] The state then used censorship, detention, and blacklisting of scholars and writers as tactics to halt the debate.[20] Nonetheless, the debate on the public intellectual persists within academic circles, albeit in a muted form, and continues online.[21]

The struggle to define the intellectual in the last three decades, like the one that occurred under Chinese Communism, has a prominent linguistic dimension. As the state ended its Marxian emphasis on class struggle and use of related classifications of people, other terms denoting educated persons and populations reemerged from under the umbrella classification of *zhishifenzi*. Table 4 summarizes the usage of various terms in *People's Daily* at ten-year intervals since the death of Chairman Mao in 1976. Even as the number of articles has increased dramatically in the official organ, for instance, from roughly 1,200 articles in January 1976 to 4,000 articles in January 2003, the usage of *zhishifenzi* has continued to decline. Meanwhile, the words *xuezhe* (scholars) and *zhuanjia* (experts), both of which carry positive meanings of knowledge, status, and influence, have become very popular in the newspaper, thanks to the CCP's emphasis on economic growth, technological development, and higher education. Other terms referring to educated persons have also seen varying degrees of revival.

Some scholars and writers have even chosen to replace *zhishifenzi* in their writings altogether with a term rarely used in the past. The term, *zhishi ren,* which literally means persons with knowledge, is part of the Japanese language and, like *zhishifenzi,* can serve as a singular, plural, or collective noun. *Zhishi ren* has been used in various kinds of analysis of Chinese society and even research on other societies. Between 1997 and 2006, at least 60 journal and newspaper articles used *zhishi ren* in their titles. The number increased to 149 in the following decade.[22] The term even appears occasionally in *People's Daily.*[23] Two of the early adopters offered an explanation of why they used *zhishi ren* instead of *zhishifenzi.* They argue correctly that the latter is a historically specific term, one that developed during China's transition to socialism. The term signals the inferior political and sometimes social status of the educated population. To these authors, it is therefore an obstacle to understanding that educated people have become the backbone of a "knowledge-based economy" that has since emerged on the Mainland.[24] More recently, another scholar has furnished a completely different reason for his switch to *zhishi ren* when writing about Chinese history. He associates the use of *zhishifenzi,* not with the Mao era or the project of Chinese Communism, but with the Dreyfus affair and the pursuit of social justice, the defense of human dignity, and other positive meanings embedded in the French term *les intellectuels.*

TABLE 4 Numbers of *People's Daily* Articles with Specific Terms for Educated Persons, 1976–2016

	1976	1986	1996	2006	2016
Zhishifenzi (intellectuals)	565	536	243	197	205
Xuezhe (scholars)	67	842	987	1,215	1,821
Zhuanjia (experts)	440	2,036	2,402	3,551	3,480
Wenren (literati)	48	71	76	79	134
Wenhua ren (cultural personnel)	4	16	28	31	79
Dushu ren (men of letters)	4	8	20	16	57

SOURCE: *People's Daily–Renmin Ribao (1946–Present).*

He contends that premodern China did not have many *zhishifenzi* because its political and social environment did not promote the above critical qualities in the individual. Literati were merely *zhishi ren,* or educated men; they were *not* intellectuals.[25] Other scholars and writers who use *zhishi ren* in their works rarely explain this linguistic choice of theirs. Nonetheless, they, too, alter the use of *zhishifenzi* through removing the social classification from their analysis of Chinese and other societies.

Finally, it is not difficult to find scholars and writers who regard themselves as intellectuals and, at the same time, attack this category of people for what they have been doing since the decline of Chinese Communism. Unlike their peers, these scholars and writers apparently refuse to redefine intellectuals as a morally responsible or politically mistreated group of people or even as indispensable to China's development. Like the critics of the intellectual class during the May Fourth movement, they observe that greed and selfishness as well as political apathy and cowardice plague the population of intellectuals. Their complaints, like those that appeared a century ago, are indictments of what they see as a wretched state of Chinese politics, culture, and society. The state encourages professionalization and consumerism, condones economic inequality and corruption, and suppresses social activism and political dissent. Under these circumstances, many intellectuals seek to profit themselves first and foremost. The latest example of such attacks comes from a sensational essay, "Ten Symptoms of Depravity of Chinese Intellectuals," which has been reposted repeatedly on the internet since 2016.[26] An excerpt from a recent novel, the essay features virtually all of the criticisms previously leveled against the intellectual class almost a century ago. Intellectuals, especially those who are highly educated, brag about their advanced degrees, professional expertise, and individual talents. They emphasize that they are sensitive, principled, and compassionate. Some highlight their intellectual innovations, comprehension of cutting-edge research, or love and grasp of Chinese culture. As a matter of fact, the author claims, China's intellectuals generally lack honesty, sincerity, social conscience, and ability. They produce little scholarship of value and add little understanding to anything, let alone Chinese culture. The author does not mention how CCP rule, past or present, contributes to this state of affairs. However, there is no mistaking that he thinks the regretable behavior of intellectuals is an outcome of a system of governance that rewards precisely braggadocio, self-aggrandizement, and deceitfulness.

To sum up, the struggle to define the intellectual in twenty-first-century China involves, once again, official representation and identification of the subject as well as unofficial reinterpretations of what the intellectual represents, even though the content of each of these three dimensions has changed dramatically since the demise of Chinese Communism. The struggle continues to affect official governance, social identity, and political resistance. No one knows how far into the future the classification will continue to have critical impact on Chinese politics, culture, and society, let alone whether the classification will regain life-and-death implications or become once more a rallying cry against official domination and even CCP rule. Nor can anyone tell whether the future of the classification will converge with what has happened to its counterparts in Western Europe or the United States, that is, *zhishifenzi* becomes a multifarious concept deployed primarily within academic circles for analytical purposes. One thing is clear, though. The intellectual as a classification of people has traveled a distinct path in China since the CCP's founding. A century later, the impact of the classification on Chinese society is still quite visible.

CHARACTER GLOSSARY

PINYIN	CHINESE CHARCTERS
a'ge	阿哥
Ai Qing	艾青
Bai mao nü	白毛女
Beida	北大
benren chushen	本人出身
Bian Zhongyun	卞仲耘
biji	笔记
Bo Gu	博古
Buju xiaojie de ren	不拘小节的人
Cai Yi	蔡仪
caidiao	彩调
canguan tuan	参观团
Changchun dianying zhipian chang	长春电影制片厂
Chen Chengze	陈承泽
Chen Duxiu	陈独秀
Chen Huangmei	陈荒煤
Chen Xuezhao	陈学昭
Chen Yi	陈毅
Cheng Fangwu	成仿吾
chengfen	成分

chun jingji guandian	纯经济观点
Cihai	辞海
cubao	粗暴
da maozi	大帽子
dangwai zhishifenzi gongzuochu	党外知识分子工作处
daoyi	道义
Dazhong dianying	大众电影
Dongbei renmin zhengfu	东北人民政府
Dongfang zazhi	东方杂志
duige	对歌
dushu ren	读书人
eba	恶霸
fanxing biji	反省笔记
Fanyou yundong	反右运动
fazhi	法治
Fei Xiaotong	费孝通
Feng Kexi	冯克熙
fengjian zhuyi	封建主义
fenzi	分子
Fu Sinian	傅斯年
fu xiangzhang	副乡长
Fu Zhongsun	傅钟孙
ganbu gongrenhua	幹部工人化
gaoji	高级
geming de zhishi jieji	革命的知识阶级
geming de zhishifenzi	革命的知识分子
geming junren	革命军人
geren yingxiong zhuyi	个人英雄主义
Gong Canguang	龚灿光
Gongchandang	共产党
gonggong zhishifenzi	公共知识分子
gongnong zhishifenzi	工农知识分子
gongren	工人
gongren jieji zhishifenzi	工人阶级知识分子
He Qifang	何其芳
hongjun zhanshi	红军战士

Hu	沪
Hu Feng	胡风
Huadong junzheng daxue	华东军政大学
Huadong renmin geming daxue	华东人民革命大学
Huai	淮
Huang Shaohong	黄绍竑
Huang Yaomian	黄药眠
Huangmei	黄梅
huixiang fe	回乡费
Hushi riji	护士日记
Jiang Nanxiang	蒋南翔
Jiang Tingfu	蒋廷黻
Jiang Xingren	蒋兴仁
jiao laoshi	较老实
jiaorou de zuozuo	娇柔的做作
jiating chengfen	家庭成分
jie	界
Jiefang ribao	解放日报
jieji	阶级
jieji yizifenzi	阶级异己分子
jinggao	警告
jishu renyuan	技术人员
jituan	集团
jiu	旧
jizhong ying	集中营
Juben	剧本
juewu	觉悟
junren	军人
Kang Sheng	康生
lao ganbu	老干部
laodong	劳动
laonian	老年
li	里
Li Dazhao	李大钊
Li Shaolin	李绍林
Liang Shuming	梁漱溟

liangmian xing	两面性
lianxi huiyi	联席会议
lilong shiye renyuan dengji weiyuanhui	里弄失业人员登记委员会
Lin Xiling	林希翎
Liu Sanjie	刘三姐
Liu Shaoqi	刘少奇
Liu Xiaobo	刘晓波
Liuzhou	柳州
lixiang zhe	理想者
Long Yinghua	龙英华
Lu Ge	鲁歌
Lü Ban	吕班
Lu Xun yishu xueyuan	鲁迅艺术学院
Ma Hong	马洪
Ma Yunfeng	马云风
Mei Lanfang	梅兰芳
Malie xueyuan	马列学院
Mao Dun	茅盾
Mao Zedong	毛泽东
mingfang	鸣放
Minzhu qingnian jinxingqu	民主青年进行曲
minzu zhenxing	民族振兴
Nanfang renwu zhoukan	南方人物周刊
ningque wulan	宁缺毋滥
nonghou de fengjian zhuyi secai	浓厚的封建主义色彩
nongmin	农民
pa chiku	怕吃苦
paidui	排队
Pang Zhuoheng	庞卓恒
Peng Pai	澎湃
Peng Shuzhi	彭述之
pingyi	评议
Qian Ruping	钱如平
Qiangjiu yundong	抢救运动
qiansan fe	遣散费
qianzhuang	钱庄

Qiao Yu	乔羽
Qingliang shan	清凉山
Qingnian zazhi	青年杂志
Qu	区
Qu Qiubai	瞿秋白
qunzhong luxian	群众路线
Renmin ribao	人民日报
renmin tuanti	人民团体
Shaanbei gongxue	陕北公学
shangdian	商店
shan'ge	山歌
Shanghai ganbu xuexiao	上海干部学校
Shanghai xinjiaoyu xueyuan	上海新教育学院
Shanghaishi chuli shiye zhishifenzi weiyuanhui	上海市处理失业知识分子委员会
Shanghaishi jiaoyuju	上海市教育局
shehui guanxi	社会关系
Shen Xia	沈霞
shi	士
shidafu	士大夫
shiye gongren	失业工人
shiye renyuan tongyi dengji	失业人员统一登记
shiye zhishifenzi	失业知识分子
shiying	使用
Sibu	四部
sishu	私塾
sixiang jie	思想界
sixiang luohou	思想落后
sixiang qingkuang	思想情况
Song Meiling	宋美龄
Subei	苏北
Sun Yatsen	孙逸仙/孙中山
Tan Tianrong	谭天荣
tanbai	坦白
tanbai congyan yinman congkuan	坦白从严，隐瞒从宽
Tao Lan	陶岚
toujiang	投降

Wang Guangqi	王光祈
Wang Ming	王明
Wang Shiwei	王实味
Wei Jingsheng	魏京生
Wei Junyi	韦君宜
Wei wancheng de xiju	未完成的喜剧
Wenhua gou	文化沟
wenhua ren	文化人
Wenhui bao	文汇报
wenren	文人
Wenxue pinglun	文学评论
Wenyi bao	文艺报
Wo sui siqu	我虽死去
Wu Jialin	吴家麟
Wu Jinnan	伍晋南
Wuben nüzi zhongxue	务本女子中学
wunü	舞女
Xi	锡
Xi Jinping	习近平
Xia Yan	夏衍
xiandaihua	现代化
xiang wenshu	乡文书
xiansheng	先生
Xiao Jianqiu	萧涧秋
xiao zichan jieji qingtiao jiaonong	小资产阶级情调较浓
xiaodu	消毒
Xin qingnian	新青年
xinggan	性感
xingqing jizao	性情急躁
xinwen jie	新闻界
Xu Jilin	许纪霖
Xu Yixin	徐一新
Xu Zhongnian	徐仲年
xueshu jie	学术界
xuexi renzhen	学习认真
xuezhe	学者

xunshi tuan	巡视团
xunyu zhidu	训育制度
Yan Fu	严复
Yan Zhongqiang	严仲强
Yan'an zhongyang yiyuan	延安中央医院
Yang Guangchi	杨光池
Yang Shangkun	杨尚昆
Yang Zhaolong	杨兆龙
yaoqiu jinbu	要求进步
yituan heqi	一团和气
yixue jie	医学界
youhong youzhuan	又红又专
Yu Guangyuan	于光远
Yu Jie	余杰
Yu Pingbo	俞平伯
Yue	越
Yun Daiying	恽代英
Zaochun eryue	早春二月
Zhang Bojun	章伯钧
Zhang Dongsun	张东荪
Zhang Guotao	张国焘
Zhang Naiqi	章乃器
Zhang Ruxin	张如心
Zhang Taiyan	章太炎
Zhang Wentian	张闻天
Zhao Chaogou	赵超构
Zheng Yimei	郑逸梅
Zheng Zhenduo	郑振铎
Zhengfeng yundong	整风运动
zhengzhi qingkuang	政治情况
zhishi	知识
zhishifenzi	知识分子
zhishifenzi de fengcai	知识分子的风采
zhishi jieji	知识阶级
zhishi qingnian	知识青年
zhishi ren	知识人

Zhonggong zhongyang zhong xuexi weiyuanhui	中共中央总学习委员会
Zhongguo guomindang	中国国民党
Zhongguo minzhu cujinhui	中国民主促进会
Zhongguo minzhu jianguohui	中国民主建国会
Zhongguo minzhu tongmeng	中国民主同盟
Zhongguo renmin kangri junshi zhengzhi daxue	中国人民抗日军事政治大学
Zhongnanhai	中南海
Zhongyang dangxiao	中央党校
Zhongyang lujun junguan xuexiao	中央陆军军官学校
Zhongyang shuiwu xuexiao	中央税务学校
Zhou Dajue	周大觉
Zhou Enlai	周恩来
Zhou Yang	周扬
Zhu De	朱德
Zhu Shouzhong	朱守忠
zhuanjia	专家
zhuguan zhuyi	主观主义
zhuti	主体
zichan jieji zhishifenzi	资产阶级知识分子
zijue	自觉
zizhuan	自传
zuofeng zhengpai	作风正派
zuoguan dang laoye	做官当老爷

ABBREVIATIONS

LSZ   *Zhongguo dangdai wenxue yanjiu ziliao: Liu Sanjie zhuanji*
PDRR   *People's Daily–Renmin Ribao (1946–Present)* database
RMRB   *Renmin Ribao*
SMA   Shanghai Municipal Archives

1. REEXAMINING THE INTELLECTUAL AND CHINESE COMMUNISM

1. Wang Youqin, *Wenge shounanzhe*, 35–62. A valuable, mid-2000s documentary about Bian's murder is available online, with her husband and others recounting events surrounding her death; see Hu Jie, *Wo sui siqu*.

2. *Oxford English Dictionary*, s.v. "objectify," accessed August 9, 2017, www.oed.com/view/Entry/129625?redirectedFrom = objectify.

3. From here onward, I use "the intellectual" or "intellectuals" instead of *zhishifenzi* to anchor this book in the literature on the intellectual, unless the context requires use of the Chinese term for clarity.

4. Kurzman and Owens, "Sociology of Intellectuals," 63.

5. Kritzman, *Michel Foucault*, 324.

6. Browning and Siegelbaum, "Frameworks for Social Engineering," 231.

7. For examples on the Soviet Union, see Alexopoulous, *Stalin's Outcasts*; Fitzpatrick, "Ascribing Class." For examples on China, see Kraus, *Class Conflict*; Kuhn, "Chinese Views of Social Classification"; Zhang, "Land Reform in Yang Village."

8. Smith, "Global History of Communism," 4.

9. For example, Chen, *Thought Reform;* Goldman, *Literary Dissent;* Goldman, *China's Intellectuals;* Cheek, *Propaganda and Culture;* Ip, *Intellectuals in Revolutionary China;* Cheek, *Intellectual in Modern Chinese History,* chaps. 2–4.

10. For example, West and Zimmermann, "Doing Gender"; Lamont, *Money, Morals, and Manners;* Bowker and Star, *Sorting Things Out;* Brubaker et al., "Ethnicity as Cognition."

11. Fitzpatrick, *Tear Off the Masks,* 3, 7.

12. Datta, "New Approaches to Intellectuals"; Forth, "Body Politics of the Dreyfus Affair."

13. Bauman, *Legislators and Interpreters,* 8.

14. Kochetkova, *Myth of the Russian Intelligentsia,* 5–6.

15. Townsley, "Public Intellectual Trope," 47.

16. Müller, "Literature of Action," 11.

17. Hall, *Representation,* 1.

18. Bourdieu, *On the State,* 164.

19. Bourdieu, *Language and Symbolic Power,* 166.

20. Loveman, "Primitive Accumulation of Symbolic Power," 1655.

21. Bourdieu, *Language and Symbolic Power,* 74.

22. Ibid., 170.

23. For example, Apter and Saich, *Revolutionary Discourse;* Knight, *Rethinking Mao;* Yu, "Maoist Discourse."

24. For example, Cheek, *Propaganda and Culture;* Chang, "Mechanics of State Propaganda"; Evans, "Language of Liberation"; Hung, *Mao's New World.*

25. For example, Holm, *Art and Ideology;* Clark, *Chinese Cinema.*

26. Perry, *Anyuan,* 4.

27. Brubaker and Cooper, "Beyond 'Identity,'" 15.

28. Bourdieu, *Language and Symbolic Power,* 120.

29. Lamont and Molnár, "The Study of Boundaries," 168.

30. For example, Bowker and Star, *Sorting Things Out;* Stagier, *Learning Difference;* Szreter et al., *Categories and Contexts.*

31. For example, Friedman et al., *Chinese Village, Socialist State;* Ruf, *Cadres and Kin,* chap. 3; Zhang, "Land Reform in Yang Village."

32. For example, Cochran, *Capitalist Dilemma;* Pepper, *Radicalism and Education Reform,* chaps. 7–13; Yang, "Campaign to Suppress Counterrevolutionaries"; Vogel, "From Friendship to Comradeship"; Croll, "Marriage Choice and Status Groups"; Diamant, *Revolutionizing the Family.*

33. Chen, *Thought Reform.*

34. Bowker and Star, *Sorting Things Out,* 11.

35. Brubaker et al., *Nationalist Politics and Everyday Ethnicity,* 35.

36. Bourdieu, *Language and Symbolic Power,* 220.

37. Bowker and Star, *Sorting Things Out,* 16.

38. Friedman et al., *Chinese Village, Socialist State,* chap. 4.

39. Zhang, "Land Reform in Yang Village."

40. For example, Whyte, *Small Groups and Political Rituals;* Esherick, "The Ye Family"; U, "Dangerous Privilege."

41. Ip, *Intellectuals in Revolutionary China;* Perry, *Anyuan.*

42. This difference had grave implications on the forms of violence and discipline condoned, instigated, and sanctioned by the party against those identified as intellectuals.

43. Gramsci, *Prison Notebooks,* 419–25.

44. Bourdieu, *Practical Reason,* 11.

45. Bourdieu, *Pascalian Meditations,* 2.

2. THE BIRTH OF A CLASSIFICATION

1. Liu Xiaobo, *Zhongguo zhishifenzi;* Xu Jilin, *Zhishifenzi shilun;* Yang Lian and Wei Jingsheng, "Wenhua yu zhishifenzi"; Yu Jie, *Panghuang yingxiong lu.*

2. Bowker and Star, *Sorting Things Out,* 5.

3. Kritzman, *Michel Foucault,* 324.

4. For example, Xu Jilin, *Zhishifenzi shilun,* 2–6; Huang Ping, "Zhishifenzi."

5. For examples of the positive and negative interpretations, see Forth, "Body Politics of the Dreyfus Affair"; Brower, "Russian Intelligentsia."

6. For example, Chow, *May Fourth Movement;* Schwarcz, *Chinese Enlightenment;* Schwartz, *May Fourth Movement.*

7. Dirlik, *Chinese Communism.*

8. Wang Zengjin, *Houxiandai yu zhishifenzi,* 12.

9. These numbers are from a search in *Dacheng laozhoukan quanwen shujuku,* accessed October 30, 2015.

10. Wang Zengjin, *Houxiandai yu zhishifenzi,* 16–18.

11. Liu, *Translingual Practice,* 302.

12. For example, see Sun, "From Literati to Legal Professionals."

13. Müller, "Literature of Action"; Kawamura, "Sociology and Socialism."

14. *Dacheng laozhoukan quanwen shujuku,* accessed October 30, 2015.

15. Wang Zengjin, *Houxiandai yu zhishifenzi,* 16–18.

16. Belgion, "Banda lun zhishi jieji."

17. Sun, "From Literati to Legal Professionals"; Culp, "Culture Work."

18. Fung, *Intellectual Foundations,* 191.

19. Chow, *May Fourth Movement.*

20. Perry, *Shanghai on Strike.*

21. Dirlik, *Chinese Communism;* Fung, *Intellectual Foundations.*

22. Kuhn, "Chinese Views," 18.

23. Grieder, *Intellectuals and the State,* 15–16.

24. Li Huaxing, *Minguo jiaoyushi,* 621.

25. Zhang Guotao, "Zhishi jieji."

26. Qu Qiubai, "Zhengzhi yundong."

27. *Wang Yunwu da cidian* (Shanghai: Shangwu yinshuguan, 1930).

28. Jiang Tingfu, "Zhishi jieji yu zhengzhi," 15.

29. *Cihai* (Shanghai: Zhonghua shuju, 1940).

30. Nor was the term included in *Baihua cidian* (Vernacular dictionary) or *Guoyin changyong cihui* (Common phrases in standard Chinese), published by the famous Commercial Press in 1938 and 1949, respectively. The exception is the 1937 edition of *Guoyu cidian* (National language dictionary), published by the same press.

31. Wang Zengjin, *Houxiandai yu zhishifenzi,* 18.

32. For example, Ying Zhun, "Hu Sha suibi"; "Tuanjie de zengjin"; Ying Sun, "Guonan xiaoshuo conghua"; Wu Jing, "Mingzhe de zhuxi."

33. Fei Xiaotong, "Lun zhishi jieji"; Zhang Pijie, "Lun zhishi jieji"; Dong Weichuan, "Zhonghua zhishi jieji."

34. Qu Qiubai, "Zhengzhi yundong."

35. For example, Mao Zedong, "Fandui benben zhuyi"; Qu Qiubai, "'Women' shi shei"; Wang Ming, "Shisan nian lai."

36. Van de Ven, *From Friend to Comrade,* 101.

37. Ibid., chap. 5.

38. The term *zhishi jieji* seldom appeared in *People's Daily* (*Renmin ribao*), the official organ of the CCP. Between 1949 and 1951, it was used only in eight articles. It resurfaced in 1957 and appeared in another 19 articles during the rest of the Mao era. Most of the appearances, however, are from the authors quoting phrases and sentences from works of Mao or other famous people published before the 1930s. The evidence is based on a search in PDRR, accessed October 20, 2017.

39. Wang Xunsen, "Jindai zhishifenzi."

40. Chen Duxiu, *Chen Duxiu zhuzhu xuan,* vol. 1, 145.

41. Fu Sinian, "Zhongguo xueshu sixiang."

42. Furth, "Intellectual Change," 32.

43. Peng Yueyu, "Du le ailuo xianke," 43.

44. Grieder, *Intellectuals and the State,* 9–10.

45. Ling Guang, "Zhishi jieji," 1.

46. Ru Wei, "Tan zhishi jieji," 34.

47. Jian Hu, "Zhishi jieji," 2.

48. Grieder, *Intellectuals and the State,* 14.

49. Zarrow, *Anarchism,* 4; Dirlik, *Chinese Communism,* 90.

50. Zheng Zhenduo, "Zailun," 1.

51. Zheng Zhenduo, "Shehui gaizao yundong," 3.

52. Qu Qiubai, "Shehui yundong," 3.

53. Zhang Dongsun, "Zhongguo zhishi jieji."

54. Gu, "Who Was Mr. Democracy?"

55. Wang Guangqi, "Shaonian Zhongguo," 6.

56. Yun Daiying, "Shaonian Zhongguo," 3.

57. Chen Chengze, "Zhishi jieji."

58. Chow, *May Fourth Movement,* chaps. 3 and 7; Schwarcz, *Chinese Enlightenment,* chap. 2.

59. Zhang Guotao, "Zhishi jieji," 99.

60. Dirlik, *Chinese Communism,* 95–120.

61. Ibid., 195–245.

62. Giddens, *Modern Social Theory,* 37

63. Gouldner, *Against Fragmentation,* 8.

64. Marx and Engels, "Manifesto of the Communist Party."

65. Gouldner, *Against Fragmentation,* 145.

66. Karabel, "Question of Intellectuals," 14, 17, 22.

67. Karabel, "Problem of the Intelligentsia," 271.

68. Ibid., 273, 275.

69. Lenin, *On the Intelligentsia.*

70. Lenin, *Selected Works,* vol. 1, 326.

71. Van de Ven, *From Friend to Comrade,* chap. 3.

72. Chen Duxiu, "Zhongguo guomin geming," 561–62.

73. Peng Shuzhi, "Geming zhi lingdao zhe," 12–13.

74. Qu Qiubai, "Shijie de shehui gaizao" and "Xiandai laodong zhanzheng."

75. Lozovsky, "Gongchan zhuyi," 87, 101.

76. For example, "Xuanchuan wenti yijue an" and "Duiyu zuzhi wenti yijue an."

77. Qu Qiubai, "Shijie de shehui gaizao," 17.

78. Peng Shuzhi, "Geming zhi lingdao zhe."

79. "Zhongguo gongchandang dierci quanguo dahuo xuanyan."

80. Brower, "Russian Intelligentsia."

3. VISIBLE SUBJECTS IN THE COUNTRYSIDE

Epigraph: Mao Zedong, *Selected Works,* vol. 3, 73.

1. Ma Hong, "Qinxue sannian."

2. Ma Ya, "Daonian fuqin ma hong."

3. Ma Hong, "Qinxue sannian."

4. Bourdieu and Wacquant, *Reflexive Sociology,* 105.

5. For example, Selden, *Yenan Way;* Holm, *Art and Ideology.*

6. For example, Cheek, "Fading of Wild Lilies."

7. Bourdieu and Wacquant, *Reflexive Sociology,* 239.

8. For a theoretical and in-depth account of this process, see Apter and Saich, *Revolutionary Discourse.*

9. Van de Ven, *From Friend to Comrade,* 162; Saich, "Chinese Communist Party."

10. "Zhongyang ju baogao."

11. Yang Fengcheng, *Zhishifenzi lilun,* 50.

12. "Zhongyang ju baogao."

13. Hofheinz, *Broken Wave,* chap. 4.

14. "Zhonggong tonggao diqihao."

15. Quoted in Michael Luk, *Chinese Bolshevism,* 211–12.

16. Van de Ven, *From Friend to Comrade,* chaps. 3 and 4.

17. Hofheinz, *Broken Wave,* chap. 4.

18. Averill, "Jiangxi Communist Movement"; Averill, "Chinese Revolution"; Ip, *Intellectuals in Revolutionary China,* 48, 56.

19. Ip, *Intellectuals in Revolutionary China,* 65.

20. Ibid., chaps. 3 and 4.

21. Yang Fengcheng, *Zhishifenzi lilun,* 51.

22. Kampen, *Mao Zedong, Zhou Enlai,* chap. 1.

23. Yang Fengcheng, *Zhishifenzi lilun,* 49–56; He Fang, *Dangshi biji,* 244–45.

24. Yu Boliu and Ling Buji, *Zhonggong suqu shi,* 772–81, 797–809.

25. Li Guoqiang, *Zhongyang suqu jiaoyu,* 36; Pepper, *Radicalism and Education Reform,* 121.

26. Guo, *China's Security State*, 13.

27. Zeng Chenggui and Xu Kaixi, *Hubei xin minzhu gemingshi*, 272; Zhou Chunyun and Zhang Yongchun, *Yunluo de hongxing*, 61, 86.

28. Zhou Chunyun and Zhang Yongchun, *Yunluo de hongxing*, 57.

29. Quoted in Hu Ping, *Chanji*, 10.

30. Xia Daohan and Chen Liming, *Jiangxi suqu shi*, 286–311; Li Guoqiang, *Zhongyang suqu jiaoyu*, 33–37.

31. Zhu Hongzhao, *Yan'an richang shenghuo*, 4–5.

32. Guo, *China's Security State*, 46.

33. Mao Zedong, "Fan toujiang tigang."

34. Karabel, "Problem of the Intelligentsia."

35. Wen Si, *Huiguo kangzhan*.

36. Zhu Hongzhao, *Yan'an richang shenghuo*, 5.

37. Zhang Junbo et al., *Yan'an suiyue*.

38. Ibid.

39. Wang Peiyuan, *Yan'an luyi*, 7, 12.

40. Ibid., chaps. 1–3.

41. Quoted in Wang Peiyuan, *Yan'an luyi*, 31.

42. Holm, *Art and Ideology*, chaps. 1 and 2; Wang Peiyuan, *Yan'an luyi*, 29–31, 52–56, 128–144; Zhu Hongzhao, *Yan'an richang shenghuo*, 95.

43. For example, Wu Jiemin, *Yan'an Malie xueyuan;* Liu Baoguan, *Xue yu huo de xili*.

44. Cheng Zhongyuan, *Zhang Wentian zhuan*.

45. Wang Peiyuan, *Yan'an luyi*, 31.

46. Li Zhimin, *Geming ronglu*, 22–23.

47. Guo Bixuan et al., *Yan'an jingshen tanyuan*, 35–37; Yang Changchun, *Yige lianluoyuan*, 21–22.

48. Zhang Junbo et al., *Yan'an suiyue*, 25.

49. Zhu Hongzhao, *Yan'an richang shenghuo*, 93; Zhao Yan, "Yanshui changliu."

50. Apter and Saich, *Revolutionary Discourse*, xvi.

51. Ibid., 54–59; Dai Moulin and Cao Zhongbin, *Wang Ming Zhuan*, 243–45.

52. Gao Xinmin and Zhang Shujun, *Yan'an zhengfeng*, chaps. 1–3.

53. Mao Zedong, *Selected Works*, vol. 3, 14–16, 35–52, and 53–68.

54. Ibid., vol. 3, 21.

55. Zhang Wentian, *Zhang Wentian xuanji*, 7–13, 71–79.

56. Ibid., 313–14.

57. Ibid., 329–30.

58. Wang Peiyuan, *Yan'an luyi*, chap. 6.

59. Stranahan, *Molding the Medium*, chaps. 2 and 3.

60. Liu Shaoqi, *Selected Works*, vol. 1, 107–68.

61. Yang Fengcheng, *Zhishifenzi lilun*, 61–74; *Zhengfeng wenjian huiji*.

62. Gao Xinmin and Zhang Shujun, *Yan'an zhengfeng*, 159–65.

63. Stranahan, *Molding the Medium*, chap. 2.

64. Gao Xinmin and Zhang Shujun, *Yan'an zhengfeng*, 164–203; Yan'an zhongyang dangxiao zhengfeng yundong bianxiezu, *Yan'an zhongyang dangxiao*.

65. Apter and Saich, *Revolutionary Discourse*, 263.

66. Cheek, "Making Maoism," 304–27.

67. Smedley, *Great Road*, 2.

68. Quoted in Zhu Hongzhao, *Yan'an richang shenghuo*, 116–17.

69. Cheng Zhongyuan, *Zhang Wentian zhuan*, 493–508.

70. Yuan Xuezhi, "Xishou youxiu zhishifenzi rudang," 131.

71. Foucault, *Discipline and Punish*, 135.

72. Wang Zhongfang, *Yan'an fengqing hua*, 19.

73. Wei Wei, "Wo de yinlu ren," 120–21.

74. The CCP validated such self-refashioning through policy. Shortly before the 1949 takeover, the party leadership declared that intellectuals and others who had served in the Red Army for a year or more were eligible to change their personal status (*chengfen*) to revolutionary soldier (*geming junren*). See "Zhongyang guanyu dizhu funong zhishifenzi ruwu gaibian chengfen de guiding."

75. For example, see Zhu Hongzhao, *Yan'an richang shenghuo*, 337–55.

76. Zhu Hongzhao, *Yan'an hebian*, 199.

77. Wang Peiyuan, *Yan'an luyi*, 289–90; Zhu Hongzhao, *Yan'an hebian*, 201.

78. Chen Xuezhao, *Yan'an fangwen ji*, 258, 398, 402.

79. Yan'an zhongyang dangxiao zhengfeng yundong bianxiezu, *Yan'an zhongyang dangxiao*, vol. 1, 26.

80. Quoted in Li Hui, *Hu Feng jituan*, 40–41.

81. Zhang Junbo et al., *Yan'an suiyue*, 56.

82. Ibid., 77–79.

83. Ibid., 22–31.

84. Shen Xia, *Yan'an sinian*, 63.

85. Bourdieu, *On the State*, 3.

4. THE SELF-FULFILLING PROPHECY OF A REGISTRATION DRIVE

1. For example, see Yang, "Campaign to Suppress Counterrevolutionaries"; Rawnsley, "Resist America and Assist Korea"; Chen, *Thought Reform*; Dikötter, *Tragedy of Liberation*.

2. For example, Gao Dashuai, "Shiye zhishifenzi de dengji."

3. Howe, *Employment and Economic Growth*, 34.

4. Zhang, *Economic Cold War*; O'Brien, *American Editor*.

5. Zhongguo shehui kexue yuan and Zhongyang dang'an guan, *Jingji dang'an ziliao*, 158.

6. Shanghaishi laodongju, "Shiye laodong jiuye renshu," 1.

7. Howe, *Employment and Economic Growth*, 96.

8. Shanghaishi laodongju, "Shiye renyuan anzhi qingkuang," 2–3.

9. The figures are based on a workforce of 1.76 to 1.85 million people in urban Shanghai between 1952 and 1955; see Guojia tongjiju, *Tongji ziliao huibian*, 340.

10. Wu Li, "Jianguo chuqi," vol. 52, 67–68.

11. Zhonggong Shanghai shiwei dangshi yanjiushi, *Zhongguo gongchandang zai Shanghai*, 369.

12. Shanghaishi jiaoyuju, "Putong jiaoyu gaikuang."

13. Wu Li, "Jianguo chuqi," 68–69.

14. Shanghishi jiaoyuju, "Yangshupu zhongxue qingkuang," 7.

15. "Shanghaishi renmin zhengfu gongshangju 1950 nian gongzuo zongjie," 95.

16. Zhongguo renmin yinhang Shanghaishi jinrong yanjousuo, "Shanghai siying jinrongye," 1092–100.

17. Zhonggong Shanghaishi duiwai jingji maoyi gongzuo weiyuanhui, "Shanghai siying jinchukou," 1114–15.

18. Xiong Yuezhi, *Shanghai tongshi*, vol. 14, 233–35, 277–80.

19. "Jiefang chuqi Shanghai pujiao xitong de jieguan zhengdun he gaizao," 31.

20. Shanghai wufan yundong zhuanti bianxie xiaozu, "Shanghai wufan yundong," 875.

21. Howe, *Employment and Economic Growth*, 96.

22. "Shanghai wufan yundong," 875.

23. Yang, "Campaign to Suppress Counterrevolutionaries."

24. Song Lanfang, "Shijiao de tudi gaige," 178.

25. An early 1930s survey shows that almost half of the men in the countryside had received some schooling. Among them, two-thirds had gone to traditional tutor school for an average of four years. Pepper, *Radicalism and Education Reform*, 77.

26. Ibid., 412.

27. "Huadong junzheng daxue Shanghai zhaosheng weiyuanhui tonggao."

28. "Shanghai zhishi qingnian suijun nanxia fuwutuan zhaosheng tonggao."

29. "Zhongguo renmin jiefangjun huadongqu songhu jingbei budui wenhua ganbu xunliantuan zhaosheng jianzhang."

30. "Wenyichu disici zhao wenyi gongzuozhe tonggao."

31. "Zhongguo renmin jiefangjun dijiu bingtuan zhishi qingnian xunlianban zhaosheng jianzhang."

32. "Huadong renmin geming daxue zhaosheng weiyuanhui fabang tonggao."

33. "Zhongyang shuiwu xuexiao huadong fenxiao zhaosheng jianzhang."

34. "Shanghai ganbu xuexiao shoutuo zhaokao zhongyang renmin zhengfu jiguan gongzuo renyuan jianzhang."

35. "Dongbei renmin zhengfu zhaopin zhuanjia jiaoshou ji ge bumen gongzuo renyuan jianzhang."

36. "Zhongyang renmin zhengfu zhong gongyebu gongzuo renyuan xunlianban zhaosheng jianzhang."

37. "Dongbei renmin zhengfu gongyebu pinqing zhuanjia jiaoshou gongchengshi yishi kuaijishi ji geji jishu renyuan tonggao."

38. Guojia tongjiju, *Tongji zilian huibian*, 190–91.

39. Ibid., 157–75, 199–203.

40. Ibid., 190–91.

41. Shanghaishi renmin zhengfu, "Choujian chuli shiye zhishifenzi weiyuanhui"; Shanghaishi chili shiye zhishifenzi weiyuanhui, "Yi nian lai zongjie," "Gongzuo renyuan jinxing zongjie de zongjie baogao," and "Zuzhi chengli chuli shiye zhishifenzi weiyuanhui."

42. Gao Dashuai, "Shiye zhishifenzi," 15, fn. 2.

43. Shanghaishi renmin zhengfu, "Choujian chuli shiye zhishifenzi weiyuanhui," 56.

44. For example, "Zhengwuyuan guanyu laodong jiuye wenti," 178–79.

45. Shanghaishi renmin zhengfu, "Choujian chuli shiye zhishifenzi weiyuanhui," 57.

46. Ibid., 56–59.

47. Ibid.; Shanghaishi chili shiye zhishifenzi weiyuanhui, "Gongzuo renyuan jinxing zongjie de zongjie baogao," 20.

48. Foucault, *Discipline and Punish,* 190, 192.

49. Shanghaishi renmin zhengfu, "Choujian chuli shiye zhishifenzi weiyuanhui," 56.

50. Shanghaishi chili shiye zhishifenzi weiyuanhui, "Shizhi wuzhengjian zhe."

51. Shanghaishi renmin zhengfu, "Choujian chuli shiye zhishifenzi weiyuanhui," 104.

52. Shanghaishi laodong jiuye weiyuanhui, "Shiye renyuan tongyi dengji."

53. Shanghaishi laodong jiuye weiyuanhui, "Gongzuo renyuan shouce."

54. Shanghaishi laodong jiuye weiyuanhui, "Laodong jiuye dengji wenti," 8–16.

55. "Gongzuo renyuan shouce," 4–9.

56. Shanghaishi laodongju, "Shiye renyuan anzhi qingkuang," 13; Shanghaishi renmin zhengfu, "Choujian chuli shiye zhishifenzi weiyuanhui," 103.

57. Shanghaishi chili shiye zhishifenzi weiyuanhui, "Yi nian lai zongjie," 5.

58. Ibid., 6.

59. Shanghaishi renmin zhengfu, "Choujian chuli shiye zhishifenzi weiyuanhui," 103.

60. Shanghaishi chili shiye zhishifenzi weiyuanhui, "Gongzuo renyuan jinxing zongjie de zongjie baogao," 1.

61. Ibid., 17–19.

62. Ibid., 4.

63. Shanghaishi renmin zhengfu, "Choujian chuli shiye zhishifenzi weiyuanhui," 106.

64. Shanghaishi chili shiye zhishifenzi weiyuanhui ji bangongshi, "Jiesu gongzuo baogao," 12–13.

65. Shanghaishi chili shiye zhishifenzi weiyuanhui, "Yi nian lai zongjie," 8.

66. Shanghaishi chili shiye zhishifenzi weiyuanhui, "Waifu laihu zhaopin shizhi."

67. Shanghaishi chili shiye zhishifenzi weiyuanhui, "Jiesu gongzuo baogao," 14.

68. Shanghaishi chili shiye zhishifenzi weiyuanhui, "Yi nian lai zongjie," 10–11.

69. Ibid., 13–14.

70. Shanghaishi chili shiye zhishifenzi weiyuanhui, "Waifu laihu zhaopin shizhi."

71. Shanghaishi chili shiye zhishifenzi weiyuanhui, "Yi nian lai zongjie," 14.

72. Shanghaishi chili shiye zhishifenzi weiyuanhui, "Gongzuo renyuan jinxing zongjie de zongjie baogao," 18–19.

73. Shanghishi jiaoyuju, "Xin jiaoyu xueyuan dibaqi xuexiban," 9.

74. Ibid., 10–11.

75. Ibid., 14.

76. Qin Yi, *Xiao zichan jieji,* 40–41, 45.

77. Shanghishi jiaoyuju, "Xin jiaoyu xueyuan dibaqi xuexiban," 9.

78. Ibid., 9–12.

79. Foucault, *Discipline and Punish,* 190–92.

80. Ibid., 173.

81. Shanghishi jiaoyuju, "Xin jiaoyu xueyuan dibaqi xuexiban."

82. U, *Disorganizing China,* chap. 2.

83. Shanghishi jiaoyuju, "Xueyuan fenpei gongzuo yijian," 1–2.

84. Bowker and Star, *Sorting Things Out,* 42.

5. CLASSIFICATION AND ORGANIZATION IN
A SCHOOL SYSTEM

1. For a summary of this episode, see Walder, *China under Mao*, 27–31. For an analysis of why the Rescue Campaign happened, see Wu, "Yan'an's Iron Bodhisattva."

2. Wei Junyi, *Sitong lu*, 7–20.

3. Ibid., 24

4. Goffman, *Stigma*.

5. U, *Disorganizing China*.

6. Smith, *Conceptual Practices of Power*, 15.

7. Ma Feihai, "Shanghai jiaoshi yundong," 165.

8. Shanghai lishi yanjiusuo jiaoshi yundong lishizu, *Shanghai jiaoshi huiyilu*.

9. Shanghshi jiaoyuju, "Wuben Nüzhong qingkuang," 12.

10. Shanghshi jiaoyuju, "Jiaozhiyuan sixiang gaizao xuexi."

11. For example, see the spring, summer, and winter issues of *Wenhui bao* published in 1952.

12. Shanghshi jiaoyuju, "Jiaozhiyuan sixiang gaizao xuexi."

13. Ibid., 29–30.

14. Shanghshi jiaoyuju, "Xingzheng renyuan pinzhi elie tanwu deng wenti," 47.

15. U, *Disorganizing China*, 37, 125–29.

16. Shanghshi jiaoyuju, "Nanyang mofan zhongxue sixiang gaizao," 38–43.

17. Xin minzhu zhuyi qingniantuan Shanghaishi weiyuanhui, "Jiaozhiyuan jinxing sixiang gaizao," 43–44.

18. Shanghshi jiaoyuju, "Diyiqi sixiang gaizao xuexiban," 36.

19. Ibid., 32–39.

20. Shanghshi jiaoyuju, "Chufen wenti de pifu." Zhu found himself attacked repeatedly and put into labor reform by the authorities because of his background and conduct. During the Cultural Revolution, his defense of the fallen CCP vice chairman Liu Shaoqi and criticism of other leaders brought about his "execution by shooting" as an "active counterrevolutionary and unrepentant criminal." See also Li Yaosong, *Ningxia geming yinglie*, vol. 2, chap. 22.

21. Xiang Bolong, *Jiaoyu weisheng tiyu xitong*, 24–25.

22. Shanghshi jiaoyuju, "Chuli jiu renyuan gongzuo," 8.

23. Ibid., 9, 13.

24. Shanghshi jiaoyuju, "Jiaoyu shiye linian tongji," 39.

25. Shanghshi jiaoyuju, "Jiaozhi yuangong zhengzhi qingkuang," 2.

26. U, *Disorganizing China*, 74–75.

27. Lü Xingwei, *Shanghai putong jiaoyushi*, 29–32.

28. Culp, *Articulating Citizenship*, 165.

29. Lü Xingwei, *Shanghai putong jiaoyushi*, 40, 45; Shanghshi jiaoyuju, "Jiaoyu shiye linian tongji," 16.

30. U, *Disorganizing China*, 62–67.

31. Shanghshi jiaoyuju, "Ganbu peibei qingkuang."

32. Shanghshi jiaoyuju, "Zhengzhi taidu jiating chushen diaocha," 2.

33. Bourdieu, *Outline*, 189–90.

34. Shanghshi jiaoyuju, "Zhengzhi jiaoshi shuqi xunlianban," 18.

35. Bourdieu, *Logic of Practice*, 122.

36. Shanghishi jiaoyuju, "Zhongdeng jiaoyu dangyuan peibei," 39.

37. Shanghishi jiaoyuju, "Zhixing dang dui zhishifenzi zhengce de qingkuang," 3.

38. Westphal and Khanna, "Keeping Directors in Line."

39. Shanghishi jiaoyuju, "Jiaoyuju gongzuo jihua," 55.

40. Zhonggong Shanghai shiwei xuanchuan bu, "Xuexiao gongzuo de zhishi tongzhi baogao," 38–39.

41. Ibid., 39.

42. Shanghishi jiaoyuju, "Xuexiao jiaoyu zhiliang de diaocha," 54.

43. Shanghishi jiaoyuju, "Putong jiaoyu gongzuo jiancha," 59.

44. Ibid., 34–37.

45. Shanghishi jiaoyuju, "Zhixing dang dui zhishifenzi zhengce de qingkuang," 36.

46. Ibid., 76–80.

47. Shanghishi jiaoyuju, "Chuli jiu renyuan gongzuo," 11–12.

48. Ibid.

49. Shanghishi jiaoyuju, "Jieguan gongzuo zongjie," 124, 133.

50. Shanghishi jiaoyuju, "Yi yue ban xuehui zongjie," 8.

51. Ibid.

52. Shanghishi jiaoyuju, "Waizi jintie xuexiao qingkuang," 4.

53. Wakeman, "'Cleanup,'" 56–57.

54. Zhonggong Shanghaishi jiaoqu gongzuo weiyuanhui, "Zhenya fangeming de qizhong qingkuang."

55. Goffman, *Stigma*, 102.

56. Qin Yi, *Xiao zichan jieji*, 44–45.

57. Jun Mo, "Sixiang jiancha."

58. Ibid.

59. He Yurun, "Women fangwen."

60. Qin Yi, *Xiao zichan jieji*, 47.

61. Zhang Hanzheng, "Sanzhong jiantao de leixing."

62. Qin Yi, *Xiao zichan jieji*, 44.

63. Ibid., 45–46.

64. Du Ming, "Jiuzheng ziwo piping."

65. Shanghishi jiaoyuju, "Jiaozhiyuan sixiang gaizao xuexi."

66. Wu Yue, "Gaizao sixiang."

67. Qin Yi, *Xiao zichan jieji*, 45–46.

68. Ibid., 32, 45–46, 49.

69. Wu Yue, "Gaizao sixiang."

70. Qin Yi, *Xiao zichan jieji*, 45.

71. Ibid., 47–48.

72. Smith, *Conceptual Practices of Power*, 93–94.

73. Blecher and White, *Micropolitics in Contemporary China*; Walder, *Communist Neo-Traditionalism*; Frazier, *Chinese Industrial Workplace*.

74. Kraus, *Class Conflict*; Ruf, *Cadres and Kin*; Zhang, "Land Reform." For a summary, see Walder, *China under Mao*, 108–13.

75. Foucault, *Discipline and Punish*, 251.

6. AN OPEN STRUGGLE OF REDEFINITION

1. For a close look at issues raised by ordinary professional workers and factory hands, see Huadong shifan daxue zhongguo dangdai shi yanjiu zhongxin, *Chachang 1957.*

2. Teiwes, *Politics and Purges;* U, "Dangerous Privilege."

3. Meisner, *Mao's China and After,* 134; Walder, *China under Mao,* 134–35.

4. Bauman, *Legislators and Interpreters.*

5. Schwarcz, *Chinese Enlightenment,* 4.

6. Quoted in Zhu Zheng, *Fanyoupai douzheng shimo,* vol. 1, 84.

7. Van Slyke, *Enemies and Friends,* chap. 10.

8. U, "Dangerous Privilege," 41–49.

9. Teiwes, *Politics and Purges,* 267.

10. MacFarquhar, Wu, and Cheek, *Secret Speeches,* 225–26.

11. Huang Yaomian, "Wo de kanfa," 392–93.

12. Gong Canguang, "Dang yu zhishifenzi."

13. Feng Kexi, "Zhishifenzi de wenti."

14. Fu Zhongsun, "Zhonggong shice zhiyi."

15. Xu Zhongnian, "Qianlun zhishifenzi."

16. Zhang Naiqi, "Minjian hui gongshang lian."

17. Teiwes, *Politics and Purges,* 265–71.

18. Rule of law, for example, was not mentioned in "On the Correct Handling of Contradictions among the People."

19. Cohen, *Criminal Process.*

20. Yang Zhongye, "Dangqian sifajie"; Huang Shaohong, "Dang buying zhijie."

21. Yang Zhaolong, "Woguo zhongyao fadian."

22. Wu Jialin, "Zhongyang zuigao lingdao"; "Faxuejie renshi."

23. Zhang Bojun, "Guanyu chengli."

24. Grieder, *Intellectuals and the State,* 4.

25. "Guangchang fakan ci," 20.

26. Bauman, *Legislators and Interpreters,* 21.

27. Weston, *Power of Position,* 177.

28. Schwarcz, *Chinese Enlightenment.*

29. Zhang Yuanxun, *Beida yi jiu wu qi,* chap. 2.

30. Tan Tianrong, "Diyizhu ducao"; Tan Tianrong, "Dierzhu ducao"; Tan Tianrong, "Disizhu ducao"; Tan Tianrong, "Liangdian lun."

31. "Zailun wuchan jieji zhuanzheng de lishi jingyan."

32. MacFarquhar, *Cultural Revolution,* vol. 1, 172–73.

33. Tan Tianrong, "Jiaotiao zhuyi."

34. Yan Zhongqiang, "Weiwu zhuyi."

35. Djilas, *New Class.*

36. Wang, *Memoirs,* 230.

37. Zhou Dajue, "Wo dui muqian."

38. Zhou Dajue, "Lun 'jieji'"; Zhou Dajue, "Zailun 'lingdaozhe jieji.'"

39. The other classes are workers, peasants, intellectuals, disappearing capitalists and supportive democratic personages. He considered the last category as part of the leadership class. Pang Zhuoheng, "Lun shehui zhuyi."

40. The May 1957 issues of *People's Daily* and other newspapers together contain numerous complaints against the state.

41. Zhou Dajue, "Buchong."

42. Qian Ruping, "Zailun 'jieji.'"

43. For an account of her background and activities, see Qian Liqun, *Jujue yiwang,* 109–50.

44. Lin Xiling, "Xiancun zhidu."

45. Jiang Xingren, "Minzhu xuanju wenti."

46. Qian Liqun, *Jujue yiwang,* 118.

47. Maksimovic, "Constitutional Socialism."

48. Long Yinghua, "Beijing daxue yinshuachang."

49. Jiang Xingren, "Minzhu xuanju"; Zhang Jingzhong, "Baogaohui shang."

50. Long Yinghua, "Baihua xueshe huiyi."

51. Lin Xiling, "Zhongguo renmin daxue"; Long Yinghua, "Shijie wang hechu qu"; Long Yinghua, "Beijing daxue yinshuachang."

52. One student at People's University openly supported competitive elections in the countryside. Li Yachun, "Xuanju shang de bu minzhu."

53. Ma Yunfeng, "Zuzhi shouduan guoshi le."

54. Jiang Xingren, "Lun dang tianxia."

55. Li Shaolin, "Youguan minzhu."

56. Fung, *Intellectual Foundations.* 5.

57. Yang Fengcheng, *Zhishifenzi lilun,* 143–50; Leung and Kau, *Mao Zedong,* 591–613.

58. Teiwes and Sun, *China's Road to Disaster,* chap. 3.

59. PDRR, accessed August 20, 2016.

60. Karabel, "Revolutionary Contradictions," 147, 150–51.

61. Yang Fangcheng, *Zhishifenzi lilun,* 143–50.

62. For example, Zhang Jingfu, "Jianli gongren jieji de kexue duiwu."

63. "Zuo yige mingfu qishi."

64. Cheek, "Making Maoism," 307.

65. Jiang Nanxiang, "Qinghua daxue"; also, "Weile shehui zhuyi."

66. "Dao gongnong qunzhong zhong"; "Helongjiang sheng jueding"; "Jianli gongren jieji."

67. Yu Guangyuan, "Woguo kexue shiye."

68. "Wei kexue yanjiu."

69. Jiang Nanxiang, "Dierci kexue taolunhui."

70. Jiang Nanxiang, "Yingjie biyesheng."

71. Andreas, *Red Engineers,* 53.

72. Jiang Nanxiang, "Yingjie biyesheng."

73. Andreas, *Red Engineers,* 52.

74. Zhonggong Shanghai shiwei jiaoyu weisheng gongzuobu, "Peiyang youhong youzhuan zhishifenzi."

75. "Zhenyang jianli gongren jieji."

76. Andreas, *Red Engineers,* 36.

77. Lu Ge, "Jin yibu Guanche."

78. Boggs, *Two Revolutions,* 16.

79. Ibid, 226.

80. For example, Dikötter, *Mao's Great Famine;* Su, *Collective Killings;* Walder, *Fractured Rebellion.*

7. UGLY INTELLECTUALS EVERYWHERE

1. *LSZ,* 1–3.

2. Tang Changfeng and Pan Boyu, *Liu Sanjie.*

3. Yang Fengcheng, *Zhishifenzi lilun,* 144.

4. Schram, *Mao Tse-tung,* 126.

5. Meisner, *Mao Zedong,* 146, 149; Walder, *China under Mao,* 155–56, 185–86.

6. Walder, *China under Mao,* 178.

7. Liu Jialing, "Liu Sanjie," 147.

8. *LSZ,* 1.

9. Zhongguo xiquzhi bianji weiyuanhui, *Zhongguo xiquzhi guangxi juan,* 122–23; *LSZ,* 1.

10. Chen, "Multiplicity in Uniformity"; Yen, "Folklore Research."

11. Fokkema, *Literary Doctrine,* 196–198; McDougall, "Writers and Performers," 290–91; Clark, *Chinese Cinema,* 64–65.

12. Blake, "Love Songs"; Yen, "Folklore Research," 25–27.

13. *LSZ,* 1, 14.

14. Chen, "Multiplicity in Uniformity," 5–7.

15. Liu, "Folksong Immortal."

16. Liu Sanjie *ziliao huibian diyiji.*

17. Zheng Tianjian, "Guanyu Liu Sanjie," 15; He Qifang, "Youmei de geju," 30–31; Loh, "Romantic Love to Class Struggle," 167–69.

18. Jia Zhi, "Minjian chuanshuo," 102; Li Huizhong, "Geju *Liu Sanjie,*" 52.

19. *LSZ,* 1.

20. Li Huizhong, "Geju *Liu Sanjie,*" 45

21. MacFarquhar, *Cultural Revolution,* vol. 2, 24–26.

22. Wu Jinnan, "Qunzhong yundong."

23. Jiang Bo and Song Chen, "Gewuji *Liu Sanjie.*"

24. *LSZ,* 2, 11.

25. Wu Jinnan, "Qunzhong yundong."

26. Liu, "Folksong Immortal," 574.

27. Zhonggong Shanghai shiwei xuanchuan bu, "Gejuyuan fanyou qianhou," 25.

28. Mei Lanfang, "Ge Liu Sanjie."

29. *"Liu Sanjie* lai Hu"; "Mingwan dianshi jiemu."

30. "Huanle de gesheng"; "Yinyue shudian kaimu."

31. Wang Shiyi, "Kewai xingqu huodong zhanlan"; "Dazhuan xuesheng jinian Wusi."

32. MacFarquhar, *Cultural Revolution,* vol. 3, 90–120.

33. "Nongcun dianying."

34. Liu, "Folksong Immortal," 554.

35. Liu Jialing, "Liu Sanjie," 147.

36. U, "Dangerous Privilege."

37. Gao Huamin, *Gonghe guo nianlun,* 289–318.

38. For a discussion of movies about Chinese intellectuals in the early and mid-1950s, see Meng Liye, *Xin zhongguo dianying,* 25–29, 81–83, 201–13.

39. *Buju xiaojie de ren* (feature film).

40. *Wei wancheng de xiju* (feature film).

41. Li Duoyu, *Zhongguo dianying bainian,* 271.

42. Yin Hong and Ling Yan, *Xin zhongguo dianying,* 53–58.

43. Sha Sha, "Duige."

44. Liu, "Folksong Immortal," 581–83.

45. Wu Jinnan, "Qunzhong yundong."

46. Liu Sanjie zhengli xiaozu, *Liu Sanjie,* 101–02.

47. Qiao Yu, "Ermu yixin," 69.

48. He Qifang, "Youmei de geju," 31.

49. Cai Yi, "Lun *Liu Sanjie,*" 84–85.

50. MacFarquhar, *Cultural Revolution,* vol. 3, 51.

51. For example, Xi Gao, "Shiqu guangze de mingzhu"; A Yi, "Lixiang he xianshi."

52. Gao Zhenhe, "Teding de ticai," 20.

53. Jia Ji, "Guanyu yingpian *Liu Sanjie,*" 22.

54. Xi Gao, "Shiqu guangze de mingzhu."

55. Jia Ji, "Zhenjia xushi zhijian," 3.

56. Jing Wenshuai, "*Zaochun eryue.*"

57. Teiwes, *Politics and Purges,* chap. 10; Goldman, *China's Intellectuals,* 18–60.

58. Yang Fengcheng, *Zhishifenzi lilun,* 170–77.

59. Pickowicz, "Limits of Cultural Thaw," 98–100.

60. Yan Ping, "Xia Yan weihe pokou dama Zhou Yang?"

61. Goldman, *China's Intellectuals,* 39.

62. Li Duoyu, *Zhongguo dianying bainian,* 338; Yan Ping, "Xia Yan weihe pokou dama Zhou Yang."

63. Yan Ping, "Chen Huangmei."

64. Jing Wenshuai, "*Zaochun Eryue.*"

65. Yan Ping, "Xia Yan weihe pokou dama Zhou Yang."

66. Shanghaishi renwei wenjiao bangongshi, "Dui 'zaochun eryue' dianying de fanying," 152–53.

67. Ibid., 154–55.

68. Shanghaishi wei zhishu jiguan weiyuanhui xuanchuanbu, "Dui *Zaochun eryue* dianying de fanying," 82.

69. Shanghaishi renwei wenjiao bangongshi, "Qingkuang tiaocha huibao," 156.

70. Shanghaishi qingnian gong, "Qingnian zai yishi xingtai douzheng zhong," 46–48, 63–65.

8. THE INTELLECTUAL AND CHINESE SOCIETY

1. Fitzpatrick, *Tear Off the Mask,* 33.

2. Kurzman and Owens, "Sociology of Intellectuals."

3. Bourdieu and Wacquant, *Reflexive Sociology,* 12.

4. Foucault, *Power/Knowledge,* 194–95.

5. Ibid., 195.

6. Zhou Enlai, "Zhishifenzi de gaizao."

7. "Xi Jinping: Woguo guangda zhishifenzi."

8. See the April to July 2017 issues of *Renmin ribao* in PDRR.

9. Ong, "National People's Congress."

10. Gan, "Chinese Universities."

11. Human Rights Watch, "China 2016."

12. Haas, "US Joins Growing Calls"; Buckley, "Liu Xiaobo"; Sui, "Liu Xiaobo."

13. Keyword search on Baidu, Liu Xiaobi (in Chinese), accessed December 28, 2017, www.baidu.com.

14. "Xi Jinping: Woguo guangda zhishifenzi."

15. For example, Xu Jilin, *Zhishifenzi shilun;* Fei Yiran, *Zhishifenzi de xuanze;* Chen Mingyuan, *Zhishifenzi yu renminbi.*

16. For example, Li Jialin and Chen Siyu, *Wang Shiwei;* Xiao Feng, *Hu Feng.*

17. Marinelli, "Public Commitment of Intellectuals."

18. "Yingxiang zhongguo gonggong zhishifenzi 50 ren."

19. Ji Fangping, "'Gonggong zhishifenzi' lun."

20. Marinelli, "Public Commitment of Intellectuals," 428.

21. For example, Feng Zhexue and Sun Jin, "Gonggong zhishifenzi."

22. The numbers are based on a search in *Zhongguo qikan quanwen shujuku* (China Academic Journals Database), accessed September 25, 2017, http://gb.oversea.cnki.net/kns55/.

23. Between 2006 and 2016, the term has appeared in 13 articles. The figure is from a search in PDRR, accessed September 25, 2017.

24. Zhang Xiaode and Zhang Xu, *Zhishi ren,* 120–25.

25. Li Junping, "Gudai shehui de zhishi ren?"

26. Xin Ke, "Zhongguo zhishifenzi."

BIBLIOGRAPHY

ENGLISH-LANGUAGE SOURCES

Alexopoulous, Golfo. *Stalin's Outcasts: Aliens, Citizens, and the Soviet State, 1926–1936.* Ithaca, NY: Cornell University Press, 2003.

Andreas, Joel. *Rise of the Red Engineers: The Cultural Revolution and the Origins of China's New Class.* Stanford: Stanford University Press, 2009.

Apter, David, and Tony Saich. *Revolutionary Discourse in Mao's Republic.* Cambridge, MA: Harvard University Press, 1994.

Averill, Stephen. "Party, Society, and Local Elite in the Jiangxi Communist Movement." *Journal of Asian Studies* 46, no. 2 (1987): 279–303.

———. "The Transition from Urban to Rural in the Chinese Revolution." *China Journal* 48 (2002): 87–121.

Bauman, Zygmunt. *Legislators and Interpreters: On Modernity, Post-Modernity, and Intellectuals.* Cambridge, UK: Polity Press, 1987.

Blake, Fred. "Love Songs and the Great Leap Forward." *American Ethnologist* 6, no. 1 (1979): 41–54.

Blecher, Marc, and Gordon White. *Micropolitics in Contemporary China: A Technical Unit during and after the Cultural Revolution.* New York: M. E. Sharpe, 1979.

Boggs, Carl. *The Two Revolutions: Gramsci and the Dilemmas of Western Marxism.* Boston: South End Press, 1999.

Bourdieu, Pierre. *Language and Symbolic Power.* Cambridge, MA: Harvard University Press, 1991.

———. *The Logic of Practice.* Stanford: Stanford University Press, 1992.

———. *On the State: Lectures at the Collège de France, 1989–1992.* Cambridge, UK: Polity Press, 2014.

———. *Outline of a Theory of Practice.* Cambridge, UK: Cambridge University Press, 1977.

———. *Pascalian Meditations.* Stanford: Stanford University Press, 2000.

———. *Practical Reason.* Stanford: Stanford University Press, 1998.

Bourdieu, Pierre, and Loïc Wacquant. *An Invitation to Reflexive Sociology.* Chicago: University of Chicago Press, 1992.

Bowker, Geoffrey, and Susan Leigh Star. *Sorting Things Out: Classification and Its Consequences.* Cambridge, MA: MIT Press, 2000.

Brower, Daniel. "The Problem of the Russian Intelligentsia." *Slavic Review* 26, no. 4 (1967): 638–47.

Browning, Christopher, and Lewis Siegelbaum. "Frameworks for Social Engineering: Stalinist Schema of Identification and the Nazi Volkgemeinschaft." In *Beyond Totalitarianism: Stalinism and Nazism Compared,* edited by Michael Geyer and Sheila Fitzpatrick, 231–65. Cambridge, UK: Cambridge University Press, 2009.

Brubaker, Rogers, and Frederick Cooper. "Beyond 'Identity.'" *Theory and Society* 29, no. 1 (2000): 1–47.

Brubaker, Rogers, Margit Fieschmidt, Jonathan Fox, and Liana Grancea. *Nationalist Politics and Everyday Ethnicity in a Transylvanian Town.* Princeton: Princeton University Press, 2004.

Brubaker, Rogers, Mara Loveman, and Peter Stamatov. "Ethnicity as Cognition." *Theory and Society* 33, no. 1 (2004): 31–64.

Buckley, Chris. "Liu Xiaobo, Chinese Dissident and Nobel Laureate, Is Cremated." *New York Times,* July 15, 2017. www.nytimes.com/2017/07/15/world/asia/liu-xiaobo-cremation-china.html?mcubz=0.

Chang, Julian. "The Mechanics of State Propaganda: The People's Republic of China and the Soviet Union in the 1950s." In *New Perspectives on State Socialism in China,* edited by Timothy Cheek and Tony Saich, 76–124. Armonk, NY: M. E. Sharpe, 1997.

Cheek, Timothy. "The Fading of Wild Lilies: Wang Shiwei and Mao Zedong's Yan'an Talks in the First CPC Rectification Movement." *Australian Journal of Chinese Affairs* 11 (1984): 25–58.

———. *The Intellectual in Modern Chinese History.* Cambridge, UK: Cambridge University Press, 2015.

———. "Making Maoism: Ideology and Organization in the Yan'an Rectification Movement, 1942–1944." In *Knowledge Acts in Modern China: Ideas, Institutions, and Identities,* edited by Robert Culp, Eddy U, and Wen-hsin Yeh, 304–27. Berkeley: Institute of East Asian Studies, 2016.

———. *Propaganda and Culture in Mao's China: Deng Tuo and the Intelligentsia.* Oxford: Clarendon Press, 1997.

Chen, S. H. "Multiplicity in Uniformity: Poetry and the Great Leap Forward." *China Quarterly* 3 (1960): 1–15.

Chen, Theodore. *Thought Reform of the Chinese Intellectuals.* Hong Kong: Hong Kong University Press, 1960.

Chow, Tse-tsung. *The May Fourth Movement: Intellectual Revolution in Modern China.* Cambridge, MA: Harvard University Press, 1960.

Clark, Paul. *Chinese Cinema: Culture and Politics since 1949.* Cambridge, UK: Cambridge University Press, 1987.

Cohen, Jerome. *The Criminal Process in the People's Republic of China.* Cambridge, MA: Harvard University Press, 1968.

Croll, Elisabeth. "Marriage Choice and Status Groups in Contemporary China." In *Class and Stratification in Post-Revolution China,* edited by James Watson, 175–97. Cambridge, UK: Cambridge University Press, 1984.

Culp, Robert J. *Articulating Citizenship: Civic Education and Student Politics in Southeastern China, 1912–1940*. Cambridge, MA: Harvard University Asia Center, 2007.

———. "Culture Work: Industrial Capitalism and Socialist Cultural Production in Mao-Era China." Paper presented at Conference on Organized Knowledge under State Socialism, University of California, Berkeley, 2013.

Datta, Venita. "New Approaches to Intellectuals and the Dreyfus Affair." *Historical Reflections/Réflexions Historiques* 24, no. 1 (1998): 1–6.

Diamant, Neil. *Revolutionizing the Family: Politics, Love, and Divorce in Urban and Rural China, 1949–1968*. Berkeley: University of California Press, 2000.

Dikötter, Frank. *Mao's Great Famine: The History of China's Most Devastating Catastrophe, 1958–1962*. New York: Walker, 2001

———. *The Tragedy of Liberation: A History of the Chinese Revolution 1945–1957*. New York: Bloomsbury Press, 2013.

Dirlik, Arif. *The Origins of Chinese Communism*. Oxford: Oxford University Press, 1989.

Djilas, Milovan. *The New Class: An Analysis of the Communist System*. New York: Praeger, 1957.

Esherick, Joseph. "The Ye Family in China." In *Dilemmas of Victory: The Early Years of the People's Republic of China*, edited by Jeremy Brown and Paul Pickowicz, 311–36. Cambridge, MA: Harvard University Press, 2007.

Evans, Harriet. "The Language of Liberation: Gender and *Jiefang* in Early Chinese Communist Party Discourse." In *Twentieth-Century China: New Approaches*, edited by Jeffrey Wasserstrom, 194–220. London: Routledge, 2003.

Fitzpatrick, Sheila. "Ascribing Class: The Construction of Social Identity in Soviet Russia." *Journal of Modern History* 65, no. 4 (1993): 745–70.

———. *Tear Off the Masks! Identity and Imposture in Twentieth-Century Russia*. Princeton: Princeton University Press, 2005.

Fokkema, D. W. *Literary Doctrine in China and Soviet Influence, 1956–1960*. The Hague: Morton, 1965.

Forth, Christopher. "Intellectuals, Crowds and the Body Politics of the Dreyfus Affair." *Historical Reflections/Réflexions Historiques* 24, no. 1 (1998): 63–91.

Foucault, Michel. *Discipline and Punish: The Birth of the Prison*. Translated by Alan Sheridan. New York: Viking Penguin, 1985.

———. *Power/Knowledge: Selected Interviews and Other Writings, 1972–1977*. Edited by Colin Gordon. Translated by Colin Gordon et al. New York: Random House, 1980.

Frazier, Mark. *The Making of the Chinese Industrial Workplace: State, Revolution, and Labor Management*. Cambridge, UK: Cambridge University Press, 2002.

Friedman, Edward, Paul Pickowicz, and Mark Selden. *Chinese Village, Socialist State*. New Haven: Yale University Press, 1991.

Fung, Edmund. *The Intellectual Foundations of Chinese Modernity: Cultural and Political Thought in the Republican Era*. Cambridge, UK: Cambridge University Press, 2010.

Furth, Charlotte. "Intellectual Change: From the Reform Movement to the May Fourth Movement, 1895–1920." In *An Intellectual History of Modern China*, edited by Merle Goldman and Leo Lee, 13–96. Cambridge, UK: Cambridge University Press, 2002.

Gan, Nectar. "Chinese Universities Tighten Ideological Control of Teaching Staff." *South China Morning Post*, August 28, 2017. www.scmp.com/news/china/policies-politics/article/2108597/china-universities-tighten-ideological-control-of-teaching.

Giddens, Anthony. *Capitalism and Modern Social Theory.* Cambridge, UK: Cambridge University Press, 1971.

Goffman, Erving. *Stigma: Notes on the Management of Spoiled Identity.* New York: Simon and Schuster, 1963.

Goldman, Merle. *China's Intellectuals: Advise and Dissent.* Cambridge, MA: Harvard University Press, 1981.

———. *Literary Dissent in Communist China.* Cambridge, MA: Harvard University Press, 1967.

Gouldner, Alvin. *Against Fragmentation: The Origins of Marxism and the Sociology of Intellectuals.* Oxford: Oxford University Press, 1985.

Gramsci, Antonio. *Selections from the Prison Notebooks.* Minneapolis, MN: University of Minneapolis Press, [1929–1935] 1971.

Grieder, Jerome. *Intellectuals and the State in Modern China.* New York: The Free Press, 1981.

Gu, Edward. "Who Was Mr. Democracy? The May Fourth Discourse of Populist Democracy and the Radicalization of Chinese Intellectuals (1915–1922)." *Modern Asian Studies* 35, no. 3 (2001): 589–621.

Guo, Xuezhi. *China's Security State: Philosophy, Evolution, and Politics.* Cambridge, UK: Cambridge University Press, 2012.

Haas, Benjamin. "US Joins Growing Calls for China to Allow Liu Xiaobo Cancer Treatment Abroad." *The Guardian,* June 27, 2017. www.theguardian.com/world/2017/jun/27/us-joins-growing-calls-for-china-to-allow-liu-xiaobo-cancer-treatment-abroad.

Hall, Stuart, ed. *Representation: Cultural Representations and Signifying Practices.* London: Sage Publications, 1997.

Hofheinz, Roy, Jr. *The Broken Wave: The Chinese Communist Peasant Movement, 1922–1928.* Cambridge, MA: Harvard University Press, 1977.

Holm, David. *Art and Ideology in Revolutionary China.* Oxford: Oxford University Press, 1991.

Howe, Christopher. *Employment and Economic Growth in Urban China, 1949–1957.* Cambridge, UK: Cambridge University Press, 1971.

Human Rights Watch. "China: Events of 2016." Accessed September 10, 2017. www.hrw.org/world-report/2017/country-chapters/china-and-tibet.

Hung, Chang-Tai. *Mao's New World: Political Culture in the Early People's Republic.* Ithaca, NY: Cornell University Press, 2011.

Ip, Hung-yok. *Intellectuals in Revolutionary China, 1921–1949: Leaders, Heroes, and Sophisticates.* London: RoutledgeCurzon, 2005.

Kampen, Thomas. *Mao Zedong, Zhou Enlai, and the Evolution of the Chinese Communist Leadership.* Copenhagen: Nordic Institute of Asian Studies, 2000.

Karabel, Jerome. "Lenin and the Problem of the Intelligentsia." *Current Perspectives in Social Theory* 17 (1997): 261–312.

———. "Marx and the Question of Intellectuals." Unpublished manuscript in possession of author, date unknown.

———. "Revolutionary Contradictions: Antonio Gramsci and the Problems of Intellectuals." *Politics and Society* 6, no. 2 (1976): 123–72.

Kawamura, Nozomu. "Sociology and Socialism in the Interwar Period." In *Culture and Identity: Japanese Intellectuals during the Interwar Years,* edited by J. Thomas Rimer, 61–82. Princeton: Princeton University Press, 1990.

Knight, Nick. *Rethinking Mao: Explorations in Mao Zedong's Thought*. Lanham, MD: Lexington Books, 2007.

Kochetkova, Inna. *The Myth of the Russian Intelligentsia*. New York: Routledge, 2010.

Kraus, Richard. *Class Conflict in Chinese Socialism*. New York: Columbia University Press, 1981.

Kritzman, Lawrence, ed. 1988. *Michel Foucault: Politics, Philosophy, Culture*. Translated by Alan Sheridan et al. New York: Routledge.

Kuhn, Philip. "Chinese Views of Social Classification." In *Class and Stratification in Post-Revolution China*, edited by James Watson, 16–28. Cambridge, UK: Cambridge University Press, 1984.

Kurzman, Charles, and Lynn Owens. "The Sociology of Intellectuals." *Annual Review of Sociology* 28 (2002): 63–90.

Lamont, Michelle. *Money, Morals, and Manners: The Culture of the French and American Upper-Middle Class*. Chicago: University of Chicago Press, 1992.

Lamont, Michelle and Virag Molnár. "The Study of Boundaries in the Social Sciences." *Annual Review of Sociology* 28 (2002): 167–95.

Leung, John, and Michael Kau, eds. *The Writings of Mao Zedong*. Armonk, NY: M. E. Sharpe, 1992.

Liu, Lydia. "A Folksong Immortal and Official Popular Culture in Twentieth-Century China." In *Writings and Materiality in China*, edited by Judith Zeitlin and Lydia Liu, 553–609. Cambridge, MA: Harvard University Asia Center, 2003.

———. *Translingual Practice: Literature, National Culture, and Translated Modernity— China, 1900–1937*. Stanford: Stanford University Press, 1995.

Liu Shaoqi. *Selected Works of Liu Shaoqi*, vol. 1. Beijing: Foreign Languages Press, 1984.

Loh, Wai-fong. "From Romantic Love to Class Struggle: Reflections on the Film *Liu Sanjie*." In *Popular Chinese Literature and Performing Arts in the People's Republic of China, 1949– 1979*, edited by Bonnie McDougall, 165–76. Berkeley: University of California Press, 1984.

Loveman, Mara. "The Modern State and the Primitive Accumulation of Symbolic Power." *American Journal of Sociology* 110, no. 6 (2005): 1651–83.

Luk, Michael. *The Origins of Chinese Bolshevism*. Hong Kong: Oxford University Press, 1990.

McDougall, Bonnie. "Writers and Performers, Their Works, and Their Audiences in the First Three Decades." In *Popular Chinese Literature and Performing Arts in the People's Republic of China, 1949–1979*, edited by Bonnie McDougall, 269–304. Berkeley: University of California Press, 1984.

MacFarquhar, Roderick. *The Origins of the Cultural Revolution*, vol. 2. New York: Columbia University Press, 1983.

———. *The Origins of the Cultural Revolution*, vol. 3. New York: Columbia University Press, 1997.

MacFarquhar, Roderick, Eugene Wu, and Timothy Cheek, eds. *The Secret Speeches of Chairman Mao: From the Hundred Flowers to the Great Leap Forward*. Cambridge, MA: Harvard University Press, 1989.

Maksimovic, Ivan. "Constitutional Socialism in Yugoslavia." *Annals of the American Academy of Political and Social Science* 358, no. 1 (1965): 159–69.

Mao Zedong. *Selected Works of Mao Tse-tung*, vols. 2 and 3. Beijing: Foreign Languages Press, [1937–1945] 1967.

Marinelli, Maurizio. "On the Public Commitment of Intellectuals in Late Socialist China." *Theory and Society* 41, no. 5 (2012): 425–49.

Marx, Karl, and Friedrich Engels. "Manifesto of the Communist Party." In *The Marx-Engels Reader,* edited by Robert Tucker, 469–500. New York: W. W. Norton, [1848] 1978.

Meisner, Maurice. *Mao's China and After.* New York: Free Press, 1986.

———. *Mao Zedong: A Political and Intellectual Portrait.* Cambridge, UK: Polity Press, 2007.

Müller, Simone. "The 'Debate on the Literature of Action' and Its Legacy: Ideological Struggles in 1930s Japan and the 'Rebirth' of the Intellectual." *The Journal of Japanese Studies* 41, no. 1 (2015): 9–44.

O'Brien, Neil. *An American Editor in Early Revolutionary China: John William Powell and the China Weekly/Monthly Review.* New York: Routledge, 2003.

Ong, Lynette. "China Just Held Its National People's Congress. Here Are Three Key Points." *Washington Post,* March 21, 2017. www.washingtonpost.com/news/monkey-cage/wp/2017/03/21/china-just-held-its-national-peoples-congress-here-are-three-key-points/?utm_term=.d6dd68019ab5.

Pepper, Suzanne. *Radicalism and Education Reform in 20th-Century China.* Cambridge, UK: Cambridge University Press, 1996.

Perry, Elizabeth. *Anyuan: Mining China's Revolutionary Tradition.* Berkeley: University of California Press, 2012.

———. *Shanghai on Strike: The Politics of Chinese Labor.* Stanford: Stanford University Press, 1991.

Pickowicz, Paul. "The Limits of Cultural Thaw: Chinese Cinema in the Early 1960s." In *Perspectives on Chinese Cinema,* edited by Chris Berry, 97–148. Ithaca, NY: Cornell China-Japan Program, 1985.

Rawnsley, Gary. "The Great Movement to Resist America and Assist Korea: How Beijing Sold the Korean War." *Media, War, & Conflict* 2, no. 3 (2009): 285–315.

Ruf, Gregory. *Cadres and Kin: Making a Socialist Village in West China, 1921–1991.* Stanford: Stanford University Press, 1998.

Saich, Tony. "The Chinese Communist Party during the Era of the Comintern." Date unknown. Accessed February 3, 2016. www.hks.harvard.edu/fs/asaich/chinese-communisty-party-during-comintern.pdf.

Schram, Stuart. *The Thought of Mao Tse-tung.* Cambridge, UK: Cambridge University Press, 1989.

Schwarcz, Vera. *The Chinese Enlightenment: Intellectuals and the Legacy of the May Fourth Movement of 1919.* Berkeley: University of California Press, 1986.

Schwartz, Benjamin, ed. *Reflections on the May Fourth Movement.* Cambridge, MA: Harvard University East Asia Research Center, 1973.

Selden, Mark. *The Yenan Way in Revolutionary China.* Cambridge, MA: Harvard University Press, 1971.

Smedley, Agnes. *The Great Road: The Life and Times of Chu Teh.* New York: Monthly Review Press, 1956.

Smith, Dorothy. *The Conceptual Practices of Power: A Feminist Sociology of Knowledge.* Boston: Northeastern University Press, 1990.

Smith, Stephen A. "Toward a Global History of Communism." In *The Oxford Handbook of the History of Communism,* edited by S. A. Smith, 1–34. Oxford: Oxford University Press, 2014.

Stagier, Annegret. *Learning Difference: Race and Schooling in the Multiracial Metropolis.* Stanford: Stanford University Press, 2006.

Stranahan, Patricia. *Molding the Medium: The Chinese Communist Party and the Liberation Daily.* Armonk, NY: M. E. Sharpe, 1990.

Su, Yang. *Collective Killings in Rural China during the Cultural Revolution.* Cambridge, UK: Cambridge University Press, 2011.

Sui, Cindy. "Liu Xiaobo: Censored by China, Supporters Take to Social Media." *BBC News,* July 19, 2017. www.bbc.com/news/world-asia-china-40656483.

Sun, Huei-min. "From Literati to Legal Professionals: The First-Generation Chinese Law School Graduates and Their Career Patterns." In *Knowledge Acts in Modern China: Ideas, Institutions, and Identities,* edited by Robert J. Culp, Eddy U, and Wen-hsin Yeh, 89–113. Berkeley: Institute of East Asian Studies, 2016.

Szreter, Simon, Hania Sholkamy, and A. Dharmalingam, eds. *Categories and Contexts: Anthropological and Historical Studies in Critical Demography.* Oxford: Oxford University Press, 2004.

Teiwes, Frederick. *Politics and Purges in China: Rectification and the Decline of Party Norms 1950–1965.* White Plains, NY: M. E. Sharpe, 1979.

Teiwes, Frederick, and Warren Sun. *China's Road to Disaster: Mao, Central Politicians, and Provincial Leaders in the Unfolding of the Great Leap Forward, 1955–1959.* Armonk, NY: M. E. Sharpe, 1999.

Townsley, Eleanor. "The Public Intellectual Trope in the United States." *American Sociologist* 37, no. 3 (2006): 39–66.

U, Eddy. "Dangerous Privilege: The United Front and the Rectification Campaign of the Early Mao Years." *China Journal* 68 (2012): 32–57.

———. *Disorganizing China: Counter-Bureaucracy and the Decline of Chinese Socialism.* Stanford: Stanford University Press, 2007.

Van de Ven, Hans. *From Friend to Comrade: The Founding of the Chinese Communist Party, 1920–1927.* Berkeley: University of California Press, 1991.

Van Slyke, Lyman Page. *Enemies and Friends: The United Front in Chinese Communist History.* Stanford: Stanford University Press, 1967.

Vogel, Ezra. "From Friendship to Comradeship: The Change in Personal Relations in Communist China." *China Quarterly* 21 (1965): 46–60.

Wakeman, Frederic, Jr. "'Cleanup': The New Order in Shanghai." In *Dilemmas of Victory: The Early Years of the People's Republic of China,* edited by Jeremy Brown and Paul Pickowicz, 21–58. Cambridge, MA: Harvard University Press, 2007.

Walder, Andrew. *China under Mao: A Revolution Derailed.* Cambridge, MA: Harvard University Press, 2015.

———. *Communist Neo-Traditionalism: Work and Authority in Chinese Industry.* Berkeley: University of California Press, 1986.

———. *Fractured Rebellion: The Beijing Red Guard Movement.* Cambridge, MA: Harvard University Press, 2009.

Wang, Fanxi. *Memoirs of a Chinese Revolutionary.* New York: Columbia University Press, 1991.

West, Candace, and Don Zimmermann. "Doing Gender." *Gender and Society* 1, no. 2 (1987): 125–51.

Weston, Timothy. *The Power of Position: Beijing University, Intellectuals, and Chinese Political Culture.* Berkeley: University of California Press, 2004.

Westphal, James, and Poonam Khanna. "Keeping Directors in Line: Social Distancing as a Control Mechanism in the Corporate Elite." *Administrative Science Quarterly* 48, no. 3 (2003): 361–98.

Whyte, Martin. *Small Groups and Political Rituals in China.* Berkeley: University of California Press, 1974.

Wu, Yidi. "Yan'an's Iron Bodhisattva: Hunting Spies in the Rectification Campaign." In *1943: China at the Crossroads,* edited by Joseph Esherick and Matthew Combs, 203–41. Ithaca, NY: Cornell University East Asian Program, 2015.

Yang, Kuisong. "Reconsidering the Campaign to Suppress Counterrevolutionaries." *China Quarterly* 193 (2008): 102–21.

Yen, Chun-chiang. "Folklore Research in China." *Asian Folklore Studies* 26, no. 2 (1967): 1–62.

Yu, Liu. "Maoist Discourse and the Mobilization of Emotions in Revolutionary China." *Modern China* 36, no. 3 (2010): 329–362.

Zarrow, Peter. *Anarchism and Chinese Political Culture.* New York: Columbia University Press, 1990.

Zhang, Shu Guang. *Economic Cold War: America's Embargoes against China and the Sino-Soviet Alliance, 1949–1963.* Stanford: Stanford University Press, 2001.

Zhang, Xiaojun. "Land Reform in Yang Village: Symbolic Capital and the Determination of Class Status." *Modern China* 30, no. 1 (2004): 3–45.

CHINESE-LANGUAGE SOURCES

Abbreviations

DZDY   *Dazhong dianying* [Popular cinema].

JFRB   *Jiefang ribao* [Liberation daily].

LSZ   *Zhongguo dangdai wenxue yanjiu ziliao: Liu Sanjie zhuanji* [Research material on contemporary Chinese literature: special volume on Third Sister Liu]. Guilin: Guangxi shifan xueyuan, [1960] 1979.

LYX   *Liuyue xue: jiyi zhong de fanyoupai yundong* [June snow: remembering the antirightist movement], edited by Niu Han and Deng Jiuping. Beijing: Jingji ribao chubanshe, [1957] 1998.

PDRR   People's Daily–Renmin Ribao (1946–Present) database. www.oriprobe. com/peoplesdaily.shtml.

RMRB   *Renmin ribao* [People's daily].

WHB   *Wenhui bao* [Wenhui daily].

XQN   *Xin qingnian* [New youth].

YSC   *Yuanshangcao: jiyi zhong de fanyoupai yundong* [Grass on a plain: remembering the antirightist movement], edited by Niu Han and Deng Jiuping. Beijing: Jingji ribao chubanshe, [1957] 1998.

ZFYS   *Zhongguo fanyou yundong shujuku 1957-* [Chinese antirightist campaign database 1957–], edited by Song Yongyi. Hong Kong: Universities Service Center, 2010.

ZZGSG   *Zhongguo zibenzhuyi gongshangye de shehuizhuyi gaizao Shanghai juan* [The socialist transformation of China's capitalist industries and commerce—Shanghai volume], edited by Li Qing, Chen Wenbin, and Lin Zhicheng. Beijing: Zhonggong dangshi chubanshe, [1951] 1993.

Books, Newspapers, and Articles

A Yi. "Lixiang he xianshi" [Ideals and reality]. *DZDY* 10 (1961): 20–21.

Belgion, Montgomery. "Banda lun zhishi jieji de zui'e" [Benda on the sins of the intellectual class]. *Dongfang zazhi* [Eastern miscellany] 26, no. 1 (1929): 89–93.

Cai Yi. "Lun *Liu Sanjie*" [On *Third Sister Liu*]. In *LSZ*, 74–86.

Chen Chengze. "Zhishi jieji yingyou de juewu" [The awakening that the intellectual class needs]. *Xueyi* [Art of learning] 2, no. 4 (1920): 1–11.

Chen Duxiu. *Chen Duxiu zhuzuo xuan* [Selected works of Chen Duxiu], vol. 1. Shanghai: Shanghai renmin chubanshe, [1897–1919] 1993.

———. "Zhongguo guomin geming yu shehui ge jieji" [The various social classes and the Chinese national revolution]. In *Chen Duxiu zhuzuo xuan,* vol. 2, 557–68. Shanghai: Renmin chubanshe, [1923] 1993.

Chen Mingyuan. *Zhishifenzi yu renminbi de shidai* [Intellectuals and the renminbi era]. Shanghai: Wenhui chubanshe, 2006.

Chen Xuezhao. *Yan'an fangwen ji* [My visit to Yan'an]. Guangzhou: Guangdong renmin chubanshe, [1940] 2001.

Cheng Zhongyuan. *Zhang Wentian zhuan* [The biography of Zhang Wentian]. Beijing: Dangdai zhongguo chubanshe, 1993.

Dacheng laozhoukan quanwen shujuku [Dacheng old periodicals full content database]. www.dachengdata.com.

Dai Moulin and Cao Zhongbin. *Wang Ming Zhuan* [The biography of Wang Ming]. Beijing: Zhonggong dangshi chubanshe, 2008.

"Dao gongnong qunzhong zhong luohu Shenyang zuojia xiaxiang xiachang" [Shenyang writers going to factories and villages]. *RMRB,* November 14, 1957.

"Dazhuan xuesheng jinian Wusi" [Postsecondary students' commemoration of the May Fourth Movement]. *Xinmin wanbao* [Xinmin evening news], May 4, 1961.

Dong Weichuan. "Zhonghua zhishi jieji zhi mingyun" [On the fate of China's intellectual class]. *Xin Zhonghua* [New China] 6, no. 19 ([1933] 1948): 3–7.

"Dongbei renmin zhengfu gongyebu pinqing zhuanjia jiaoshou gongchengshi yishi kuai-jishi ji geji jishu renyuan tonggao" [Public notice from the bureau of industry of the people's government of northeast China on recruitment of experts, professors, doctors, accountants, and technical personnel of various levels]. *JFRB,* February 16, 1950.

"Dongbei renmin zhengfu zhaopin zhuanjia jiaoshou ji ge bumen gongzuo renyuan jian-zhang" [Guidelines for recruitment of experts and professors and personnel for various departments of the people's government of northeast China]. *JFRB,* September 26, 1949.

Du Ming. "Jiuzheng ziwo piping zhong de liangzhong pianxiang" [Rectifying two undesirable trends in self-criticism]. *WHB,* August 15, 1952.

"Duiyu zuzhi wenti yijue an" [Resolution on organization (by the fifth national party congress)]. May 1927. Accessed on July 31, 2007. http://data.people.com.cn.

"Faxuejie renshi zai zhongguo zhengzhi falü xuehui zhaokai de zuotanhui shang tichu dui woguo falü zhidu de yijian" [The opinions expressed by legal circles personnel in the symposium organized by the Chinese political law study society]. *RMRB,* May 29, 1957. In ZFYS.

Fei Xiaotong. "Lun zhishi jieji" [On the intellectual class]. *Guancha* [Observations] 3, no. 8 (1947): 11–15.

Fei Yiran. *Zhongguo zhishifenzi de xuanze yu tansuo* [The explorations and decisions of China's intellectuals]. Kaifeng: Henan daxue chubanshe, 2006.

Feng Kexi. "Zhishifenzi de wenti zai nali?" [What are the issues regarding intellectuals?].
    Chongqing ribao [Chongqing daily], May 23, 1957. In ZFYS.
Feng Zhexue and Sun Jin. "Zhongguo gonggong zhishifenzi de chansheng ji qi tezhen" [The
    emergence of public intellectuals in China and their characteristics]. *Lilun guancha*
    [Theoretic observation] 7 (2013): 63–64.
Fu Sinian. "Zhongguo xueshu sixiang jie zhi jiben wumiu" [Fundamental mistakes of
    Chinese academic thought]. *XQN* 4, no. 9 (1918): 328–36.
Fu Zhongsun. "Zhonggong shice zhiyi" [One of the misjudgments of the party]. *Shida
    jiaoxue* [Pedagogy at Beijing Normal University] 121. In LYX, 443–46.
Gao Dashuai. "Shanghai dui shiye zhishifenzi de dengji he chuli gongzuo yanjiu 1951–1953"
    [A study of how Shanghai registered and handled unemployed intellectuals, 1951–1953].
    Master's thesis, Huadong shifan daxue, 2012.
Gao Huamin. *Gonghe guo nianlun 1955* [The year 1955 in the PRC]. Hebei: Hebei renmin
    chubanshe, 2001.
Gao Xinmin and Zhang Shujun. *Yan'an zhengfeng shilu* [True records of the rectification
    campaign in Yan'an]. Hangzhou: Zhejiang renmin chubanshe, 2000.
Gao Zhenhe. "Yao cong teding de ticai he renwu chufa" [We need to begin with already
    specified themes and characters]. *DZDY* 3 (1962): 19–20.
Gong Canguang. "Wo ye tantan dang yu zhishifenzi jian de guanxi wenti" [I, too, want to
    discuss the relations between the party and intellectuals]. 1957. In ZFYS.
"Guangchang fakan ci" [Foreword to *The Square*]. 1957. In YSC, 19–20.
Guo Bixuan, Yang Yanghu, and Ren Xueling. *Yan'an jingshen tanyuan* [Researching the
    origins of the Yan'an spirit]. Beijing: Hongqi chubanshe, 2005.
Guojia tongjiju [National Bureau of Statistics]. *Xin zhongguo wushi nian tongji ziliao
    huibian* [Collections of fifty years of statistical data of new China]. Beijing: Zhongguo
    tongji chubanshe, 1999.
He Fang. *Dangshi biji: Cong Zunyi huiyi dao Yan'an zhengfeng* [Notes on CCP history: from
    the Zunyi conference to the rectification campaign in Yan'an]. Hong Kong: Lee Man
    Publisher, 2005.
He Qifang. "Youmei de geju *Liu Sanjie*" [*Third Sister Liu*: an elegant song and drama]. In
    LSZ, 29–44.
He Yurun. "Women fangwen le canjia sixiang gaizao de laoshimen" [We visited our teachers
    in thought reform]. *WHB*, August 16, 1952.
"Helongjiang sheng jueding jinyibu jinsuo jigou choudiao shi'er wan ganbu shangshan
    xiaxiang" [Helongjiang Province transferring 120,000 cadres to rural areas]. *RMRB*,
    November 25, 1957.
Hu Ping. *Chanji: 1957 kulan de jitan* [Subtle lessons: the 1957 altar of bitterness and tragedies].
    Guangdong: Guangdong luyou chubanshe, 2004.
"Huadong junzheng daxue Shanghai zhaosheng weiyuanhui tonggao" [Public notice from
    the student recruitment commission of the East China Military and Political University].
    JFRB, June 13, 1949.
"Huadong renmin geming daxue zhaosheng weiyuanhui fabang tonggao" [Official list of
    successful candidates of recruitment of the East China People's Revolutionary University].
    JFRB, August 7, 1949.

Huadong shifan daxue zhongguo dangdai shi yanjiu zhongxin, ed. [Research center of contemporary Chinese history at the East China Normal University]. *Chachang 1957 nian zhengfeng dazibao* [Big-character posters from a tea factory in the 1957 rectification campaign]. Shanghai: Dongfang chuban zhongxin, 2011.

Huang Ping. "Zhishifenzi: zai piaobo zhong xunzhao guisu" [Intellectuals: finding a home while drifting aimlessly]. In *20 shiji zhongguo zhishifenzi shilun* 20 [Essays on intellectuals in twentieth-century China], edited by Xu Jilin, 2–4. Beijing: Xinxing chubanshe, 2005.

Huang Shaohong. "Dang buying zhijie xiang renmin fahao siling" [The party should not directly issue orders to the people]. In LYX, 372–375.

Huang Yaomian. "Wo de kanfa" [My views]. In LYX, 390–94.

"Huanle de gesheng cong zheli xiangqi" [The happy sound of singing begins here]. *WHB*, January, 2, 1961.

Ji Fangping. "Touguo biaoxing kan shizhi—xi 'gonggong zhishifenzi' lun" [See through the appearance to perceive the essence—an analysis of the debate on 'public intellectuals']. *RMRB*, November 25, 2004.

Jia Ji. "Guanyu yingpian *Liu Sanjie* taolun de zagan" [Thoughts on the discussion of the movie *Third Sister Liu*]. *DZDY* 8 (1962): 20–23.

———. "Zhenjia xushi zhijian" [Between the real and fictitious as well as the substantive and nonsubstantive]. *WHB*, May 30, 1962.

Jia Zhi. "Minjian chuanshuo Liu Sanjie de xin xingxiang" [New representations of the folk legend of Third Sister Liu]. In *LSZ*, 96–107.

Jian Hu. "Zhishi jieji de zishen gaizao" [The self-reform of the intellectual class]. *Dongfang zazhi* 19, no. 4 (1922): 1–2.

Jiang Bo and Song Chen. "Zheng Tianjian yu gewuji *Liu Sanjie*" [Zheng Tianjian and the musical drama *Third Sister Liu*]. 1995. Accessed January 26, 2017. www2. hcclib.net/lsj/web_detail.asp?id = 366.

Jiang Nanxiang. "Qinghua daxue dierci kexue taolunhui kaimuci" [Opening speech at the second science symposium of Tsinghua University]. 1957. In ZFYS.

———. "Qinghua daxue xiaozhang Jiang Nanxiang dui Qinghua daxue yingjie biyesheng de jianhua" [Chancellor Jiang's speech to the graduating class]. 1957. In ZFYS.

Jiang Tingfu. "Zhishi jieji yu zhengzhi" [The intellectual class and politics]. *Duli pinglun* [Independent review] 51 (1933): 15–19.

Jiang Xingren. "Lun dang tianxia" [On CCP domination]. 1957. In ZFYS.

———. "Minzhu xuanju lungang" [Outlines on democratic elections]. 1957. In ZFYS.

———. "Minzhu xuanju wenti dabian" [Replies to queries on democratic elections]. 1957. In ZFYS.

"Jianli gongren jieji zuojia duiwu de daolu" [The road to producing writers of the working class). *WHB*, December 30, 1957. In ZFYS.

"Jiefang chuqi Shanghai pujiao xitong de jieguan zhengdun he gaizao" [The takeover, reorganization, and reform of Shanghai's school system in the wake of liberation]. In *Zhonggong Shanghaishi jiaoyu weisheng tiyu xitong dangshi wenji* [Collections of CCP historical material on Shanghai's systems of education, health, and sports], edited by Xiang Bolong. Shanghai: Tongji daxue chubanshe, 1996.

Jing Wenshuai. "*Zaochun eryue* yao ba renmen yindao na'er qu?" [Where is *Early Spring in February* taking people to?]. *RMRB,* September 15, 1964. Accessed January 29, 2017. PDRR.

Jun Mo. "Sixiang jiancha zhong de jizhong pianxiang" [Some undesirable trends in thought reform]. *WHB,* May 16, 1952.

Li Duoyu, ed. *Zhongguo dianying bainian 1905–1976* [One hundred years of Chinese cinema 1905–1976]. Beijing: Zhongguo guangbo dianshi chubanshe, 2005.

Li Guoqiang. *Zhongyang suqu jiaoyu shi* [The history of education in the CCP's soviet bases]. Nanchang: Jiangxi jiaoyu chubanshe, 1986.

Li Huaxing.*Minguo jiaoyushi* [A history of education in the Republican era]. Shanghai: Shanghai jiaoyu chubanshe, 1997.

Li Hui. *Hu Feng jituan yuan'an shimo* [The unjust case of the Hu Feng clique]. Beijing: Renmin ribao chubanshe, 2010.

Li Huizhong. "Tan geju *Liu Sanjie*" [Thoughts on the musical drama *Third Sister Liu*]. In *LSZ,* 45–61.

Li Jialin and Chen Siyu. *Qixue danxin Wang Shiwei* [The loyal heart and weeping blood of Wang Shiwei]. Kaifeng: Henan daxue chubanshe, 2012.

Li Junping. "Jintian women ruhe kandai zhongguo gudai shehui de zhishi ren?" [How should we look at people of knowledge in ancient China?]. *Shehui kexue luntan* [Tribune of social sciences] 9 (2010): 15–27.

Li Shaolin. "Youguan minzhu de jige wenti" [A few questions on democracy]. 1957. In *YSC,* 285–88.

Li Yachun. "Xuanju shang de bu minzhu" [Undemocratic characteristics in elections]. 1957. In ZFYS.

Li Yaosong. *Ningxia geming yinglie* [Fallen revolutionaries of Ningxia], vol. 2. Yinchuan: Ningxia renmin chubanshe, 2008. Accessed December 12, 2016. http://nuoha.com/book/ 153243/00022.html.

Li Zhimin. *Geming ronglu* [The furnace of revolution]. Zhonggong dangshi ziliao chubanshe, 1986.

Lin Xiling. "Xiancun zhidu shi chansheng 'sanhai' de zhijie yuanyin" [The 'three evils' are direct products of the existing system of rule]. 1957. In ZFYS.

———. "Zai zhongguo renmin daxue bianlunhui shang de fayan" [Speech in the debate at people's university]. 1957. In ZFYS.

Ling Guang. "Tao zhongguo de zhishi jieji" [On the Chinese intellectual class]. *Gujun* [Lone army] 2 (1925): 1–4.

Liu Baoguan, ed. *Xue yu huo de xili: cong Shaanbei gongxue dao Huabei daxue huiyilu 1937–1949* [The baptism of blood and fire: remembering the transition of the North Shaanxi Academy to the North China University, 1937–1949]. Beijing: Zhongguo renmin daxue chubanshe, 2007.

Liu Jialing. "Liu Sanjie." In *Liushi niandai jiyi* [Remembering the 1960s], edited by Zhu Yong. Beijing: Zhongguo wenlian chubanshe, 2002.

"*Liu Sanjie* lai Hu" [*Third Sister Liu* coming to Shanghai]. *WHB,* January 25, 1961.

Liu Sanjie zhengli xiaozu [The small group for the reorganization of the folklore of Liu Sanjie]. *Liu Sanjie.* Nanning: Guangxi Zhuangzu zizhiqu renmin chubanshe, 1959.

Liu Sanjie *ziliao huibian diyiji* [Collected essays on *Third Sister Liu*], vol. 1. Nanning: Guangxi Zhuangzu zizhiqu renmin chubanshe, 1960.

Liu Xiaobo. *Zhongguo dangdai zhengzhi yu zhongguo zhishifenzi* [Contemporary Chinese politics and China's intellectuals]. Taipei: Tangshan chubanshe, 1990.

Long Yinghua. "Gei Beijing daxue yinshuachang yige gongren de xin" [Letter to a worker at Beida printing house]. In ZFYS, 1957 [2010].

———. "Shijie wang hechu qu, zhongguo wang hechu qu, beida wang hechu qu" [Where are Beida, China, and the world going?]. 1957. In ZFYS.

———. "Zai Baihua xueshe huiyi shang de fayan" [Speech at the meeting of the hundred flowers study association]. 1957. In ZFYS.

Lozovsky, Solomon. "Gongchan zhuyi zhiyu laodong yundong" [Labor movements and communism]. *XQN* 1 (1923): 87–104.

Lu Ge. "Jin yibu guanche gaodeng xuexiao xiang gongnong kaimen de fangzhen" [Furthering workers' and peasants' accessibility to institutions of higher learning]. *RMRB*, December 27, 1957.

Lü Xingwei, ed. *Shanghai putong jiaoyushi 1949–1989* [A history of Shanghai education, 1949–1989]. Shanghai: Shanghai jiaoyu chubanshe, 1994.

Ma Feihai. "Jiefang zhanzheng shiqi de Shanghai jiaoshi yundong" [Political activities of Shanghai schoolteachers during the liberation war]. In *Shanghai jiaoshi huiyilu* [Recollections of Shanghai schoolteachers], edited by Shanghai lishi yanjiusuo jiaoshi yundong lishizu [Editorial group on teachers' movements of the Shanghai institute of historical research]. Shanghai: Shanghai renmin chubanshe, 1984.

Ma Hong. "Qinxue sannian shouyi zhongshen" [Studying hard for three years and reaping benefits for my entire life]. In *Yan'an Malie xueyuan huiyilu* [Remembering the Marxist-Leninist institute in Yan'an], edited by Wu Jiemin, 43–59. Beijing: Zhongguo shehui kexue chubanshe, 1991.

Ma Ya. "Daonian fuqin Ma Hong" [Remembering my late father Ma Hong], 2007. Accessed February 28, 2009. www.caijing.com.cn/2007-12-04/100040210.html.

Ma Yunfeng. "Zuzhi shouduan guoshi le" [Organization as a weapon is outdated]. 1957. In YSC, 193–96.

Mao Zedong. "Fan toujiang tigang" [An outline against surrender]. In *Mao Zedong sixiang wansui Wuhan ban* [Long live Mao Zedong Thought, Wuhan edition], [1936] 1968. Accessed June 10, 2016. www.marxists.org/chinese/maozedong/1968/1-116.htm.

———. "Fandui benben zhuyi" [Oppose dogmatism]. In *Mao Zedong xuanji* [Selected works of Mao Zedong], vol. 2, 109–18. Beijing: Renmin chubanshem, [1930] 1991.

Mei Lanfang. "Ge *Liu Sanjie*" [Applauding *Third Sister Liu*]. WHB, January 27, 1961.

Meng Liye. *Xin zhongguo dianying yishu shigao 1949–1959* [A history of cinema in New China 1949–1959]. Beijing: Zhongguo dianying chubanshe, 2003.

"Mingwan dianshi jiemu" [Tomorrow evening's TV programs]. WHB, January 27, 1961.

"Nongcun dianying faxing fangying gongzuo xunsu fazhan" [Rapid development in the release of films in rural areas]. WHB, December 14, 1961.

Pang Zhuoheng. "Lun shehui zhuyi shehui de jieji douzheng" [On class struggle in socialist societies]. 1957. In ZFYS.

Peng Shuzhi. "Shui shi zhongguo guomin geming zhi lingdao zhe?" [Who are the leaders of the Chinese national revolution?]. *XQN* 4 (1924): 1–14.

Peng Yueyu. "Du le ailuo xianke 'Zhishi jieji de shiming' de ganxiang" [Reflections on Eroshenko's 'The Mission of the Intellectual Class']. *Jinri* [Today] 1, no. 3 (1922): 40–46.

Qian Liqun. *Jujue yiwang: 1957 nian yanjiu biji 1957* [Refusing to forget: research notes on 1957]. Hong Kong: Oxford University Press, 2007.

Qian Ruping. "Zailun 'jieji de fazhan'" [More on 'The Development of Classes']. 1957. In ZFYS.

Qiao Yu. "Ermu yixin—tan geju *Liu Sanjie*" [Truly an innovation: thoughts on the musical drama *Third Sister Liu*]. In *LSZ*, 62–73.

Qin Yi. *Xiao zichan jieji de sixiang gaizao* [The thought reform of the petty bourgeoisie]. Shanghai: Shixi chubanshe, 1953.

Qu Qiubai. "Shehui yundong de xisheng zhe" [Martyrs of social movements]. *Xin shehui* 8 (1920): 1–3.

———. "Shijie de shehui gaizao yu gongchan guoji" [The Comintern and the remaking of the world]. *XQN* 1 (1923): 12–36.

———. "'Women' shi shei?" [Who are 'we'?]. In *Qu Qiubai wenji* [Selected works of Qu Qiubai], vol. 2, 875–878. Beijing: Renmin chubanshe, [1932] 1953.

———. "Xiandai laodong zhanzheng yu geming" [Contemporary labor-capital warfare and revolutions]. *XQN* 1 (1923): 37–56.

———. "Zhengzhi yundong yu zhishi jieji" [Political movements and the intellectual class]. *Xiangdao zhoubao* 18 (1923): 47–49.

Ru Wei. "Tan zhishi jieji—zhongguo xianzai de luanyuan dierzhong" [On the intellectual class: the second source of the chaos in China]. *Jinri* 3, no. 1 (1923): 32–38.

Sha Sha. "Duige" [Singing competition]. *WHB*, January 27, 1961.

"Shanghai ganbu xuexiao shoutuo zhaokao zhongyang renmin zhengfu jiguan gongzuo renyuan jianzhang" [Guidelines from the Shanghai Cadre Institute on recruitment of official personnel for the central government of the PRC]. *JFRB*, February 8, 1950.

Shanghai lishi yanjiusuo jiaoshi yundong lishizu [Editorial group on teachers' movements of the Shanghai institute of historical research], *Shanghai jiaoshi huiyilu* [Recollections of Shanghai schoolteachers]. Shanghai: Shanghai renmin chubanshe, 1984.

Shanghai wufan yundong zhuanti bianxie xiaozu [Shanghai editorial group on the five-anti campaign]. "Shanghai wufan yundong" [Shanghai's five-anti campaign]. In *ZZGSG*, vol. 2, 859–85.

"Shanghai zhishi qingnian suijun nanxia fuwutuan zhaosheng tonggao" [Public notice on the recruitment of intellectual youths for the southward-bound service corps]. *JFRB*, June 19, 1949.

"Shanghaishi renmin zhengfu gongshangju 1950 nian gongzuo zongjie" [The 1950 final report of the Shanghai bureau of industry and commerce]. In *ZZGSG*, vol. 1, 94–103.

Shen Xia. *Yan'an sinian 1942–1945* [My four years in Yan'an, 1942–1945]. Zhengzhou: Daxiang chubanshe, 2009.

Song Lanfang. "Shanghai shijiao de tudi gaige" [Land reform in Shanghai's countryside]. In *Lishi jubian 1949–1956* [Historic changes, 1949–1956], vol. 2, edited by Zou Ronggeng, 492–497. Shanghai: Shanghai shudian chubanshe, 2001.

Tan Tianrong. "Dierzhu ducao" [Another stalk of poisonous weed]. 1957. In *YSC*, 30–34.

———. "Disizhu ducao" [The fourth stalk of poisonous weed]. 1957. In *YSC*, 39–43.

———. "Diyizhu ducao" [My first stalk of poisonous weed]. 1957. In *YSC*, 28–29.

———. "Jiaotiao zhuyi chansheng de lishi biranxing" [The historical necessity of Marxian dogmatism]. 1957. In ZFYS.

———. "Liangdian lun" [On two points]. 1957. In ZFYS.

Tang Changfeng and Pan Boyu. *Liu Sanjie*. Beijing: Renmin meishu chubanshe, 1962.

"Tuanjie de zengjin" [Increase in solidarity]. *WHB*, May 5, 1938.

Wang Guangqi. "Shaonian Zhongguo xuehui zhi jingshen ji qi jinxing jihua" [The guiding spirit of the Young China Association and its plan]. *Shaonian Zhongguo* [Young China] 1, no. 6 (1919): 1–9.

Wang Ming. "Shisan nian lai de zhongguo gongchandang" [The first thirteen years of the CCP]. In *Gongchan guoji yu zhongguo geming ziliao xuanji 1928–1943* [Materials on the Comintern and the Chinese Revolution, 1928–1943], 393–419. Beijing: Renmin chubanshe, [1934] 1988.

Wang Peiyuan. *Yan'an luyi fengyunlu* [Changes and misfortune at the Lu Xun Academy of Arts in Yan'an]. Guilin: Guangxi shifan daxue chubanshe, 2004.

Wang Shiyi. "Kewai xingqu huodong zhanlan" [An exhibition of art works from student extracurricular activities]. *WHB*, July, 18, 1961.

Wang Xunsen. "Jindai zhishifenzi ziwo xingxiang de zhuanbian" [Changes in the self-images of contemporary Chinese intellectuals]. In *20 shiji zhongguo zhishifenzi shilun*, 107–26, 2005.

Wang Youqin. *Wenge shounan zhe—guanyu pohai jianjin he shalu de xunfang shilu* [Victims of the Cultural Revolution: an account of persecution, imprisonment, and murder]. 2004. http://ywang.uchicago.edu/history/victim_ebook_070505.pdf.

Wang Zengjin. *Houxiandai yu zhishifenzi shehui weizhi* [Postmodernity and the social locations of intellectuals]. Beijing: Zhongguo shehui kexue chubanshe, 2003.

Wang Zhongfang. *Yan'an fengqing hua* [A Yan'an picture of romance and passion]. Beijing: Zhongguo qingnian chubanshe, 2010.

Wei Junyi. *Sitong lu Lusha de lu* [Records of pain; the road taken by Lusha]. Beijing: Wenhua yishu chubanshe, 2003.

"Wei kexue yanjiu gongzuo chuangzao lianghao de tiaojian" [Creating favorable conditions for scientific research]. *RMRB*, November 10, 1957.

Wei Wei. "Wo de yinlu ren" [My guiding light]. In *Kangda xiaoyou huiyilu xuanji* [Recollections of alumni of the People's Resistance University of Political and Military Affairs], vol. 1, edited by Shanghai kangri junzheng daxue yanjiuhui [Research Society of the People's Resistance University of Political and Military Affairs), 120–121. Shanghai: Shanghai kangri junzheng daxue yanjiuhui ji xiaoyou lianyihui, 1999.

"Weile shehui zhuyi wenyi jianshe de bai'nian daji" [A hundred-year plan for developing socialist art and literature]. *Wenyi bao* [Art and literature gazette], vol. 26 (1957). In ZFYS.

Wen Si, ed. *Huiguo kangzhan benfu Yan'an* [Returning to China and rushing to Yan'an to fight against Japanese aggression]. Beijing: Zhongguo wenshi chubanshe, 2005.

"Wenyichu disici zhao wenyi gongzuozhe tonggao" [Public notice on the fourth round of recruitment of literature and art workers by the Literature and Art Department]. *JFRB*, September 24, 1949.

Wu Jialin. "Zhongyang zuigao lingdao jiguan fazhi guannian boruo" [The understanding of legality is weak at the highest level of government]. 1957. In ZFYS.

Wu Jiemin, *Yan'an Malie xueyuan huiyilu* [Remembering the Marxist-Leninist institute in Yan'an]. Beijing: Zhongguo shehui kexue chubanshe, 1991.

Wu Jing. "Mingzhe de zhuxi" [A sensible note of explanation]. *WHB*, February 22, 1947.

Wu Jinnan. "Qunzhong yundong de shengli Mao Zedong wenyi sixiang de shengli—chuangzuo he yanchu minjian gewuju Liu Sanjie de tihui" [The success of mass movement and Mao Zedong Thought on art and literature—my understanding of the creation and performance of *Third Sister Liu*]. *RMRB*, July 26, 1960. Accessed January 21, 2017. PDRR.

Wu Li. "Jianguo chuqi dang guanyu jiuye wenti de zhengce" [The CCP policy of employment in the wake of the PRC's founding]. In *Zhonggong dangshi ziliao* [Material on the CCP's history], edited by Zhonggong zhongyang dangshi ziliao zhengji weiyuanhui [Commission on Material Collection of the CCP Central Committee], vol. 52. Beijing: Zhonggong dangshi ziliao chubanshe, 1994.

Wu Yue. "Gaizao sixiang weishenme shouxian bixu baolu sixiang?" [Why is exposing one's own thought most important in thought reform?]. *WHB*, May 9, 1952.

Xi Gao. "Shiqu guangze de mingzhu" [The gem that has lost its luster]. *DZDY* 3 (1962): 20–21.

"Xi Jinping: Woguo guangda zhishifenzi yao zhudong dandang jiji zuowei wei guojia fuqiang minzu zhenxing xingfu duo zuo gongxian" [Xin Jinping: The broad population of intellectuals of our country should actively take on responsibilities and contribute abundantly to the nation's power and wealth and the revival of the Chinese race]. *Xinhua she* [New China news agency], March 4, 2017. Accessed August 20, 2017. http://news.xinhuanet.com/politics/2017–03/04/c_1120585225.htm.

Xia Daohan and Chen Liming. *Jiangxi suqu shi* [History of the Jiangxi soviet base]. Nanchang: Jiangxi renmin chubanshe, 1987.

Xiang Bolong, ed., *Zhonggong Shanghaishi jiaoyu weisheng tiyu xitong dangshi wenji* [Collections of CCP historical material on Shanghai's systems of education, health, and sports]. Shanghai: Tongji daxue chubanshe, 1996.

Xiao Feng. *Wo de fuqin Hu Feng* [My father Hu Feng]. Wuhan: Hubei renmin chubanshe, 2007.

Xin Ke. "Zhongguo zhishifenzi duoluo de shi da biaoxian" [Ten symptoms of depravity of Chinese intellectuals]. 2013. Accessed September 15, 2017. http://blog.sina.com.cn/s/blog_72853bee0102xcic.html.

Xiong Yuezhi, ed. *Shanghai tongshi* [General history of Shanghai], vol. 14. Shanghai: Shanghai renmin chubanshe, 1999.

Xu Jilin. *Zhongguo zhishifenzi shilun* [Ten essays on China's intellectuals]. Shanghai: Fudan daxue chubanshe, 2004.

Xu Zhongnian. "Qianlun zhishifenzi" [A general discussion on intellectuals]. 1957. In ZFYS.

"Xuanchuan wenti yijue an" [Resolution on propaganda (by the Enlarged Executive Committee of the CCP Central Bureau)]. October 1925. Accessed July 31, 2007. http://data.people.com.cn.

Yan Ping. "Chen Huangmei yu wenhuabu zhengfeng" [Cheng Huangmei and the rectification campaign in the Department of Culture]. 2007. Accessed July 8, 2017. www.gmw.cn/02sz/2007–01/01/content_560535.htm.

———. "Xia Yan weihe pokou dama Zhou Yang?" [Why did Xia Yan openly rebuke Zhou Yang]. 2016. Accessed July 8, 2017. http://cul.qq.com/a/20160201/043752.htm.

Yan Zhongqiang. "Weiwu zhuyi shi zongjiao" [Materialism is a religion]. 1957. In ZFYS.

Yan'an zhongyang dangxiao zhengfeng yundong bianxiezu [The rectification editorial group of the Central Party School in Yan'an]. *Yan'an zhongyang dangxiao de zhengfeng xuexi* [Rectification in the Central Party School in Yan'an], 2 vols. Beijing: Zhonggong zhongyang dangxiao chubanshe, 1998.

Yang Changchun. *Yige lianluoyuan de zishu: Yang Changchun huiyilu* [The memoirs of Yang Changchun, a liaison officer]. Beijing: Zhonggong dangshi chubanshe, 1999.

Yang Fengcheng. *Zhongguo gongchandang de zhishifenzi lilun yu zhengce yanjiu* [Research on the CCP's theory of and policies on intellectuals]. Beijing: Zhonggong dangshi chubanshe, 2005.

Yang Lian and Wei Jingsheng. "Yu Wei Jingsheng tan wenhua yu zhishifenzi" [A chat with Wei Jingsheng about culture and intellectuals]. *Beijing zhichun* [Beijing Spring], [1998] 2003. Accessed April 4, 2016. www.beijingspring.com/ bj2/1998/150/20031213170234.htm.

Yang Zhaolong. "Woguo zhongyao fadian heyi chichi hai bu banbu—shehuizhuyi zhong jianshe zhong de lifa wenti" [Why has the state repeatedly delayed issuing important legal codes? The problem of legislation amid socialist development]. 1957. In ZFYS.

Yang Zhongye. "Dangqian sifajie cunzai shenme wenti? Huang Shaohong fangwen ji" [What are the problems in the legal realm? An interview with Huang Shaohong]. 1957. In ZFYS.

Yin Hong and Ling Yan. *Xin zhongguo dianying shi 1949–2000* [A history of Chinese cinema, 1949–2000]. Hunan: Hunan meishu chubanshe, 2002.

Ying Sun. "Guonan xiaoshuo conghua" [On novels about national calamity]. *WHB*, July 26, 1938.

Ying Zhun. "Hu Sha suibi" [Hu Sha's random notes]. *WHB*, May 3, 1938.

"Yingxiang zhongguo gonggong zhishifenzi 50 ren" [The 50 public intellectuals who influence China]. *Nanfang renwu zhoukan*, September 9, 2004. Accessed September 12, 2017. www.360doc.com/content/09/0402/21/127159_3003066.shtml.

"Yinyue shudian kaimu hou sanzhou jian" [First three weeks of the new music bookstore]. *WHB*, February 26, 1961.

Yu Boliu and Ling Buji. *Zhonggong suqu shi* [History of the Chinese Soviet Republic]. Nanchang: Jiangxi renmin chubanshe, 2001.

Yu Guangyuan. "Fazhan woguo kexue shiye de liangtiao daolu" [Two roads to develop our science enterprise], *RMRB*, September 4, 1957. In ZFYS.

Yu Jie. *Panghuang yingxiong lu: zhuanxing shidai zhishifenzi de xinlingshi* [Heroes at the crossroads: the heart and spirit of intellectuals in the age of transformation]. Taipei: Lianjing chuben shiye gufen youxian gongsi, 2009.

Yuan Xuezhi. "Xishou youxiu zhishifenzi rudang" [Recruiting fine intellectuals into the party]. In *Kangda xiaoyou huiyilu xuanji*, vol. 1, 1999.

Yun Daiying. "Zhenme chuangzao shaonian Zhongguo?" [How to create a young China?]. *Shaonian Zhongguo* 2, no. 1 (1920): 1–26.

"Zailun wuchan jieji zhuanzheng de lishi jingyan" [More on the historical experience of the dictatorship of the proletariat]. *RMRB*, Dec 29, 1956.

Zeng Chenggui and Xu Kaixi. *Hubei xin minzhu gemingshi: tudi geming zhanzheng shiqi juan* [The history of the new democratic revolution in Hubei province: volume on the period of the agrarian revolutionary war]. Wuhan: Huazhong shifan daxue chubanshe, 2008.

Zhang Bojun. "Guanyu chengli zhengzhi sheji yuan de fayan" [On establishing a political design department]. *RMRB*, May 22, 1957. In LYX, 255–258.

Zhang Dongsun. "Zhongguo zhishi jieji de jiefang yu gaizao" [The emancipation and reform of the intellectual class in China]. *Jiefang yu gaizao* [Emancipation and reconstruction] 1, no. 3 (1919).

Zhang Guotao. "Zhishi jieji zai zhengzhi shang de diwei ji qi zeren" [The political status and responsibilities of the intellectual class]. *Xiangdao zhoubao* 12 (1922): 98–100.

Zhang Hanzheng. "Sanzhong jiantao de leixing" [Three types of reflection on political and ideological mistakes]. *WHB*, May 17, 1952.

Zhang Jingfu. "Jianli gongren jieji de kexue duiwu: Zhang Jingfu fuyuanzhang zai zhongguo kexueyuan Beijingqu qingnian dahui shang de jianghua" [Establishing a science troop of the working class: speech given to the mass meeting of youths from Beijing by Vice President Zhang Jingfu of the Chinese Academy of Science]. 1957. In ZFYS.

Zhang Jingzhong. "Zai baogaohui shang de fayan" [Speech at the symposium]. In *YSC*, 68–72.

Zhang Junbo, Wang Lulin, Zhao Liansan, and Zhang Yuanbao. *Yan'an suiyue* [The Yan'an years)]. Beijing: Jiefangjun chubanshe, 1990.

Zhang Naiqi. "Zai Minjian hui gongshang lian changwei lianxi huiyi shang diyici fayan" [First address to the joint meeting of the standing committees of the Association for Democratic Construction of China and the Federation of Commerce and Industry]. In *LYX*, 181–88.

Zhang Pijie. "Lun zhishi jieji yu qi zeren" [On the responsibilities of the intellectual class]. *Zhengheng* [Political reports] 1, no. 4 (1947): 23–27.

Zhang Wentian. *Zhang Wentian xuanji* [Selected works of Zhang Wentian]. Beijing: Renmin chubanshe, 1985.

Zhang Xiaode and Zhang Xu. *Zhishi ren yu zhishi zhongguo* [People of knowledge and a knowledge-based China]. Beijing: Beijing kexue jishu chubanshe, 1999.

Zhang Yuanxun. *Beida yi jiu wu qi* [Peking University in 1957]. Hong Kong: Mingbao chubanshe, 2004.

Zhao Yan. "Yanshui changliu: Mao Zedong yu Yan'an zhongyang yiyuan" [Mao and the Central Hospital of Yan'an]. 2008. Accessed October 31, 2009. www.1921.org.cn/CN/library/books_r.jsp?s=a0993efa1fe841a68931e8217d688b80.

Zheng Tianjian. "Guanyu Liu Sanjie de chuangzuo" [On the folktales of Third Sister Liu]. In *LSZ*, 13–27.

Zheng Zhenduo. "Zailun women jinhou de shehui gaizao yundong" [A further discussion of the movements to reconstruct Chinese society]. *Xin shehui* [New society] 9 (1920): 1–3.

———. "Xiandai de shehui gaizao yundong" [The current movements to reconstruct Chinese society]. *Xin shehui* 11 (1920): 1–3.

Zhengfeng wenjian huiji [Documents of the rectification campaign]. Taihang: Taihang qu dangwei, 1947.

"Zhengwuyuan guanyu laodong jiuye wenti de jueding" [The State Council's decision on labor and employment]. In *Zhonghua renmin gongheguo jingji dang'an ziliao xuanbian-laodong gongzi de zhigong fuli juan 1949–1952* [Selections of economic archival documents of the PRC: volume on workforce salaries and welfare, 1949–1952], edited by Zhongguo shehui kexue yuan [Chinese Academy of Social Science] and Zhongyang dang'an guan [CCP Central Archives], 178–179. Beijing: Zhongguo shehui kexueyuan chubanshe, [1952] 1994.

"Zhenyang jianli gongren jieji zhishifenzi duiwu? Sichuan gaodeng xuexiao fuzhe ren jiaohuan yijian" [How to establish a corps of working-class intellectuals? Exchange of ideas among leaders of Sichuan's higher education]. *WHB*, January 18, 1958.

Zhonggong Shanghai shiwei dangshi yanjiushi [Center of CCP history of the Shanghai CCP Commission]. *Zhongguo gongchandang zai Shanghai 1921–1991* [The CCP in Shanghai, 1921–1991]. Shanghai: Shanghai renmin chubanshe, 1991.

Zhonggong Shanghaishi duiwai jingji maoyi gongzuo weiyuanhui [Shanghai CCP Commission on Foreign Trade and Economics]. "Shanghai siying jinchukou ye de shehuizhuyi gaizao" [The socialist transformation of Shanghai's import-export industry]. In ZZGSG, vol. 2, 1110 –31.

"Zhonggong tonggao diqihao" [Announcement no. 7 of the CCP Central Committee]. In *Zhonggong zhongyang wenjian xuanji* [Selected documents of the CCP Central Committee], vol. 4, edited by Zhongyang dang'anguan, 639–40. Beijing: Zhonggong zhongyang dangxiao chubanshe, [1928] 1989.

"Zhongguo gongchandang dierci quanguo dahuo xuanyan" [Declaration of the CCP's second congress]. 1922. Accessed September 1, 2016. http://cpc.people.com.cn/GB/64162/64168/64554/4428164.html.

Zhongguo qikan quanwen shujuku [China academic journals database]. http://gb.oversea.cnki.net/kns55/

"Zhongguo renmin jiefangjun dijiu bingtuan zhishi qingnian xunlianban zhaosheng jianzhang" [Recruitment guidelines from the PLA's Ninth Regiment for the training camp for intellectual youths]. *JFRB*, October 19, 1949.

"Zhongguo renmin jiefangjun huadongqu songhu jingbei budui wenhua ganbu xunliantuan zhaosheng jianzhang" [Recruitment guidelines for the cultural-cadre training camp of the Shanghai garrison of the PLA's East China division]. *JFRB*, September 1, 1949.

Zhongguo renmin yinhang Shanghaishi jinrong yanjousuo [Shanghai Financial Research Institute of the People's Bank of China]. "Shanghai siying jinrongye de shehuizhuyi gaizao" [The socialist transformation of Shanghai's financial sector]. In ZZGSG, vol. 2, 1092–100.

Zhongguo shehui kexue yuan and Zhongyang dang'an guan [Chinese Academy of Social Science and the Central Archives of the Chinese Communist Party]. *Zhonghua renmin gongheguo jingji dang'an ziliao xuanbian–laodong gongzi he zhigong fuli juan 1949–1952* [Selections of economic archival documents of the PRC: volume on workforce salaries and welfare, 1949–1952]. Beijing: Zhongguo shehui kexueyuan chubanshe, 1994.

Zhongguo xiquzhi bianji weiyuanhui [Editorial commission of the Gazettes of Chinese Opera]. *Zhongguo xiquzhi guangxi juan* [The Guangxi gazette of Chinese opera]. Beijing: Zhongguo zhongxin chubanshe, 1995.

"Zhongyang guanyu dizhu funong zhishifenzi ruwu gaibian chengfen de guiding" [Regulations on class reassignment of enlisted landlords, rich peasants, and intellectuals]. 1948. Accessed July 31, 2017. http://cpc.people.com.cn/GB/64184/64186/66649/4495969.html.

"Zhongyang ju baogao shi shiyi yuefen" [October and November reports of the CCP Central Bureau]. 1926. Accessed March 11, 2007. *Renmin shujuku* [PeopleData]. http://data.people.com.cn.

"Zhongyang renmin zhengfu zhong gongyebu gongzuo renyuan xunlianban zhaosheng jianzhang" [Recruitment guidelines for the training class of the Ministry of Heavy Industry of the Central Government]. *JFRB*, January, 28, 1950.

"Zhongyang shuiwu xuexiao huadong fenxiao zhaosheng jianzhang" [Student recruitment guidelines for the East China branch of the Central Tax Administration Institute]. *JFRB*, February 1, 1950.

Zhou Chunyun and Zhang Yongchun. *Yunluo de hongxing: Suqu hongjun yuansha dajishi* [Fallen red stars: records of unjust killings of red army personnel in soviet bases]. Chengdu: Sichuan renmin chubanshe, 1995.

Zhou Dajue. "Buchong 'wo dui muqian jushi de kanfa'" [Supplement to 'My View on the Current Situation']. 1957. In ZFYS.

———. "Lun 'jieji' de fazhan" [On the development of 'classes']. In *YSC*, 166–171.

———. "Wo dui muqian jushi de kanfa" [My view on the current situation]. 1957. In *ZFYS*.

———. "Zailun 'lingdaozhe jieji' wenti" [More on the question of the leadership class]. 1957. In ZFYS.

Zhou Enlai. "Guanyu zhishifenzi de gaizao wenti" [On the question of the reform of intellectuals]. In *Zhou Enlai xuanji* [Selected works of Zhou Enlai], vol. 2, 59–71. Beijing: Renmin chubanshe, [1951] 1984.

Zhu Hongzhao. *Yan'an hebian de wenren men* [Literati on the banks of Yan'an River]. Shanghai: Dongfang chuban zhongxin, 2010.

———. *Yan'an richang shenghuo zhong de lishi 1937–1947* [Daily life in Yan'an, 1937–1947]. Guilin: Guangxi shifan daxue chubanshe, 2007.

Zhu Zheng. *Fanyoupai douzheng shimo* [The origins and conclusion of the struggle against rightists]. Hong Kong: Mingbao chubanshe, 2004.

"Zuo yige mingfu qishi de gongren jieji zhishifenzi" [To be a working-class intellectual who truly lives up to this name]. *WHB*, October 28, 1957. In ZFYS.

Documents from the Shanghai Municipal Archives (SMA)

Shanghaishi chili shiye zhishifenzi weiyuanhui ji bangongshi [Office of the Shanghai commission for handling unemployed intellectuals]. "Ben shi gequ zhengfu guanyu zuzhi chengli chuli shiye zhishifenzi weiyuanhui weiyuan ji gongzuo renyuan mingdan baosong bei'an de han" [Letter for the record of the lists of commission and staff members of the various district commissions for handling unemployed intellectuals], 1951. SMA B130–2–2.

———. "Guanyu gequ gongzuo renyuan jinxing zongjie de zongjie baogao he zenyang jinxing shiye zhishifenzi diaocha gongzuo de jianghua" [Report on reports of work from various districts and speech on how to investigate unemployed intellectuals], 1952. SMA B130–2–3.

———. "Guanyu shizhi wuzhengjian zhe keyou quji yishang huo renmin tuanti zhengming de baogao banfa deng" [Report on unemployed intellectuals with no identification getting certification from government offices or people's associations and other materials], 1951. SMA B130–1–3.

———. "Guanyu waifu laihu zhaopin shizhi gongzuo de yijian ji dongyuan shizhi yingkao Nei Menggu zhongxue jiaoshi gongzuo zongjie baogao" [Summary report on establishments from other regions arriving in Shanghai and hiring unemployed intellectuals and the work of mobilizing unemployed intellectuals to take the examination to become secondary school teachers in Inner Mongolia], 1953. SMA B130–2–6.

———. "Shifu guanyu zhubu chexiao shi shizhi zhi shiqu liangji jigou de tongzhi he shiwei jiesu gongzuo baogao" [Instruction on phasing out the two levels of offices for registering unemployed intellectuals and the report from the commission on the completion of its work], 1953–54. SMA B130–1–7.

———. "Yi nian lai zongjie baogao" [Report on one year of work], 1952. SMA B130–1–6.

Shanghishi jiaoyuju [Shanghai municipal bureau of education]. "1956–1957 xueniandu Shanghaishi zhongchudeng putong youer jiaoyu jiaozhi yuangong zhengzhi qingkuang tongji" [Statistics on the political situations of the faculty, staff, and workers in Shanghai's kindergartens and primary and secondary schools, 1956–1957], 1956–1957. SMA B105–1–1504.

———. "Chuli jiu renyuan gongzuo baogao ji chuli gaikuang biao" [Report and summary tables on the handling of holdover employees], 1949. SMA B105–1–10.

———. "Dui xuexiao xingzheng renyuan jiaozhi yuangong chufen wenti de pifu" [Replies to questions regarding disciplinary action for faculty and staff members and school workers], 1957–1958. SMA B105–2–329.

———. "Gequxian jiaoyu bumen li zhongxiaoxue zhuanren jiaozhiyuan zhengzhi taidu jiating chushen diaocha zonghebiao" [Summary tables on the political attitudes and family backgrounds of the faculty and staff in the primary and secondary schools in the districts and counties of the Shanghai municipality and the schools operated directly by the municipal department of education], 1958. SMA B105–2–395.

———. "Guanyu ganbu peibei qingkuang baogao he zhongjiaoshi renyuan dengji biao" [Report on staffing and registration records of staff members of the office for secondary education], 1950. SMA B105–1–21.

———. "Guanyu gongsili zhongxiaoxue xingzheng renyuan pinzhi elie tanwu deng wenti de pifu" [Replies on poor character, graft, and other problems of administrative personnel within public and private primary and secondary schools], 1953–1955. SMA B105–5–733.

———. "Guanyu Shanghai waizi jintie xuexiao qingkuang zonghe fenxi" [An integrated analysis of conditions within the foreign-subsidized schools in Shanghai], 1949–1950. SMA B105–5–1328.

———. "Guanyu Shanghai zhongxue deng jiuge xuexiao jiaoyu zhiliang de diaocha baogao caogao" [Draft report on the survey of instructional quality in Shanghai Secondary School and eight other secondary schools], 1954–1955. SMA B105–5–1969.

———. "Guanyu Shanghaishi jiaozhiyuan sixiang gaizao xuexi jihua yu zongjie" [Summary report on the thought reform of the faculty and staff within the Shanghai municipality and the study plans], 1952–1953. SMA B105–1–664.

———. "Guanyu xuexiao xingzheng zhixing dang dui zhishifenzi zhengce de qingkuang yu zhongxiaoxue zhishifenzi wenti de diaocha baogao" [Report on schools implementing the CCP's policy of intellectuals and the issue of intellectuals in primary and secondary schools], 1955. SMA B105–5–1354.

———. "Guanyu zhongxue zhengzhi jiaoshi shuqi xunlianban de baogao" [Reports on the summer class for secondary school politics instructors], 1951. SMA B105–5–488.

———. "Jieguan gongzuo zongjie baogao" [Final report on the work of takeover], 1949. SMA B105–1–8.

———. "Nanyang mofan zhongxue sixiang gaizao zhongdian shiyan qingkuang zongjie" [Summary report on the key trial of thought reform at Nanyang Model Secondary School], 1952. SMA B105-5-697.

———. "Shanghaishi jiaoyu shiye linian tongji ziliao huibian" [Collections of annual statistics on education in Shanghai], 1965. SMA B105-2-901.

———. "Shanghaishi putong jiaoyu gaikuang tongjibiao" [Statistical tables on the general conditions in Shanghai education], 1951. SMA B105-1-331.

———. "Shanghaishi zhongdeng xuexiao jiaozhiyuan diyiqi sixiang gaizao xuexiban dangzu huiyi jilu" [Meeting records of the party group handling the first session of the thought reform of Shanghai's secondary school faculty and staff], 1952. SMA B105-1-662.

———. "Shi jiaoyuju gongzuo jihua baogao" [Reports on work plans of the Shanghai bureau of education], 1953. SMA B105-1-660.

———. "Shifu pifu guanyu xin jiaoyu xueyuan dibaqi xueyuan fenpei gongzuo yijian ji fenpei qingkuang jilubiao" [Reply of the municipal government to the opinions of the New Education College on work assignment related to the eighth training session, and tables on ongoing work of assignment], 1952. SMA B105-5-529.

———. "Wu lian lai putong jiaoyu gongzuo jiancha ji bufen zhongxue diaocha" [An examination of the last five years of work in primary and secondary education and surveys of some of the schools], 1954. SMA B105-1-890.

———. "Wuben Nüzhong qingkuang" [Conditions at Wuben Girls Secondary School], 1949. SMA B105-5-110.

———. "Xin Jiaoyu Xueyuan dibaqi xuexiban (shiye zhishifenzi xuexiban) gongzuo zongjie" [Concluding work report on the eighth training class of the New Education College specially designed for unemployed intellectuals], 1952. SMA B105-1-614.

———. "Yangshupu zhongxue qingkuang" [Conditions at Yangshupu Secondary School], 1949. SMA B105-5-100.

———. "Yi yue ban xuehui zongjie" [Summary report from the study commission on one-and-a-half month of work], 1950. SMA B105-1-202.

———. "Zhongdeng jiaoyu dangyuan peibei baogao" [Report on the presence of party members in Shanghai secondary education], 1954. SMA B105-1-273.

Shanghaishi laodong jiuye weiyuanhui [Shanghai municipal commission on labor and employment]. "Gongzuo renyuan shouce" [Staff manual], 1952–1953. In SMA B131-1-7.

———. "Guanyu shiye renyuan tongyi dengji de banfa shixing xize de tongzhi he shi laojiuhui youguan dengji fanwei" [Regarding the implementation of rules and regulations for the unified unemployment registration and the scope of registration established by the labor and employment commission], 1952–1953. SMA B131-1-7.

———. "Shi laodongju fendangzu dui jige youguan laodong jiuye dengji wenti de yijian de qingshi" [Requests for instructions from party subgroups on certain issues regarding the registration and placement of the unemployed], 1953. SMA B131-1-8.

Shanghaishi laodongju [Shanghai municipal bureau of labor]. "Guanyu 1950–1956 nian dengji shiye renyuan anzhi qingkuang tongjibiao" [Statistics on arrangements for registered unemployed personnel, 1950–1956], 1956. SMA B127-1-78.

———. "Shanghaishi shiye laodong jiuye renshu 1950–1954" [Numbers of unemployment and reemployment in the Shanghai municipality, 1950–1954], 1954. SMA B127-1-49.

Shanghaishi qingnian gong [Shanghai youth palaces]. "Guanyu qingnian zai yishi xingtai douzheng zhong dui yixie pipan zuopin de qingkuang huibao ji zuotan jilu deng"

[Reports and symposium records on the ideological struggle among the youth in regards to their criticism of some recent works], 1964. SMA C26-2-113.

Shanghaishi renmin zhengfu [People's government of Shanghai]. "Guanyu choujian chuli shiye zhishifenzi weiyuanhui ji youguan gongzuo de wenjian" [Documents related to the preparation for the establishment of the commission for handling unemployed intellectuals], 1951–1952. SMA B1-1-1121.

Shanghaishi renwei wenjiao bangongshi [Office of culture and education of the Shanghai people's commission]. "Yijiu liusi nian qingkuang tiaocha huibao" [Reports on investigation of conditions in 1964], 1964. SMA B3-2-216.

Shanghaishi wei zhishu jiguan weiyuanhui xuanchuanbu [Propaganda division of the Shanghai commission for establishments under the direct authority of the Shanghai municipal government]. "Dui *Zaochun Eryue* dianying de fanying" [On the reactions to *Early Spring in February*], 1964. SMA A77-2-455.

Xin minzhu zhuyi qingniantuan Shnaghaishi weiyuanhui [Shanghai commission of the New Democratic Youth League]. "Zhonggong Shanghai shiwei guanyu shujia jizhong zhongdeng xuexiao jiaozhiyuan jinxing sixiang gaizao jihua" [On the Shanghai CCP Commission's plan to gather secondary school faculty and staff to undergo thought reform during the summer vacation], 1951–1952. SMA C21-2-221.

Zhonggong Shanghai shiwei jiaoyu weisheng gongzuobu [Department of education and health of the Shanghai CCP commission]. "Guanyu peiyang youhong youzhuan zhishifenzi duiwu de yijian he huiyi jilu" [Opinions and meeting records on the development of red-and-expert intellectuals], 1957. SMA A23-2-260.

Zhonggong Shanghai shiwei xuanchuanbu [Department of propaganda of the Shanghai CCP commission]. "1953 nian benbu guanyu xuexiao gongzuo de zhishi tongzhi baogao" [Instructions, notices, and reports regarding the work of the commission in schools for the year of 1953], 1953. SMA A22-1-115.

———. "Shanghai shiyan gejuyuan fanyou qianhou de qingkuang bianhua" [Changes at the Shanghai Academy of Experimental Opera after the antirightist movement], 1958. SMA A22-2-619.

Zhonggong Shanghaishi jiaoqu gongzuo weiyuanhui [Rural work committee of the Shanghai CCP commission]. "Guanyu zhenya fangeming de qizhong qingkuang tongji biao" [Statistics on the seven types of treatment of suppressed counterrevolutionaries], 1951. SMA A71-2-94.

Feature Films and Documentary

Buju xiaojie de ren. Dir. Lü Ban. Changchun: Changchun dianying zhipian chang, 1956. DVD.

Hushi riji. Dir. Tao Jin. Shanghai: Jiangnan dianying zhipian chang, 1957. DVD.

Liu Sanjie. Dir. Su Li. Changchun: Changchun dianying zhipian chang, 1961. DVD.

Minzhu qingnian jinxingqu. Dir. Wang Yi. Beijing: Beijing dianying zhipian chang, 1950. DVD.

Wei wancheng de xiju. Dir. Lü Ban. Changchun: Changchun dianying zhipian chang, 1957. DVD.

Wo sui siqu. Dir. Hu Jie. (Documentary) 2006. www.youtube.com/watch?v=eBfGc3-InrA.

Zaochun Eryue. Dir. Xie Tieli. Beijing: Beijing dianying zhipian chang, 1963. DVD.

INDEX

CPSIA information can be obtained
at www.ICGtesting.com
Printed in the USA
LVHW092254190419
614933LV00001B/87/P